GOING PUBLIC
A Practical Handbook
of Procedures and Forms

GOING PUBLIC
A Practical Handbook
of Procedures and Forms

Daniel S. Berman

PRENTICE-HALL, INC.   Englewood Cliffs, N.J.

Prentice-Hall International, Inc., *London*
Prentice-Hall of Australia, Pty. Ltd., *Sydney*
Prentice-Hall of Canada, Ltd., *Toronto*
Prentice-Hall of India Private Ltd., *New Delhi*
Prentice-Hall of Japan, Inc., *Tokyo*

This publication is designed to provide accurate and
authoritative information with regard to the subject matter covered. It is sold with the understanding that the
publisher is not engaged in rendering legal, accounting, or
other professional advice. If legal advice or other expert
assistance is required, the services of a competent professional person should be sought.

—From a Declaration of Principles jointly adopted
*by a Committe of the American Bar Association
and a Committe of Publishers and Associations*

Library of Congress Cataloging in Publication Data

Berman, Daniel S
   Going public.

    1. Securities—United States. I. Title.
KF1439.B47   332.6'42'0973   73-19766
ISBN 0-13-357848-8

Printed in the United States of America

Other books by the author:

How to Organize and Sell a Profitable Real Estate Condominium
How to Reap Profits in Local Real Estate Syndicates
Urban Renewal: Bonanza of the Real Estate Business
Tax Saving Opportunities in Real Estate Deals, (with Sheldon & Schwartz)

ABOUT THE AUTHOR

Daniel S. Berman is a New York attorney, a partner in the firm of Fink, Weinberger, Levin & Charney, practicing law in New York City for over twenty-five years. He has lectured on the subject of going public to audiences consisting of accountants, lawyers, comptrollers, stock brokers, underwriters and mortgage bankers. His first work on the subject of going public appeared in 1962, and this latest revision adds ten more years of experience, dozens of new forms, and many new ideas to the work.

WHAT THIS BOOK WILL DO FOR YOU

This handbook will do three very important things:

1. It will give you the pros and cons of going public, so that you can see for yourself if a public financing is what you need, *and* it will call your attention to alternative ways of raising capital, *if* you decide that public financing is not for you.

2. It will call your attention to the kind of preparation you need to do the job right. It will point out to you the places where decisions have to be made, and it will call your attention to disaster after disaster (as well as the successful alternative) so that you can avoid the mistakes other people have made.

3. It will lead you step-by-step through the process of taking a corporation public, so that you can organize the work load, visualize the kind of information that has to be assembled, and put together the necessary presentations and forms.

HOW THIS BOOK WILL HELP YOU MAKE BETTER DECISIONS

In other words, it will help you reach a decision by calling your attention to the pros and cons; it will help you organize the information necessary; and, if you then decide to go ahead, it will help you to get all the information down on paper so that you can "go public" as efficiently and profitably as possible.

That sounds like a tall order; how will we go about doing this? In Chapter 1 of this book we will point out the trends and tell you what kinds of corporations have had successful public offerings. We will also show why over 41 percent of the firms that have gone public were dissatisfied with their underwriters. Then we show you some alternatives, as well as some temporary "tide overs."

Chapters 2 and 3 take you through the advantages of going public. They show you how going public can benefit your firm, as well as benefit you personally (as a major executive or controlling stockholder).

How to use leverage is specifically discussed, and the more important misconceptions and traps are pointed out. You are mentally taken through the problems of being a public corporation, so that you can decide for yourself whether you are prepared (personality-wise and staff-wise) for the changes you will have to undergo. You are shown how to make money with your new public image, and advised of the changes you must make if your company is to grow as a public corporation. You are shown how to operate your business differently, after going public, and what to avoid.

AVOIDING TROUBLE SPOTS

Chapter 4 deals with the "No-Nos," so that you can decide for yourself whether being public will inhibit your major money-making opportunities. You are shown how your business will be different once you are public, so that you can ask yourself whether, because of the peculiarities of *your* operation, going public is for you.

Chapters 5 and 6 point out the specifics of what it costs to go public in detail. In fact, you are taken behind the scenes and are shown such trade secrets as what underwriters ask for and what they get, so that you can pick the right underwriter and make sure you get the best long term value.

Remember what we said before—41 percent of the companies that went public were unhappy with their underwriters. Chapters 5, 6, and 7 specifically show you what to expect from your underwriter; what to demand from your underwriter; and how to pick the underwriter that is best for your company.

FINDING THE RIGHT UNDERWRITER FOR YOU

Chapters 7, and 9 on selecting your underwriter, understanding his viewpoint and negotiating with him can be most valuable. Only by reading those three chapters carefully (and doing your homework) can you avoid being among the 41 percent of the public corporations who are unhappy with their underwriters.

It is not strange that so many companies were dissatisfied. After all, a typical company goes public once in a lifetime, and they are unprepared, by experience, for it. There is no better way to prepare for going public than to read Chapters 7, 8, and 9 of this book. Not only will these chapters tell you how to find the right underwriter and negotiate the best price with him, but they will show you how to prepare for the underwriting, by putting together the kind of information that will make your package attractive to an underwriter, thus enabling you to find the best possible underwriter at the lowest possible cost.

GUIDE YOU THROUGH UNDERWRITING

Moving on through Chapters 10, 11, and 12 we deal with the subject of what goes into the underwriting agreement, as well as some of the problems, and how to overcome them. The use of "finders" in getting an underwriter is covered. Major problems in the underwriting field are discussed (whether to do a full registration or a "Regulation A" registration); how to avoid getting trapped with a bad "finder"; and the subject of how to negotiate the more important clauses of the underwriting agreement.

Chapter 13 explains to you some of the "magic" in the use of such sophisticated securities as "convertibles," "preferreds," "hybrids," and "debentures." By taking the mystery out of these subjects, you will be less frightened by Wall Street "gobbledegook" and more able to determine whether a suggested course of action is good for you, good for Wall Street, and good for the investors.

FAMILIARIZING YOURSELF WITH SEC PROCEDURES

Chapters 14 and 15 are meant to take some of the fear out of the SEC registration process, as well as out of the state "blue sky" laws. Again, by taking the mystery out of the procedures (although they are changing from time to time) you see how to assemble the kind of information that goes into a registration, and you are taken through such gritty problems as picking the "right" accountant; how to overcome income tax problems on "hidden inventories"; and how to wade through Regulation Sx with your accountant.

While these two chapters will not make either an SEC lawyer or a certified public accountant out of you, they will deal with enough of the specific problems so that when your accountant or lawyer raises the questions, you'll be able to do more than shrug your shoulders. You'll be able to contribute some constructive thinking in the field, with your new understanding of the philosophical concepts involved.

THROUGH THE REGISTRATION, STEP-BY-STEP

Chapter 16 takes you through an actual registration literally, step-by-step. You start with the first planning conference. You are shown how to assign tasks to the various members of the team who will be working with you, and how to hold each one responsible. You are shown how to coordinate these tasks, so that no one is able to buck-pass and say he wasn't told what to do.

You are told about the typical kinds of problems which come up on a registration, and the mystery of "deficiency" letters and "delaying amendments" is explained. The chapter ends by recapitulating, and taking you through the entire procedure once again, step-by-step.

SEE HOW YOU AND YOUR LAWYER PUT
TOGETHER THE KEY FORMS

Chapter 17 is one of the most important in the book. It consists mainly of forms, but the forms have been carefully gathered from dozens of files prepared by some of the best underwriting, accounting, and legal firms in the business. We begin with a detailed corporate questionnaire which assembles in one place the kind of information needed to go public. You are shown how to put together, in one place, the information which will help you to determine your own strengths and weaknesses. You will need a lawyer to help you with the forms, but having them before you will guide you both through the rough spots.

KEY CHECKLISTS

What follows is a going public checklist, covering over eighty decision-making points. It will help you make sure you do not overlook something in your planning stages. There follows an important outline which shows you how to "sell the underwriter with facts"—a key part of that checklist. Following those points will force you to think through your financing problems, and put you in a much better negotiating posture no matter who your underwriter is going to be.

Next, the reader is provided with a form section entitled "How To Draw Up an Effective Prospectus Step-By-Step." Form S1, the full SEC registration, is torn apart and put together for you piece-by-piece. In each case, we start out with the requirements of the SEC, as reproduced from their official rule book. While the requirements are constantly changing, and while most of the examples must be updated for current practice, by seeing how other people solve their prospectus drafting problems, you begin to see that a task which looks insurmountable becomes simple when broken down piece-by-piece, especially as you see how others have solved their own drafting problems. The reader is given a list of sample prospectuses, together with information how to obtain and the general price involved.

A COMPLETE UNDERWRITING AGREEMENT

Finally, the last form in the book is a detailed, complete underwriting agreement involving a "firm" underwriting, so that you and your advisors can see in advance what will be expected of them. All can then plan their own workload, and can see what can be negotiated and what cannot be negotiated. You also can see where your own trouble spots might lie.

HERE IS A SUMMARY OF WHAT THIS BOOK IS ALL ABOUT

The author started out by telling you that he hoped to accomplish three objectives: (1) to help you decide whether to go public; (2) to avoid the pitfalls; and (3) to see how to do it, step-by step.

You are shown the advantages and disadvantages; how to go about getting the money you need; how to avoid losing control of your business; how to select the right timing and the right price for your stock; how to find the right underwriter and negotiate with him; and how to overcome the complexities of the securities law.

This book will help you prepare in a field where most companies come unprepared. Statistics published by the Small Business Administration show that there are 200,000 private companies with assets of a quarter of a million dollars, of which only 4 percent are public. Almost $50 Billion of public financing is projected for the next ten years among those 200,000 businesses. There was a time when General Motors, United States Stell, IBM and American Telephone and Telegraph were also privately held rather than publicly. But even Howard Hughes has been forced into the public market with the Hughes Tool Company by business conditions.

The author has tried to help you decide whether the public financing market is for you. He has tried to make that transition as smooth as possible for you and your company. Some of you, by using the principles set forth in this book, can become millionaires. This book will help all of you avoid the tragic mistakes of the uninformed. The best luck to you. The author hopes his experiences, and those of his clients, underwriters, lawyers, and accountants who contributed the "know-how" in this book will help you and your company "go public" successfully.

Caution: Throughout this book you will find sample forms, statements of accounting principles, and resumes of SEC regulations. This material is constantly being updated. This book is not intended as a substitute for a full looseleaf service on SEC regulations.

This book is intended to simplify and guide you in the techniques of putting together a public offering. It is not a substitute for up-to-the-minute legal and accounting advice; nor can any printed work replace checking out the latest changes with the governmental regulatory agency involved.

Daniel S. Berman

CONTENTS

17

GOING PUBLIC
A Practical Handbook
of Procedures and Forms

1

ARE YOU <u>SURE</u> YOU WANT TO GO PUBLIC?

During the last fifteen years, the number of new corporations that have "gone public" has increased well over 400 percent. Here are just a few figures:

In 1950, the number of new public offerings of stock was approximately 500. By the time the 1962 boom rolled around, there were over 1,200. In 1969, there were over 2,200. Note that these are actual offerings. As a matter of fact, the number of registrations, of course, exceeded the number of offerings.

Well over 40,000 companies all across the United States now have their stocks traded "over the counter" or on one of the various exchanges.

There are probably a number of reasons for the boom in new public issues. Unquestionably, the bull markets of 1960 and 1961 and 1968 and 1969 certainly contributed to the number of new offerings in those and the succeeding years. Investor demand for "new merchandise" literally sent underwriters all across the country seeking off-the-beaten-path "growth" stocks.

As new issue after new issue came out, and as each new issue seemed to go up immediately after the initial offering, more and more investors became attracted to the "new issue" field. Even institutions which had for many years concentrated only on "big board" stocks became attracted to the over-the-counter new issue market. Such issues as Mattel Toy, Hudson Vitamin, Stirling Homex and "Minnie Pearl" Chicken Franchises showed spectacular rises when institutional investors and mutual funds showed an interest in them.

Industries that could never have been considered worthy of public investment fifteen or twenty years ago suddenly began attracting public stock market support. Apparel, publishing, toys, service companies, real estate investment trusts, one-family home builders, and chicken and restaurant franchising all went public and found their stocks bid up to spectacular highs overnight, as industry after industry became the fad of the day.

You should note that the average size of the public issues went down at the same time that the number of issues was going up. In other words, although you had more SEC registrations, numerically the average registration was a smaller one, indicating that smaller companies were going to market. This created new paper work problems for the SEC, which found that its backlog became even more acute as smaller, less sophisticated companies sought public funds. The timetable to clear SEC stretched to three, four, and six months.

SOLVING PROBLEMS FOR THE SMALLER ISSUE

The trend toward smaller issues put a strain on the underwriting business, as older underwriting firms were forced to adopt new procedures to handle these smaller issues economically, and as entirely new firms stepped in to fill the demand of the public for these newer, smaller issues.

Even today, you can get two entirely contrary opinions among the Wall Street underwriting fraternity. Some alert investment bankers feel that the market for new small issues is saturated and that a lull in the stock market's rise will have a disastrous effect on future new issues. These underwriters look at the new issue market with a jaundiced eye and feel that once the investors learn they can get stuck in a new issue just as easily as they can make a "windfall" overnight, the new issue investors will abandon the new issue market for the older and more mature securities.

On the other hand, there are other Wall Street underwriters who feel that the market for new smaller issues has not even been scratched. They point out that while there exist today approximately 40,000 companies whose stock is public, there are almost 40,000 more with a net worth of $1 million or more which are not public, and there are over 200,000 companies with a net worth of over one-quarter of a million dollars which are not public. Many of these companies got started in the post-World War II era, and many of them are now twenty-five years old.

As the owners of these companies grow older and become more estate-planning conscious, and as these older companies seek to attract new, younger management, the pressure on these privately held companies to go public or to merge will be tremendous, say these new-issue oriented underwriters.

MARKETING THE SMALLER ISSUE

The argument of this new breed of underwriters is that the underwriting business today is at the same stage that commercial banking was in during the 1930s. They argue that those underwriters who move with the trend and who find an economical way to market the issues of the newer, smaller companies will grow. Those underwriters who insist on marketing only the public securities of multimillion dollar corporations will find their market constantly shrinking.

The new breed of underwriter argues that underwriting must become a broadly based retail business in the same way that commercial banking has become a retail business, with ten-cent checking accounts and installment loans for the smaller customer.

It is still not easy to predict which one of these two underwriting groups has the answer. It is the function of this book, however, to point out to you that if you have a small issue and if you bring it to the wrong underwriting house (to a house which feels that only the larger issues are attractive), you are wasting your time and you can be easily discouraged by such an underwriter.

You must, if you want to market a smaller issue, seek out the underwriters who are anxious to deal with the newer companies and who prefer to do a retail business rather than a wholesale business.

ARE YOU SURE YOU WANT
TO GO PUBLIC?

Why, you may ask, should I inquire whether or not you want to go public? You have proved your interest in this subject by purchasing this book. When the material in this book was given in the form of a series of workshop lectures in New York, and I asked the question: "Are you *sure* you want to go public?" I could see annoyance spreading over the faces of my audience. Of course they wanted to go public. It was so easy to raise money from the public. Everyone could use money to enhance his business. Yet, when the smoke had cleared away from the hot issue market of 1961-62 and 1968-69, questionnaires sent out by the Graduate Business School of Rutgers University, New Jersey, and by the Armour Research Foundation of the Illinois Institute of Technology disclosed a number of uncomfortable statistics.

SOME TRAPS–PITFALLS TO AVOID–

Over 20 percent of the chief executives whose corporations had gone public were disenchanted by what had happened.

Many of their firms had rushed into going public to take advantage of the earnings multiples then available, only to discover that the funds raised could not be put to good use, or that the disadvantages of going public outweighed the advantages.

Over one-third of the companies questioned considered that the cost of going public was excessive.

Over 41 percent of the firms surveyed expressed dissatisfaction with the performance of the underwriting firms which they employed.

Almost one-half of the firms that had gone public were dissatisfied with the investment banking firm with whom they probably had the most intimate business relationship during their business lifetimes.

Imagine that! It will be the function of this book to discover why these firms were disenchanted, and how you can learn from their experience to avoid their mistakes.

Bear in mind throughout this book that you should constantly be asking yourself the question: *Do I Really want to go public?* Is this my only answer? Are there alternatives?

Since the title of the book is *Going Public,* the major portion of the text is devoted to the subject of how to go public, step-by-step. As you review these steps and ask yourself: "Is it for me?" you should also be considering the alternative methods of financing and accomplishing the same results which the book outlines as alternatives.

As an appendix to this book you will find a checklist to take you through the public offering step-by-step, and you will note that the checklist offers several alternatives to public financing. We won't take the space to cover them all here, but we will deal with some of the alternatives and we will suggest ways of enhancing the time-honored techniques to see if they cannot be put to work for you.

Among the more important techniques are:

1. The private placement of equity financing with a venture capital company or through a private offering.
2. The private placement of a debenture loan with a pension fund or an insurance company.

Most of the larger investment banking houses are constantly looking for companies not yet quite ready to go public, either because they have not been in business long enough or their earnings record is not good enough or the timing is not right. These companies, if they show the proper prospects for growth or are in an industry which the investment banking house considers is "ripe" for a public offering, are good prospects for what the underwriting houses call "private placement."

In some cases, the underwriting house will buy a percentage of the growing corporation's stock for a group of insiders (such as the partners of the underwriting house) to keep the stock "on the shelf" until the time is right to sell it to the public. Since these partners in underwriting houses are sophisticated investors, they can be expected to put money into businesses which would not pass muster with the SEC or with less worldly-wise investors. Since the market is more limited, we can expect that these sophisticated investors will exact their price, by paying less for the stock than the public would, if the company were ready for a public offering.

PRIVATE PLACEMENTS: THE PROS AND CONS

On the other hand, the private investments of Wall Street banking houses have launched many a new industry to the profit of both the industry and the underwriting investors, as well as the public. Frozen foods, *Time* magazine, Transcontinental Pipelines, and the great American Telephone and Telegraph Company were originally launched as private offerings to sophisticated investors.

Entirely aside from the "in-house capabilities" most underwriters have of investing in worthwhile projects themselves, there are the possibilities of privately offering stock to such entities as "SBICs" or other publicly held venture capitalists. They exist in almost every large city in the United States, and some of the better known ones include the Heizer Corp., First Capital Corp., Creative Capital Corp., Techno-Ventures, Midland Capital Corporation, the Rockefeller Bros. Fund, Continental Capital Corporation, Citizens and Southern Capital Corporation, Business Capital Corporation, Boston Capital Corporation, American Research and Development Corp., Greater Washington Investors, Inc. and others too numerous to mention.

In approaching these venture capital companies, it is best to work through someone who knows the particular needs of each of the companies instead of going about it on a shotgun basis. Typically, underwriters, lawyers, professional finders, and accountants who have dealt with these venture capital companies before know the needs and eccentricities of each one of them. Many of these venture capitalists will make loans; others want only common stock; some take a combination of both; but all are as anxiously looking for you as you are for them.

Since these venture capitalists are in most cases putting out their own money and since they represent a fairly high level of investment sophistication, they are usually able to act quickly in deciding whether or not they want to finance your company.

As we mentioned before, the greater speed and sophistication carries with it certain other costs. In the first place, in many cases they will drive a harder bargain than the public will in a public offering. You will want to push around your pencil and paper to compare costs of public versus private financing, as well as the costs of getting funds from various venture capitalists.

You should bear in mind, of course, that there is a disadvantage, too. If you take money from the venture capitalists, you are going to wind up with a single substantial stockholder instead of distributing your stock in the hands of many people, each of whom will only own a few shares. Obviously, a single 40 percent stockholder is going to have a bigger voice in your business than 1,000 stockholders who, in total, own 40 percent of the company, most of them in the form of 100-share lots or even smaller investments.

PRIVATE PLACEMENT OF DEBENTURE LOANS WITH INSURANCE COMPANIES AND PENSION FUNDS

Now, let us take a look at the private investment of debenture loans, which is usually done with an insurance company, a large commercial banking organization, a pension fund, or other institutional investors. In looking for one of these debenture loans, you must bear in mind three facts:

1. Your loan must be large enough to be interesting to the lender, economically. They will, in most cases, be unwilling to process small loans. To many lenders, even $1 million is a small loan, and they are not interested in deals less than that.

2. Also, the private placement loan, being a loan and not an equity investment, in most cases involves a relatively short period of repayment. That means you must be prepared to pay the money back pretty quickly out of earnings. If your earnings are not going to be sufficient, then the private placement loan is not a substitute for equity financing.

3. Furthermore, most private debenture loans contain quite a number of restrictions concerning the way you can operate your business after the loan is made. These will be discussed in greater detail later, but you must take those restrictions into consideration in thinking through whether you want to obtain a private placement loan.

RESTRICTIONS IN PRIVATE DEBENTURE LOANS

Let's take a look at some of the restrictions generally found in an insurance-company debenture loan. What kind of restrictions are usually found in a private placement? Here are some typical clauses found in a number of debenture agreements which I have examined:

1. *Working capital restrictions:* The loan becomes due and payable in the event the borrower does not keep a certain working capital ratio at all times. In other words, the buyer must keep himself in a predefined liquid position in order for the loan to continue to remain in force. Such working capital restrictions are bothersome compared with the unrestricted possibilities of equity financing.

2. *Duty of supplying financial information:* While a similar duty is generally required of public corporations, the private placement generally permits the lender to require more detailed financial statements than are generally granted the public, and sometimes the duty of supplying financial information is coupled with the lender's right to audit your books and records.

3. *Limitations on debt:* Many private placements make the loan terminable in the event that the first debt exceeds a certain predetermined amount or formula. Again, a restriction on the free operating ability of your business.

4. *Dividend limitations and limitations on "insider" salaries and emoluments:* Regardless of the tax consequences to you, most private placements restrict the amount of money which may be drawn out by stockholders and officers as long as the loan is outstanding. While it is true that this is a necessary protection for the lender, the borrower must ask what the ultimate cost of this limitation may be.

5. *Limitation on right to merge, pledge, or consolidate:* Future corporate expansion in many cases depends on the corporation's ability to merge with other growing corporations or its ability to "hock" itself by pledging its assets. Severe restrictions on both of these rights are often inserted for the protection of the lender. Though these may inhibit the borrower, the borrower should ask itself if it wants a private placement, and whether the private placement is none the less worthwhile—to be replaced by equity financing at a later date. In other words, the private placement may tide you over; there is nothing to prevent your paying off a loan at a later date.

6. *Insurance requirements:* Many private placements require substantial amounts of casualty and life insurance to be taken out, which increases the cost of the loan to the borrower. This is particularly true when the lender is a casualty or life carrier.

7. *Loan, stock, and investment restrictions:* Many private placements inhibit the making of loans by the borrower and limit the investments the borrower may make in other companies. Exchanges of stock, in some cases, are also restricted.

You must weigh these restrictions against your own future plans, and, in any case, you must be prepared to negotiate on some of them. It is impossible to tell how many of these restrictions you will be able to get modified at a particular time; the result will depend on your negotiating ability, the money market at a particular time, and the size of your loan.

Do not abandon private placement without at least studying it. In many cases, long term loans available under private placement may tide you over until your company reaches a higher equity financing status. In other words, private placement may offer cheaper money for a temporary period of time while your company "grows" to a better "going public" status.

Private placement can be done more quickly, in many cases, than going public. Do not overlook this important field of long term and relatively low cost funds.

DO IT YOURSELF?

Should you try to sell your own stock to the public instead of using an underwriter? Many growing firms find themselves in the position where outsiders (such as suppliers and customers) ask to invest in the company. Using these friendly investors as a source of expansion capital has certain advantages and a number of disadvantages. In the first place, until you test these offers of capital, you cannot be sure of what they mean. Many growing firms have had friends, customers, and suppliers beg them to be permitted to make investments in the company. When the time comes to call on these sources, however, many businessmen find that their friends, customers, and suppliers back out of their promises gracefully. Some may still want to come in, but you can be sure of one thing: Everybody who was interested in the abstract will not be interested enough to put up a check.

So, if you should ever attempt to call on these funds, you may have difficulty predicting in advance exactly how much money you will be able to raise and how long it will take you. True, if you do an effective job of being your own underwriter, you will make a saving of underwriting commissions; and, if you keep the number of offerees down, you may save the cost of SEC registration together with the accounting and legal fees involved.

More about avoiding SEC registration later. At this point it is enough to point out that if you are able to avoid this, there will be a substantial saving.

SOME PROBLEMS IN "DOING IT" YOURSELF

The difficulty of predicting exactly how many of your investors will come through with money when you need it is the major problem involved in placing your own equity financing with friends, neighbors, suppliers, and relatives.

Suppose you need half a million dollars by September 15th. You plan to sell this stock to ten buyers at $50,000 each. But, further suppose that you must have this $500,000 no later than September 15th, because that is the amount of a payment you are going to need on a new plant you are planning to build.

Suppose that you start selling your stock, and you are only able to sell $250,000 worth. What have you accomplished? You are in very bad shape when you consider that you have a half-million dollar commitment to meet by September 15th. You are $250,000 short, and a miss is as good as a mile in public financing.

What is even worse, unless you have found some way of protecting yourself in advance by drawing up the proper subscription agreement, you may have $250,000 worth of stockholders, find that their funds are not sufficient to help you, and yet, since they have bought stock, they are investors—partners in your business. This gives them a voice in your business and can make them deadly nuisances.

In other words, you have had all the disadvantages of going public and none of the advantages.

If you need a definite amount of capital by a definite date, this informal sell-it-yourself type of financing is probably not your answer. On the other hand, if you don't mind taking in outsiders and plan to sell small amounts of stock over a fairly regular basis, thus building up your equity in accordance with a predetermined plan, informal financing may make sense.

You will have to decide for yourself which program you want to undertake, taking into consideration the lower cost of do-it-yourself financing as against its unpredictability.

OTHER DISADVANTAGES

Another disadvantage, aside from the uncertainty of the amount which can be raised by informal financing is the fact that you do not get broad public distribution for your stock. In other words, you are not building up a following for the next step in your expansion program.

Most companies, when they go public, sell some of their stock now because of a temporary capital need, but they look forward to selling more stock or more bonds at a later date. By running a genuine public financing, they get broad distribution and, they hope, a broad following for future issues.

NO DISTRIBUTION

If you sell your stock yourself on an informal basis to a list of friends and suppliers, you are not accomplishing broad distribution at all. You are not building a potential list of customers for future issues, in most cases. Indeed, the narrowly based do-it-yourself issue suffers from the further disadvantage that when, as, and if you decide to go truly public, you may have to buy back or otherwise get rid of the informal public stock you previously issued.

You will find, in many cases, that the kind of charter requirements suitable for informal public issues are by no means sufficient to pass the more difficult tests of Wall Street or LaSalle Street. Accordingly, should you do informal financing now, you may have trouble at a later date when you truly decide to go public.

Be sure that you have planned not only the first step in your public financing, but your second and third steps, too.

If you are only interested in raising a limited sum of money on a one-shot basis and you don't intend to do a second offering at a later date, perhaps the saving you will make on running your own informal stock sales program makes sense.

But, if you intend to do a truly public stock offering at a later date, be careful about interim informal equity raising now.

WARNING ON INFORMAL FINANCING

In any event, as a word of warning, if you intend to sell your own stock, be sure that you enter into contingent subscription agreements with your subscribers. Those contingent agreements should provide, essentially, that if a certain amount of stock is not sold, investors will get their money back and the entire deal is off.

You do not want to be in the position of selling a minimal amount of stock and tying yourself down to issuing those shares. You may find that you have gotten some public stockholders (a nuisance) without raising substantial amounts of money. Be certain to protect yourself against that eventuality.

THE MERGER ROUTE

Here is the merger or acquisition method of getting your stock before the public: A corporation can go public by exchanging its stock with the stock of a publicly held corporation so that it gets back for its owners publicly held stock. In that way it "takes the company public." You broaden your stockholder base without having to go through the complexities of a public securities offering. If you want to exchange your closely held private shares for publicly traded stock, the merger or acquisition of a publicly held corporation is a relatively simple route to follow.

Being acquired by the right company can broaden your stockholder base, give you public security, and add the acquiring company's management base to yours.

In some cases, the "up-stream" merger technique is being used, in which a small private company arranges to acquire control of a public company to broaden its investor base and control of assets. In some cases, the entire transaction can be financed with short term bank loans. The transaction, some years back, in which a smaller company acquired the huge "Ethyl" leaded gasoline company was an example of this kind of up-stream merger. The acquiring company accomplished two results: It broadens the stockholder base and it grows at the same time it goes public.

Another technique of going public which was popular some years ago, but which is now out of favor as a result of SEC hostility, was the technique of a private corporation taking over the "shell" of a listed corporation or a publicly traded corporation, and thereafter exchanging stock. Since the acquired corporation was in most cases a "shell" containing few assets and, in many cases, had a poor earnings record, the sole purpose of the shell acquisition was to avoid the time-consuming technique of a public offering of new securities. Merely by exchanging stock for the acquired shell, the acquiring corporation was able to acquire an "instant list" of public stockholders: to wit, the holders of the old (acquired) corporation's public stock (the shell).

All of these more sophisticated techniques such as mergers, acquisitions, and shell corporations require careful study and analysis by accountants, lawyers, and investment bankers, and are beyond the scope of this work, except to alert you to the possibility that there are other ways of getting your stock into the hands of the public entirely aside from coming out with a new stock issue.

2

ADVANTAGES OF GOING PUBLIC

Now that we have touched on some of the alternatives to going public, let's get back to the main stream of our thoughts. What are the advantages of going public? Most of them will be discussed in greater detail later; but let's touch on some of the major advantages now, so that when the detail picture comes in, we will see the framework on which it is to hang.

THE INSIDER'S VIEW

Let us suppose that you and several members of your family control a growing corporation in a desirable industry. Suppose you wish to offer shares to the public. You plan that the public corporation will have 150,000 shares and you intend to keep 60 percent of those shares in your own hands (or 90,000 shares for you and your group); the other 60,000 (or 40 percent) will be issued to the public. As things stand now, before the public financing, you and your group own 100 percent of the outstanding stock of the corporation.

The corporation has a present book value of $200,000. As you look around, you, as the sole stockholders of a privately held corporation, often feel "locked in." It is true that your corporation has a book value of $200,000, but you know that it would be difficult for you to sell the business to realize $200,000 if you needed the money to pay a state tax purposes estate or for some other personal reason.

Traditionally, it has been hard to sell closely held businesses for the simple reason that you must go to a single buyer and ask him to come up with $200,000. This means you are dealing with a sophisticated buyer who ordinarily is under no compulsion to buy your business; he has several other investment opportunities available to him at all times.

YOU ARE LOCKED IN

Often, such privately held businesses are unable to realize 100 cents on the dollar for their book value and have to sell at substantially below book.

However, you will be in a much better position if you should decide to sell your business in smaller pieces (in other words, if you should decide to sell 100-share lots to the public instead of trying to sell the entire business to one outfit for $200,000).

Retailing your business will put you in the driver's seat; wholesaling it limits the number of potential customers severely.

So, you decide to sell 40 percent of your 150,000 shares. In other words, you are going to sell 60,000 shares of your stock to the public. It is planned that those 60,000 shares will be sold for the account of the corporation; that is, the proceeds of this stock sale will not go into your individual pocket, but rather, into the corporate bank account.

Let's further assume that you have decided to sell those 60,000 shares for $5.00 per share. Of course, the question of how the sales price of each share should be fixed is a more complicated question and is negotiated between you and the underwriter. It will usually depend on a number of factors which will be discussed elsewhere.

But for present purposes, let's assume that you and the underwriter have agreed that the stock will get good public acceptance at $5.00 a share and that 60,000 shares, or 40 percent of the company, is the right amount to sell. The 60,000 share will gross $300,000.

Of course, you will have to deduct underwriters charges, legal and accounting fees, the printing bill, the cost of engraving certificates, hiring transfer agents, etc. Let's assume that all of these deductions total $50,000.

Therefore, although you gross $300,000, the corporation will pocket only $250,000 after the issue is completed. Note that the $250,000 is going into the corporate till; no stock has been sold for the insiders.

INSIDERS BETTER OFF

Let us now go back and look at the position of the insiders as a result of this public stock issue. If 40 percent of the stock was sold at $5.00 per share, is it unreasonable to assume that the other 90,000 shares now held by the insiders are worth $5.00 per share?

Aside from the fact that a very large block of stock will be sold at one time, it is reasonable to assume that if you have sold 40 percent of the company at $5.00 a share, if the company does well, you will be able to sell the other 60 percent at $5.00 per share, also. In fact, if the company shows an excellent record, you may even to be able to get more money for your stock on the second issue than was possible on the first.

ANOTHER LOOK AT THE FIGURES

Let us go back and look at those figures once again. You will recall that when we started out we had a group of inside stockholders who owned a business with a net worth of approximately $200,000 and that, if they sold this business to a single corporation or buyer, they would have great difficulty in getting the full $200,000.

Yet, by going public, we have pointed out that it was not unreasonable to assume that they might be able to get $300,000 for 40 percent of the business. We concluded that by retailing your business in small pieces, you might get a substantially better price for it than if you wholesaled it.

Let's take a closer look at those figures once again and at some of the ramifications of them. Note that on the first issue the public put $250,000 into the corporate till. That $250,000, when added to the old net worth of the corporation which had been $200,000, gave the corporation a new net worth of $450,000.

The public only owns 40 percent of the corporation; the insiders own 60 percent. If you examine the figures closely, you will discover that the public only owns $180,000, or 40 percent of $450,000, while the insiders own the remaining 60 percent, or $270,000 of book value.

In other words, merely by going public, the value of the insiders' stock on a book basis has increased by $70,000.

Put another way, from the insiders' viewpoint, although they have not put another dime into the corporation, as a result of going public and from the funds put up by the public investor, they have increased the book value of their own stock by some $70,000. Of course, it is true that the $70,000 increase in the book value of their stock is merely a paper profit. Nothing has been done for the insiders that can put any money in their pockets as of the present moment.

For the insiders to get some money out, they must sell all or a portion of their retained 60 percent to the public, also. Or they could liquidate the corporation, but I am assuming that they have no intention of doing that. On such a liquidation, the corporation is not likely to bring book value for the same reasons discussed before. Our insiders have decided that their sole future, their sole ability to bail themselves out of the corporation, lies in a secondary public issue. Until they sell some of their own insider stock (60 percent of the company), they have not made a dime for themselves.

SECONDARY ISSUES

Let us assume, then, that our insiders have their eye on that second public offering of stock. They are anxious to sell additional stock at at least the same $5.00 per share price, and, preferably, at an even higher price. Let us assume that our insiders, through skillful management of the business, are able to make their earnings increase.

Growth or earnings increase is obviously the key to the entire plan. Let us assume that the earnings picture is such that after a year of public ownership the reported earnings of the corporation increase the market value of the stock from $5.00 per share to $6.00 per share.

As the public looks at it, the $300,000 investment in the corporation looks like a pretty good one. In a year, the public's investment has increased some 20 percent, from $5.00 per share to $6.00 per share, and the investors have made themselves $60,000 on their $300,000 investment.

But, remember, the insiders have been standing by and watching the market, too. The insiders own the other 60 percent of the stock, and their 90,000 shares have a potential market value of $540,000 at $6.00 per share.

Whereas a year ago, before they went public, the insiders owned 100 percent of the stock of a $200,000 book value corporation, and whereas they would have been very lucky to get the $200,000 for the corporation if they had to sell, they now find themselves in the position where they own $540,000 worth of marketable stock.

GETTING A BETTER PRICE ON
THE SECONDARY ISSUE

Presumably, as a result of having a 20 percent increase in market value over the last year, the insiders have behind them a group of satisfied stockholders and a number of underwriters who would be only too happy to sell all or part of their stock to the public. Our insiders have increased their equity from a "locked in" $200,000 to a presumably readily marketable $540,000 in securities.

Of course, we have oversimplified the case here. You may argue that the insiders will not be able to sell all of their stock at $6.00; that 90,000 shares will be a pretty large block to sell; and that if the outsiders see that all the insiders are selling out, the bottom will fall out of the market.

None the less, if all our insiders wanted to do was to get out their $200,000, and if their stock were currently selling at $6.00, they would only have to sell some 33,000 shares to the public—which would leave them with all of their money out of the corporation and with approximately 60,000 shares still left in their pockets as their share of the future growth possibilities of the corporation.

This is the kind of leverage that has enabled the American economy to grow and has helped capable management get million-dollar capital gains out of healthily growing corporations.

GROWTH DYNAMICS

Stripped down to its simplest form, a plan only requires a good, rapidly growing corporation. For such corporations, the public and the institutional investor will pay a substantial premium. If yours is such a corporation, the opportunities of going public open a vast future.

PINPOINTING SOME PROBLEMS

One of the major mental blocks facing insiders when they plan to go public is the hesitancy with which they face taking in the public as a new partner. Closely held corporations which have developed a successful method of operation such as this method fear something new. However, many alert managements realize that the privately held corporation in today's money and tax markets faces certain limitations.

THE MOST COMMON PROBLEM

Will the insiders lose control if they sell any great portion of their stock to the public? If your underwriter gets broad distribution for your stock, so that you wind up with a couple of thousand shareholders each owning 100 shares or less, you may be able to issue as much as 70 or 80 percent of your voting stock, retaining only 20 or 30 percent for yourself, and still have effective voting control. The industrial giants who have several hundred thousand stockholders find that effective voting control may be as little as a few percentage points, because the public stock is so widely disbursed.

There are other ways of maintaining voting control, among them, the issuance of two classes of stock. In some cases, nonvoting stock is retained by the insiders; in other cases, two classes of stock are issued—one that has preferential voting rights over the other.

AVOID LOSING CONTROL

Thus, management stock may be permitted to elect ten directors; public stock may be permitted to elect only five. Thus, management will be assured of controlling two-thirds of the board of directors, no matter what the public does.

It is not the function of this section to discuss whether you will be better off using voting and nonvoting stock or whether you would be better off using stock that has preferential treatment on election of directors. These subtle differences will depend on the rest of your issue, and you would be well advised to discuss these features in the light of your current marketing conditions with your underwriter.

There have been times when the public has refused to accept one of these packages and, at the same time, has accepted another type. The sole point I wish to make here is that:

1. In a widely dispersed public corporation, 51 percent of the stock is not required for effective control.
2. Such devices as weighted voting rights and multiple classes of stock may limit the public's ability to elect a majority of the board.

We are often asked whether the public knows if the stock being sold to it is offered on behalf of the issuing corporation or whether it is the insiders who are selling stock. The answer is that if the stock is being sold pursuant to SEC registration, the public must be informed in the SEC prospectus whether the money is going into the corporate treasury or whether it is going into the pockets of insiders who are bailing out their own stock.

DO YOU NEED THE MONEY?

We have made it seem very simple to go public. We have stated that on your first time around you are most likely to be selling stock for the account of the corporation and putting the funds into the corporation. We also assumed that by putting these funds into the corporation skillful management automatically increased earnings.

But, can *you* do that? That is the key question. Do you really have a use for the money? We have discovered that many clients who planned to go public have not thought the problem through to the bitter end. They have dreamed about going public because their competitors have gone public. They realize that going public will give them personal estate advantages, and they have planned to go public so that they will be able at some later date to unload some of their own stock on the public.

But, will they be able to do it? We have stated before that the key to their being able to make a successful second offering of the stock depends on the first stocks going up in price. Such an increment in value can only come out of the future growth of the corporation; but, will the corporation continue to grow?

Not unless the management has a plan to use the money it is raising from the public for some successful purpose. Here, many new public corporations fall flat. If you have not planned in advance for the use of the money, do not go public. (There are some exceptions to the rule in service companies that sometimes do not require public funds.)

DON'T MAKE THIS MISTAKE

Ordinarily, if the management has made no intelligent plans for use of the money raised from the public, the market value of the stock will fall like a lead weight. I will give you two examples:

One client of mine went public and banked a substantial amount of money from the proceeds of the public sale. It was planned to use those funds to buy other businesses and to expand. However, the company neither had any specific businesses in mind, nor did it have the personnel with which to expand. For the better part of two years the funds lay in an unproductive bank account, while management ran from one unsuccessful venture to another, desperately trying to put the money out.

The result was the dissipation of management's energies, increased overhead, unsuccessful side ventures, net losses, and severe deterioration of stock prices. The possibility of a secondary issue for the benefit of the insiders was then hopeless. Why? The answer is simple: no advance planning; no personnel; no real need for the money.

EXPANSION VIA PUBLIC STOCK

On the other hand, another client had for some time been buying and merging small businesses in kindred lines into its own operation; unfortunately, such purchases depleted working capital. The client planned to go public so that it could acquire such businesses in the future with stock instead of cash—or, at least, with part stock and part cash.

The client had established a technique and a formula for buying these businesses in such a way that it recouped its investment in from two to three years—a return of from 33 1/3 to 50 percent per annum, before taxes.

SETTING THE STAGE FOR STOCK ZOOMS

The result was that when the company went public, it was able to hoard its cash and to buy additional businesses at a decreasing cost to itself, as its stock zoomed in the market. Here was a client that had both the plan and the personnel to utilize the proceeds of the public issue.

Indeed, the publicity and improved credit standing of the second client as a result of going public has resulted in his receiving offers of businesses for sale that he could not have gone near a couple of years ago. The result was a healthy, thriving, growing business, with wonderful opportunities for a secondary issue and excellent enhancement of the client's own stock holdings.

The first client, without a plan, will be lucky if it can ever straighten out its mess. It did not truly need the money; or, if it needed the money, it had no plan to use it.

HOW TO FINANCE CORPORATE GROWTH—
A RECAPITULATION OF THE VARIOUS POSSIBILITIES

A public offering of securities, in the right market, can provide additional funds for expansion. It also provides a new kind of paper (stock) for the acquisition of additional companies, and the same paper can be used to keep key executives happy (stock options). The issuance of a public stock fixes the market value for estate tax purposes of the insiders' holdings and offers a more liquid market for the estate to unload the stock when the time comes.

Finally, a public offering creates a built-in market for secondary offerings by the insiders at such later dates as they decide to unload their stock in the company.

As mentioned above, there are disadvantages, too. To the uninitiated, the requirements of a public offering involving the disclosure of insider arrangements and secret business contracts is a difficult burden to carry. Difficulties of calculating the best time to market the issue and the amount of time it takes to prepare the prospectus and other material, as well as the absorption of executive personnel in this task are all problems for the new company facing the public market for the first time.

The difficulty of reversing the situation once you have decided to go public, even if you decide it is a mistake, is an important consideration. You can go public only once during your business lifetime. To get the stock back from the public afterwards, if you decide to "go private" again is an extremely difficult and expensive task. Some companies have done it and have survived—but not many.

The added responsibility to public stockholders and the necessity of opening an entire new line of communications with the public (public relations) are also tasks foreign to many efficient businessmen who are used to running one-man companies and accounting to no one. Stockholders and their lawyers ask difficult, penetrating questions that many managers feel are none of their business; they demand results; they expect dividends; they are disenchanted with long-range projects which involve extensive and expensive research and development (even though these may be in the best interests of the company in the long run).

There are continual responsibilities to the public such as the responsibility of disclosing favorable and unfavorable information to the public promptly (Texas Gulf Sulphur case). There are continuing financial reporting requirements, and there will be ultimately the impact of the proxy rules and the liabilities under §16(b) of the Securities Act.

Being public is an entirely new way of life. It adds an overlay of public relations and communications people; it requires extensive time on the part of upper echelon executives; it requires high initial and continuing costs in time and money and in consultation with lawyers, accountants, and other professionals in coping with the myraid of state, Federal, and local regulatory requirements and reporting responsibilities.

To avoid some of these problems, the private placement has been considered. We have listed in the chapter some of the venture capitalists, including the public venture corporations and the private ones, such as J.H. Whitney, Payson and Trask, Davis and Rock, and W.A. Burden.

The private placements are faster and generally have a lower legal and accounting paper work cost. You are not tied to the workload of the SEC, nor to the expensive requirements of specially audited financial statements in a form acceptable to the SEC. You do not have either the extensive legal or printing bills involved. There is nothing that the public can see; all your business secrets are still intact, except to your new venture capital stockholder.

But watch this: If you plan to have a private offering and avoid SEC registration, you must be certain that the offering is really "private" and that you have met the legal requirements of exemption from the SEC statute. It is clear that you can avoid them, if the acquirer is a single investment banking house which buys for its insiders or places it with a single insurance company or other professional.

It is by no means as clear, however, if the investment banking house goes out and contacts fifty or sixty investors and puts together a group for you. In that event, you and the investment banking house may both be underwriters; and afterwards, of course, if the deal does not turn out too well, the offerees may decide to sue both of you on the theory that this was a public offering or that they were entitled to some of the protections of the SEC statutes.

Furthermore, while you may be avoiding an SEC registration now, you may just be deferring the problem. In many cases, the private investors may want to get out of the stock by selling it to the public and, as part of the investment package, they may make you contract with them to register the stock at a later date. In addition, they may exact additional pounds of flesh by requiring you to bank portions of the money with them, to retain them as financial consultants, or to lock yourself into their use in any future underwriting; and they may require of you a greater dilution of your stock than the public would; and they may offer you a lower price than the public would.

If you are looking for a private placement, many of the tests would be the same as if you were going public. Private investors want to know how they are going to bail out their stock and they view your stock in terms of its future "romance" value to the public. Are you in a "hot industry"? What is your growth rate? When do you expect to go public? Obviously, they want you to be as close to going public as possible; to be as ready to go public as possible; and they want to buy your stock at a price less than the public would.

In general, private placements have been weak where the public market has been weak; and they have been strong where the public market has been strong.

I suppose that is about it. You have now seen the major differences between private placement and public placement of your securities.

3

SPECIAL ADVANTAGES OF GOING PUBLIC

Another advantage of having publicly traded stock is that the stock value is readily ascertainable. To some, there is a substantial estate tax advantage in having readily marketable securities with a definable value. However, many small businessmen who have all or a major portion of their estate locked into a single privately held corporation leave their estates with a difficult administrative problem.

SOLVING ESTATE PROBLEMS

The question of what your stock was worth for estate tax purposes involves almost certain litigation. You are dealing merely with an opinion—the opinion of the government's appraiser against the opinion of your estate's appraiser.

On the other hand, when you have publicly held stock, you are dealing in most cases not with an opinion but with a reasonably ascertainable fact.

Of course, if the stock is traded on a major exchange, there can be little or no dispute. One merely looks on the stock market page on the date of death and, aside from the concept of a discount for large blocks, one is able to ascertain the fair market value of the stock. However, I have had clients who felt that they might do better if the fair market value of their stock were not as readily ascertainable and if they were able to litigate what the stock was worth.

Such clients are the exception that proves the rule. Most clients would like to know where they stand in advance and would like to avoid the uncertainties of tax litigation, particularly since public stock is ordinarily readily marketable with the result that it can be self-liquidating on death.

Going public, then, has two estate advantages: First, the value can be fixed with greater ease; and, second, money can be raised for the stock with greater ease.

GIFT TAX PROBLEMS

These are similar to the estate tax problems discussed above. When you have privately held stock there is always a question as to what the value is on any particular day. If you own 100 percent of a closely held corporation and if you give some shares to your children, what are they worth? Shall you use book value? Shall you capitalize earnings? Is there hidden good will?

VALUATION PROBLEMS

Whatever you do, if you are dealing with closely held stock, you are going to have a problem with the tax examiner. There is no absolute certainty concerning the fair market value of a closely held corporation (unless you can demonstrate that the company was recently purchased or sold). In most cases you are dealing with a successful business owned by the person who built it up. If you look at the history of the business, you will see that it started with two thin dimes, and now, after a quarter of a century of work, it has a book value of a quarter-million or half-million dollars.

The growth rate has been 15, 20 or 30 percent a year—even after taxes. As a matter of fact, the first question that comes up is: Have all the earnings been reported on the books?

Now, the successful businessman wants to give away control of the company to a trust for his children; or he wants to give some stock to a university; or he wants to make some shares available to his key employees. What are they worth? Valuation questions, for tax purposes, involve constant litigation with the government, because two honest men's opinions on value can differ, and the expert you hire is almost certain to differ from the government's expert.

AN EXPENSIVE PROBLEM

Nor is the problem—whether estate or gift tax—an inexpensive one to cope with. Gift tax rates are almost 20 percent at $50,000. They are almost 30 percent at $1 million. Estate taxes are 22 percent at $100,000; almost 40 percent at $1 million.

Suppose you own 100 percent of the stock of a corporation that has a half-million dollar book value and earns $100,000 a year after taxes. Is your business worth ten times earnings (a million dollars)? In some industries, public corporations that do not earn as much as 20 percent on their book value are being valued at 15 and 20 times earnings.

If your business is in one of these "hot" industries, is it worth $500,000 (book value) or $2 million (20 times earnings)? If you give away 25 percent of the stock to your son or daughter, the gift tax will be entirely different if the 25 percent is valued at book value ($125,000) or at 20 times earnings ($500,000).

The gift tax on $125,000 is only $20,000; but on one-half million, it is $109,000. If you were to leave this stock to a member of your family through your estate and if you were taxed at the 40 percent bracket, a difference between one value and another could be 40 percent of $375,000 or $150,000.

Not only does owning closely-held corporation stock leave you with estate and gift tax problems, but it leaves you with the problem of financing the payment of the tax. Closely-held stock is hard to sell. There is no ready market for it. If the tax agent tells you that you own $150,000 on a gift of stock you gave to your son, you may find it hard to raise the money by selling some of the stock. If you own publicly held stock, there can be little dispute as to what the value is; you just look at the stock pages in your local newspaper. Also with publicly held stock there is no problem in selling some to raise the money to pay the tax.

ONE PRACTICAL TIP

If you intend to go public, it is often advisable to make gifts of stock *before* going public, rather than afterwards. In spite of the fact that you have a valuation problem, you have a ceiling on your tax risk. Certainly, closely held stock is worth less than publicly traded stock. So, if you make a gift of your stock *before* you go public or, better yet, before you even start drawing up the prospectus or have an underwriting agreement, you will be giving away an asset which would appreciate above book value when you go public. While private, book value plus a smaller earnings multiplier is appropriate.

While there is a risk of litigation in this gift of private stock prior to going public you often can make substantial gift and estate tax savings by giving the stock away while it is closely held and there is no market for it, instead of waiting to give it away after the stock has gone public, when there is iron clad evidence as to its value.

In other words, if you are prepared to take some tax risk, you have a ceiling on the up side (equal to the issue price), and there may be a substantial tax saving by making a gift before you have gone public. Even if you have guessed wrong on valuation, you can always sell some of the stock to liquidate the tax.

ATTRACTING OUTSIDE MANAGEMENT

The publicly held corporation has a very substantial advantage in attracting good second echelon management, and that substantial advantage is the opportunity of offering these people stock option plans and capital gains instead of ordinary income.

Top drawer executives making $30,000 and $40,000 a year find themselves in the 50 to 60 percent tax bracket. Ordinarily, their present income is adequate for their current living expenditures and they cannot be lured away from their present secured jobs to new jobs merely by offering them $10,000 a year more.

To attract these men you must have something more. These top people upon whom the future growth of your business depends are interested mainly in capital gains. Capital gains of less than $50,000 are taxed at half ordinary tax rates, with a maximum ceiling of 35 percent.

When offered a plan which gives them long term capital gains, these top drawer men can see themselves building their own retirement program for their later years, and they can see themselves accumulating estates for the benefit of their families. They cannot see themselves doing this out of ordinary income rates, even with increased pay checks. Thus, any business which cannot offer a sensible stock plan to its employees is constantly in the position of losing its best employees. It is a parasitic business, weakening itself by destroying its strongest members, ultimately to go to its own death.

As a result, progressive businesses find that stock option plans are imperative. In order to mean anything, the stock offered these executives must be marketable. In other words, it must be the stock of a publicly held corporation. In addition, it is almost impossible to set up a stock option plan that means anything in a private corporation.

IMPORTANCE TO KEY PEOPLE

The importance of offering key people capital gains cannot be overstated. If you examine any ten young, growing corporations, you will find that they are working out all kinds of capital gains opportunities for their top people.

One case I recently ran across was that of a publicly held corporation which offered its important junior executives the opportunities of buying up the stocks of supplier corporations (which were gradually being acquired by the parent) with practically guaranteed capital gains opportunities for these key men. Those capital gains opportunities came out of the almost guaranteed growth of the supplier corporation through its relationship with the parent.

In another situation where a corporation was not quite ready to go public, most of its key secondary executives were none the less given opportunities at stock options which would offer great possibilities when the corporation went public in the near future.

When I asked the president of this company why he felt obliged to offer stock to these secondary executives, he said:

> If you have a plan to expand your organization, you've got to make darn sure that the key parts don't fall out while you're busy building the grand scheme. You must lock them in. All of my employees can get a couple of thousand dollars a year more elsewhere, but, once I've got them tied in as stockholders they think twice about leaving. Many of them can go into business for themselves, but they find that the risk of starting up from scratch becomes too great a long shot when assured against their almost guaranteed stock growth if they stay here. Give one of our executives a couple of good years under our stock plan and he'll never leave.

Organizations that plan to expand must recognize the importance of stock option plans to their key men. They must also recognize that the failure to offer these plans to the key men is almost certain to result in their leaving, should such plans be offered to them by a competitor.

On the other hand, now that the tax rules have changed and now that there is an income tax ceiling of 50 percent on earned income, and, since stock market performance during the last couple of years has not been so great, as of the date of this writing many executives prefer to receive cash rather than stock. We cannot predict what will happen at the time you decide to go public, but always keep in the back of your mind that stock options are useful incentives to keep your employees interested in the growth of the company, whether there are tax benefits or not.

Sometimes the tax benefits are more important than the growth incentives; sometimes the growth incentives are more important than the tax benefits; but, in any case, publicly held stock makes both of these incentives more meaningful.

SOME MORE DISADVANTAGES

First of all, remember that if you're going to become a public corporation, you owe the public a duty to run your corporation as though the public owned it. No longer can you charge your wife or your girlfriend off on the corporate books. The public corporation finds that its travel and entertainment expenses must now be limited to travel and entertainment expenses involving corporate business. The company yacht must have a bona fide company purpose; it cannot be used for the boss's vacation fling.

If you violate these simple rules, you will find yourself faced with stockholder's derivative suits which are expensive to defend and are disastrous, public relations-wise. Even worse, should you lose, you may have to pay back to the corporation out of your own pocket judgments running to six figures, together with fantastic legal costs.

Face up to it: As soon as you go public, special privileges for insiders must be discarded. If you cannot face up to this new duty, then remain private—do not go public.

Most clients reconcile themselves to giving up these special privileges as part of the cost of going public. They heave a sigh and yearn for the good old days, but they realize that these special privileges are becoming more difficult to get; they are undergoing increasing scrutiny by the Internal Revenue Service, and they can be replaced by greater advantages in the form of stock opportunities at capital gains rates when the corporation goes public.

"YOU ARE IN A GOLD FISH BOWL"

The public corporation must operate in the open. Its contracts, if they are of major importance, will have to be revealed in the SEC prospectus. While it is true that theoretically it is possible to keep a bona fide confidential contract outside of the prospectus with special SEC permission, the right to do so is largely theoretical; the SEC rarely grants such permission, except under the most unusual of circumstances.

WHAT MUST BE REVEALED

Ordinarily, all major contracts become part of the public record, or, at least abstracts from them become part of such record. For example, some of the confidential information you might ordinarily not want to give out involves the expiration dates and terms of major leases in connection with a piece of real estate owned by the corporation or the details of certain "insider" transactions in which majority stockholders sold or conveyed certain properties to the corporation in exchange for stock or cash.

Fairly detailed financial statements become part of the SEC registration. If you list your corporation on a stock exchange, regular statements will have to be issued thereafter, and such statements must give fairly detailed financial data.

Many corporations which never gave financial statements to their major creditors—indeed, never gave financial statements to anyone except possibly their banks—are reluctant to reconcile themselves to the necessary information that must now be exposed.

We suggest that if you are at all reluctant to do this, that you read half a dozen annual reports of competitors of yours and half a dozen recent SEC prospectuses in your field. Look at them carefully and ask yourself whether you are content to reveal the same kind of information about your company. If you have any hesitancy, now is the time to find out.

OTHER CHANGES YOU MUST FACE

Remember that once you become a public corporation, if you are a substantial stockholder in it, your future success depends very much on your helping increase the value of the public stock. Accordingly, the kind of financial information you will issue to the public and the image you will project to the public must be viewed in a new light.

THE IMPORTANCE OF GIVING FINANCIAL INFORMATION

This is a difficult transition for many businessmen to make. One of the wisest businessmen I know spent quite a few months (after he had gone public) bitterly ejecting from his office financial reporters and other "busybodies" who were "prying into" his private business.

These people asked embarrassing questions: Why were my client's sales off 8 percent; what was he doing about closing up an unprofitable plant and was the union going to let him; was there any truth to the rumor that one of the company's product lines had turned out to be a "dog" and that several suits had been started by discontented purchasers?

To someone who never answered questions such as these before—particularly to members of the press who had promptly and gleefully spread his answers across the print where all of his competitors and disgruntled stockholders might read them—the change was a dramatic one. As I mentioned before, this wise businessman spent the first several months stating "no comment" and considering most of his inquirers irritations, time wasters, and pests.

The result was that by refusing to give out information, this businessman deteriorated the value of his stock; people began to think the worst of the company, and analysts, unable to get satisfactory answers, "dumped" the stock.

Since the president and his family own 60 percent of the stock, the net result of his refusal to give out information to "busybodies" was a cool loss to himself of over $100,000 in market value.

Moral: The public corporation depends on the good will of the public. A constant public relations campaign with frank disclosure of management mistakes and realistic appraisal of future management policies is indispensable to a stable market. Good news must be well publicized and bad news explained. Silence is equated with potential bankruptcy proceedings.

GETTING THE MOST FROM OUTSIDE DIRECTORS

The public corporation is going to have one or more outside directors; some of them will be nominees of the underwriter. If you are prepared to put these directors to work and have chosen them wisely, these outside directors can take your business to new heights.

If you continue to run your business as a private little shop and seek to make your directors merely rubber stamps, withholding information from them and treating them as necessary evils, you will fritter away what benefits they might be and you will destroy the future of your stock.

Again, two specific examples will be helpful. A friend of mine, connected with a Wall Street underwriter, is a director of a corporation that recently went public. At his first two meetings of the board of directors, he found the old management quite annoyed at the questions he asked.

How dare he, an outsider, question the decisions of management to enter into new fields of endeavor. He was asking the management why they were buying certain companies; how they intended to finance those purchases; and how long it would take them to get their money out. When the outside director explained to the management that he was inquiring, not to be hostile, but to put his Wall Street experience at their disposal, he met reluctant but nevertheless cooperative answers from the management.

HOW DIRECTORS CAN HELP YOU

As a result, the insiders obtained new insight into what the public looks for in its growth stocks. The management rejected deals suitable for its old corporate history and took on deals much better suited to its new corporate purpose. Deals which overtaxed present management were rejected; deals which offered new expansion possibilities were taken on.

By tapping the know-how of its newly expanded board of directors, this company gradually changed in outlook from a closely held, inside-dominated corporation to a truly public corporation with a long, growing future ahead of it.

BUT HERE IS THE "OTHER SIDE"

Here is an example on the other side of the fence. Another closely held family business worth several million dollars was owned by four brothers where one brother for years had dominated the other three, although all were equally capable in their specialized fields. Some years ago, the three younger brothers, thinking about their own estate plans and the futures of their children, began to talk about going public, over the vigorous objections of the oldest brother.

The three younger men pointed out to the senior brother the advantages of going public—estate liquidity, ability to attract younger second echelon management, stock options and pension plans, and ability to diversify their own personal investment portfolios by liquidating some of the money now tied up in the family corporation and investing it in other securities.

The senior brother opposed this. He argued that the timing was not right; that unless he could get twenty-five times earnings for the stock, the underwriters would be stealing the stock. Reluctantly, he permitted the younger brothers to explore "going public." Several houses were consulted. When the offering price for the new issue stock got to twenty times earnings, the senior brother rudely rejected it and broke off negotiations. They were coming too close to twenty-five times earnings—the asking price.

The problem was that the senior brother was not temperamentally suited for "going public." Under no circumstances was he willing to permit outsiders on the board of directors.

As things now stand, it is he who asks his associates why earnings are off and what they are doing to keep up profits in their departments. If the company had gone public, these questions would be asked by the banks, the underwriters, and third party directors. While this senior brother lives, since he dominates the company and is temperamentally suited only to run the business by himself, his pattern will continue, and the company will not go public.

DO YOU REALLY WANT TO BE PUBLIC?

Who can say he is wrong? Of course, his younger brothers who have different objectives for the corporation can argue that he is ruining the business; wiping out future growth; preventing the acquisition of good second line men and making, for the rest of the family, a difficult estate problem.

On the other hand, senior brother has his own way of life and is happy as he is. He does not want to be the chairman of the board of a public corporation.

You must decide for yourself which of these two corporate examples you will follow. If you feel you cannot live with outsiders on your board of directors, if you feel you must lock them in and if you feel you do not want to maximize their participation in your firm's affairs, perhaps you should abandon all thoughts of going public.

THE FINE POINTS OF DISCLOSURE REQUIREMENTS

Annual financial reports to the SEC for public corporations that qualify (known as Form 10K reports), beginning with January 1, 1971, must be filed within ninety days after the end of the fiscal year. (It used to be 120 days.)

There are a whole batch of new accounting requirements calling for separation according to "various lines of business," if the company operates several divisions.

In addition, Form 10Q, quarterly reports to the SEC, are required which show profit and loss information on a comparative basis, including earnings and dividends per share.

Form 7Q, a special quarterly report for real estate companies to the SEC, has been required since January 1, 1971. The Accounting Principles Board of the American Institute of Certified Public Accountants is now considering a proposal to require financial statements showing the application of funds.

The thrust of these and many more reports (insider trading, proxy solicitations, etc.) is to represent an additional drain on executive time and an additional cost in terms of legal and printing bills, as well as accounting statements for the company that plans to go public to consider.

Since the accounting profession itself is in the midst of a soul-searching review concerning what constitutes "generally accepted accounting principles," with Securities and Exchange Commission stating that it, too, wants a newer, more up-to-date approach, it would be well to check with your accounting firm on the latest regulations in the field. A book such as this cannot possibly keep on top of them; only the looseleaf services and the current releases of the accounting profession itself, through the American Institute of Certified Public Accountants and the SEC, can bring you completely up to date on the subject.

4

DUTIES AND RESPONSIBILITIES
OF PUBLIC CORPORATIONS

This chapter will deal with some of the responsibilities imposed by the courts and the law upon the officers and directors of a public corporation. To owners of closely held corporations who are wont to run their businesses as their private pocketbooks, the change-over to becoming a public corporation can be a startling one. In private corporations, directors' meetings are almost never held. Profit-making opportunities are shifted around from corporation to corporation and from the corporation to its private stockholders based solely on the selfish interests and tax motivations of the insiders.

Once the corporation has gone public, all of this must be a thing of the past. The legal standards imposed on corporate officers and directors are rigid, and severe penalties will be imposed on the pocketbooks of officers and directors who neglect them.

The officers and directors of a public corporation are expected to exercise reasonably prudent care in managing the corporate affairs. Honest intentions, ignorance, and lack of experience do not excuse lack of care.

While it is true that officers and directors are permitted mistakes of business judgment, there comes a point where honest but unwise conduct results in personal liability on the part of the officers and directors. Because the point of no return, where errors of judgment become "negligence," is difficult to define, corporate directors must spread across the corporate minutes evidence of their investigation of all unusual transactions.

It is important to note that corporate officers and directors must be scrupulously honest in all their dealings with the corporation and they must not put themselves in a position where they may act in conflict with the corporation's interests. Extreme care should be used if officers and directors find that they must buy from or sell to the corporation.

CONTROLLING STOCKHOLDERS

Note that special duties to the general stockholders are owed by those stock-holders who "control" the corporation. As we mentioned before, it is entirely possible that control may be exercised by a group of stockholders who own only a few percentage points. When such stockholders are in the position of dominating the corporation and electing its officers and directors with their minority stock holdings, they owe to the rest of the stockholders and to the corporation the same kind of duties as directors and officers do—the duty similar to that of a trustee.

So, if the controlling stockholders deal in an unfair way with the corporation even though they may not be directors or officers, they, too, may find themselves responsible at law for damages.

Of course, *complete* stockholder ratification will avoid any problems, but complete stockholder ratification may mean as much as 100 percent stockholder consent. Thus, a single objecting stockholder may hold the insiders liable if there has been a dissipation of corporate assets, a gift of them, or some fraud.

No ratification of the acts of the insiders can be effective unless that ratification is based on full disclosure. In an attempt to get stockholders to ratify all of the acts done by the officers and directors for the past year, proxy statements often merely state that a blanket endorsement of all the actions by the officers and directors will be approved at the next annual meeting. Such a blanket ratification is worthless.

If there has been a secret transaction, unless it is revealed in the proxy statement, it cannot be released by a blanket ratification. In any case where there have been dealings between the insiders and the corporation, a considerable burden will be put on the insiders to show that the transaction between themselves and the corporation was eminently fair to the corporation. Interested officers and directors should abstain from voting and, indeed, often cannot be counted as part of the quorum in ratifying dealings between themselves and the corporation.

SELLING "CONTROL"

While it is true that the controlling stockholders (and you will remember that the controlling stockholders need not own a majority of the stock) have a right to sell their stock to anyone they choose, sales of "controlling stock" ordinarily command a premium, since the sale of such stock ordinarily means that the buyer will similarly be able to control the corporation.

The right of the insiders to "sell this control" has been limited by the courts. Thus, where the controlling stockholders sell their stock to a buyer who is known to be a "looter of corporate assets," the controlling stockholders may be liable for the damages resulting from such sale.

The higher the premium above market at which control stock is sold, the more likely it is that the insiders will be held to account to the public for their profit. As soon as it becomes apparent that control of the corporation is the object of the sale, instead of a mere block of stock, the sellers may be accountable to the remaining stockholders for their excess profit.

It has been held for many years that if the corporate officers or directors resign for a cash consideration, they are in the position of selling their office, and they must account to the outside stockholders for the proceeds of that sale. This is true even though the sale is disguised as a sale of stock.

If an excess over market value has been paid for the shares and if the stock sale is coupled with a resignation of the inside directors, an almost certain case has been made out that there has been a sale of control for the excess price, with the result that the excess price may be recovered by the other stockholders.

Where the insiders or controlling stockholders are asked to "set up" the corporation so that it will be more liquid and where this setting up of the corporation is made at the request of a purchaser who is without ascertainable means by which said purchaser will finance the purchase of the stock, the sellers are put on guard in the event that the purchaser intends to loot the corporation of its liquid assets as a means of raising the money to pay off the seller.

Setting up the corporation for such a looting prior to the sale of the stock is the legal equivalent of looting the corporation yourself, with the result that a recovery may be made for the corporation or its stockholders who have suffered therefrom.

TAKING ADVANTAGE OF CORPORATE OPPORTUNITIES

Officers, directors, and controlling stockholders are responsible to the corporation and its stockholders if they pocket for themselves an opportunity which came to the attention of the corporation and which the corporation is financially able to undertake.

Often, investigation shows that not only has the insider pre-empted for himself a deal more properly belonging to the corporation, but that corporate funds have been used to investigate the deal and corporate personnel used to exploit it. In the famous Loft-Pepsi Cola case, the court found that Guth used corporate facilities to exploit promotion of the soft drink from which he intended to profit on his own.

REIMBURSEMENT OF EXPENSES
OF STOCKHOLDER LITIGATION

Many corporate charters and by-laws provide that in the event minority stockholder suits are brought against officers and directors, the officers and directors may be reimbursed for their legal expenses in their capacity as officers or directors. Such reimbursement of an officer's or director's expenses by the corporation or the corporate treasury may be made only if the officer or director is not found guilty of negligence or misconduct. Reimbursement of the officer's expenses may not be made where the defendant is found guilty of misconduct.

WHAT YOU MUST DISCLOSE
AND WHAT YOU SHOULD NOT DISCLOSE
TO STOCKHOLDERS, ONCE YOU ARE PUBLIC

The disclosure field has become extremely complicated in the last half-dozen years as a result of both the activities of the Securities and Exchange Commission and the results of certain stockholder litigation such as the famous Texas Gulf Sulpher case.

In general, what both the courts and the SEC are trying to do is to get the insiders to reveal to the public, almost the very minute they learn about it, any factual information or news which might affect the market value of the stock. Insiders cannot be permitted to use their inside knowledge to either buy or sell stock for their own accounts. In addition, there are quite a number of rules propounded by the SEC to prohibit "gun jumping" of an offer in registration—which means that the SEC does not want the management to leak favorable information to the press at the time it has a registration pending, because such outside-of-the-prospectus news has the effect of touting the issue in registration without giving the investors the full facts thought to have been disclosed by the prospectus.

Therefore, we run into a number of problems: You must disclose good and bad news promptly, but you must avoid doing anything outside of the prospectus, if you have a registration pending. The rules look simple, and they appear to be logical; their application, however, is often difficult.

Thus, at a recent annual stockholders' meeting to which many hundreds of stockholders came, the management was forced to tell the stockholders that they could not tell them anything or even hand out the usual quarterly earnings report, because there was a prospectus pending, and the SEC would forbid management to talk until the prospectus was issued and the marketing completed.

What should a public corporation disclose, and what should it abstain from disclosing, in order to put its stockholders in a position to make intelligent decisions about buying? The SEC tells us that the information to be disclosed to the public is information which the stockholders would deem "material." Neither the courts nor the SEC have any kind of objective test to determine what is or what isn't "material," and sometimes it is very difficult to tell in advance.

The insiders in the famous Texas Gulf Sulphur case found themselves in a difficult dilemma in applying the rules. You may recall (since the case was given extensive publicity) that what happened in Texas Gulf Sulphur was that the corporation was carrying on mining explorations in Canada, and the geological team discovered through its test borings what appeared to be a very rich mineral find. They faced a number of difficult decisions. If they revealed this information immediately, they would be harming the company because other prospectors might be encouraged to buy up adjacent lands' rights, to the detriment of the company.

Furthermore, at an early stage it was difficult to tell just how rich the vein was. To be unduly optimistic would be unfair to stockholders. They might purchase additional stock at inflated value only to discover later that the vein was not as rich as they had expected, to their detriment as investors. Thus, the management decided to "sit on the news."

I suppose that if that was all that had happened, there would never have been a Texas Gulf Sulphur case. However, certain insiders in the management took the opportunity of buying "a little stock" as soon as they found out the good news and before it was released to the public. The SEC and certain stockholders sellers sued to recover from the insiders who had purchased the stock on the theory that the insiders had utilized information about the company for their own selfish purposes to the detriment of the other stockholders.

The kinds of information that are generally considered material and which should be disclosed as promptly as available are: earnings; projected earnings; financings and proposed new financings; acquisitions and proposed acquisitions (or divestures); new products and new discoveries.

Generally, management has a right to decide when to disclose information about new discoveries, except when this is coupled with some kind of pattern of purchasing the stock which works to the detriment of third party stockholders. I suppose you might put the rule on an informal basis and say that it is reasonably O.K. to keep a new discovery a secret, if there is some business for it, but God help you if you are buying stock at the same time!

Sales and purchases of stock by insiders should be disclosed; important purchases of stock by insiders *must* be disclosed and, as a matter of fact, the SEC has a special reporting form for it. Litigation, if important, must be disclosed. News on casualty losses (fire or earthquake, etc.) should be disclosed, as should changes in control of the corporation's stockholdings of any importance, as well as important changes in the officers and directors of a corporation.

HOW DO YOU MAKE A DISCLOSURE?

Since a broad distribution of the news is important and since timing is also important, it will not do you much good to send out a letter to the stockholders revealing the news. Generally, one seeks to release the news as quickly as possible, once it is decided that the news is material, and this is accomplished by preparing a press release which goes to such publications as Reuters, the Associated Press, important local newspapers, the *Wall Street Journal*, Dow Jones, etc.

If the stock of the corporation is traded on an exchange, generally, the exchange has rules, too. For example, the New York Stock Exchange has a procedure on disclosure of information which offers guidelines whether you are on the New York Stock Exchange or not.

WHEN DO YOU MAKE DISCLOSURE?

As soon as you decide that something is material, it should be disclosed.

The problem then arises as to whether you have your information straight, before you issue your press release. For example, in the Texas Gulf Sulphur case, a press release could have claimed an important mineralogical discovery before it was absolutely certain and before all the tests were in. Would that have been fair to the stockholders? What if it turned out afterwards that initial tests were wrong and that there had been no important mineralogical discovery? One of the things management should do while it is trying to make up its mind whether the information is accurate or not and whether it warrants a press release is to make sure that maximum security is kept over the information. In other words, as few people as possible should have access to the business secret. The more people who have such access, the greater is the possibility that some parties will be the beneficiaries of this secret information and use it for trading in the stock, while others will be kept from it. I suppose that if no one knows and no one acts on it, that is all right. It is just that if some people act, and others do not, on the basis of such secret information, you have a Texas Gulf Sulphur-type of situation.

SUMMARY

The public corporation must be dealt with fairly by its officers and directors. Even controlling stockholders may not take advantage of the corporation. When in doubt, don't do it. Even successful defenses of stockholder suits are costly and make for poor public relations. If you are not prepared to lean over backwards, you are not temperamentally suited to run a public corporation.

5

HOLDING DOWN THE COSTS
OF GOING PUBLIC

Obviously, the cost of selling a large bond or common stock issue to the public varies with the complexity of the deal and its size. A very complicated combination of stock and bond financing involving the preparation of the long debenture agreement together with the additional printing bill involved will cost much more in legal, printing, and accounting fees than a simple common stock issue.

A company which requires the auditing of sixty branches and the preparation of complicated consolidated financial statements will have a substantially higher accounting bill than a newly organized company where the sole asset is cash in the bank.

WHAT KINDS OF EXPENSE?

Let us, however, examine some averages; but, before we do that, let's first see the types of expenses which go into a public stock or bond offering.

First, there are legal bills; there are fees in connection with the preparation of the prospectus; fees in connection with the preparation of an agreement with the underwriters; fees in connection with such work as recapitalization of the corporation and redrawing or modification of the corporate by-laws, etc.

There are the underwriter's legal expenses which are either directly or indirectly paid by the corporation going public. They are paid directly by contracts providing for a lump sum payment to the underwriter's counsel; or they are paid indirectly by an increase in the underwriting commission to cover legal expenses.

There are also accounting expenses, covering the cost of certified audits.

There are also printing costs for long, carefully printed prospectuses involving quite a bit of overtime work, and, in many cases, a number of revisions or amendments. In addition, there are the costs of preparing stock cerificates which may be simple printed certificates or steel engravings.

There are transfer agent's fees and registrar's fees, which are required to pay the independent banking organization that will handle the issuing and transferring of your stock certificates.

LESSONS TO BE LEARNED FROM SEC STUDIES

Studies have been made both by the SEC and private foundations of the cost of public offerings. The costs were expressed as percentages of the total issue. Included in those costs were underwriting commissions, accounting fees, issuer's legal fees, and printing costs. Generally, the percentage which the costs of the offering will take depends upon the size of the issue. In other words, there were a number of brackets: A common stock issue from $1 million to $2 million; a common stock issue from one-half million dollars to $1 million; a common stock issue of $300,000, etc.

The SEC's study showed that a number of underwriting commissions, legal and accounting costs, and printing bills on common stock issues during a five-year period were as follows:

Size of Issue	*Percentage of Expenses*
$1,000,000 to $2,000,000	11½ percent
$500,000 to $1,000,000	15 percent
$300,000 to $500,000	22 percent
$300,000 or less	25 percent

It is important to note that those percentages represent cash expenses on the part of the issuers. They do not represent the expenses of giving away "cheap stock" or "stock options" to the underwriters.

Also take into consideration the fact that the figures compiled above are averages which are a blend of all the highs and all the lows so that if you have an average at about 11½ percent, there must be some people in there at 3 percent and a number of people in there at 20 percent.

Also, the expenses are those of common stock issues. Underwriting commissions on bonds have historically been substantially less than common stock issues. Thus, a good bond issue might go at 1½ or 2 percent underwriting commission, while a good common stock issue may command as much as 7½ percent or more.

Expenses start to climb spectacularly, when expressed as percentages, on the smaller size issues. You knew this even before you began looking at the table, and the reasons are obvious: the printing bill is the same on a small issue as on a larger one; legal fees are higher in proportion to the total issue on small issues than on large issues; and the underwriter has certain fixed costs on even the smallest of issues, with the result that percentages on small issues are higher than on large issues.

BREAKING DOWN THE EXPENSES

Now that we have determined the total percentage within certain ranges, let us examine the expenses more closely, to get an estimate of what is involved as to each of the items going into the expense schedule. To begin with, you will have accounting and auditing costs. Most of you know that a full registration requires three years of fully audited figures and two years of unaudited figures. Of course, accounting costs will vary with the complexity of the enterprise, and they may be less if your books have been supervised by a good accounting firm and audited regularly, so that your going public requires only a limited extra effort.

Usually, however, most closely held corporations do not have their books in shape to go public and, as a result, accounting costs will range from $10,000 to $20,000 or more, depending upon the size of the company and the complexity of the job involved.

We come now to legal costs. There are attorneys for the company (and there may be two of them—the company's regular counsel and a special SEC counsel hired to help out in the preparation and speeding up of the prospectus) and lawyers for the underwriters. Since the company (the issuer) pays for the underwriter's counsel one way or the other, we thought it best to lump the legal fees of both sides together. The range on a typical common stock issue for *both* sides might run from $20,000 to $30,000 or more.

Then there are the printing costs. Obviously, a fifty-page prospectus that has had to be changed thirteen times will cost much more than a fifteen-page prospectus that has required only one amendment. For small issues, the printing bill may run as low as $5,000, but on a larger, more complicated debenture or convertible issue for a company such as General Motors or Ford, the printing bill may go as high as $100,000. A large portion of the printing bill will depend on how many changes there are in the copy.

Underwriting commissions in today's market may run from 10 to 15 percent in the $500,000 range; from 8 to 11 percent in the $500,000 to $1,500,000 range; and from 7 to 9 percent or less in the above $1,500,000 range. Bond offerings are underwritten at a relatively low cost (as little as a few percentage points), and issues in the $300,000 or less area, at a very high cost of 25 to 30 percent or even more when stock options are taken into consideration.

There are also SEC Filing Fees (which are very small when compared to the other expenses—only one-fiftieth of one percent of the offering price, with a minimum fee of $100). There will also be the cost of printing stock certificates and the charges of the registrar and transfer agent. There may also be the expenses of the underwriters which can range in the $10,000 to $20,000 area. There may be special fees for blue sky law work (which means qualifying the securities issue in a number of states) and these can run in the $3,000 to $5,000 area or more, depending upon the number of states and the difficulty of qualifying therein.

What does it all add up to? Well, if you add up all of the figures we have set forth above, on a typical new issue, ranging in the $500,000 to $1 million area, expenses alone, exclusive of the underwriting commission, run in the $50,000 to $100,000 area, with very few running below $25,000, or $30,000 and some, depending upon difficulties and printing costs, will run in the $100,000 to $150,000 area.

CONTROLLING UNDERWRITING CHARGES

Since underwriter's hate to be "shopped" and lose confidence in you and do not want to handle your transaction if you tell them you are going from house to house, you have to do your homework in advance.

The costs of going public in a typical year for companies of roughly the same size have ranged from a low of 10 percent to a high of 30 percent. On a $1 million underwriting, that is $200,000.

The dilution involved in the high sales costs gets the issue off to a bad start. To the extent you can, you should plan your underwriting costs in advance and attempt to cut them.

Let us understand what is involved in the underwriter's mind in fixing his fees. You only go public once in a lifetime; underwriters may go public every other week. From the underwriter's viewpoint, the fees he charges are a combination of service charge for professional skills, plus a charge for capital risk (on a firm offering). The greater the marketing difficulty, the higher the charge.

Here are some of the things that go through the underwriter's mind in fixing your fee:

1. Timing and fashionability: Is the market moving upward and looking for merchandise; or is it slow and stagnant and risky, from the underwriter's viewpoint?

   Will your stock move easily (because there is a demand for that kind of stock) or are you in a tough industry where the underwriter has an uphill battle in putting together an investment syndicate?

2. Track record: Is yours a company of many years' standing that has gone before the public many times before with successful issues, or are you a new issue, and is yours a new business?

   The better the track record, the more seasoned the company, the more favorable the histories of earlier offerings—the lower will be the charge to you, because you have a proven product with ready acceptance. It is like any other kind of sales transaction; the manufacturer of the product which has the best actual sales record can pay his salesman a smaller commission than the man who has a new, untried product—both because the manufacturer is in a better bargaining position and because the salesman can sell the superior product more easily; many smaller commissions overcome the large but difficult commission.

3. Future growth: If yours looks like growth stock, it should sell more easily than if you are in a static industry or yours is a static share of the market.

4. Pricing: If the price for your stock is out of line with the rest of the market, it will be harder to sell and it will be a riskier transaction, from an underwriter's viewpoint, than if it had a reasonable price. There is a longer discussion on pricing in a separate chapter of this book.

5. Amount of the issue: The larger the issue, the lower the percentage, because the fixed costs remain the same. Theoretically, larger issues should demand higher prices, because there is a higher underwriting risk (more capital is involved), but it never seems to work like that.

You, your financial adviser, your lawyer, or your accountant should have prepared for you a list of recent issues in your field comparable to yours in size, together with the names of the underwriting houses and a study of their charges, so that when you are told "We will have to get a 15 percent commission to sell your deal" instead of saying "I have to walk around Wall Street and see what other people will offer me" (which is bad form) you will be able to say "Well, I think that schedule might be suitable for some other issue, but I notice you have done a number of issues at 10 percent, for example, the recent offering of XYZ stock, and I feel ours is a better security for the market place, and I think we should be able to have our stock offering done for a 10 percent commission, also," (that is good form and impresses the underwriter and it shows you have done your homework).

SUMMARY

Underwriters can stay in business only if they keep their investors happy. In normal markets investors are more important to the underwriter than prospects looking to go public. As a result, each underwriting firm has a policy about the type of issue it is looking for for its customers. Some underwriters will deal in wildly speculative issues, but this is what their customers are looking for.

Offering a few more percentage points of underwriting commission will not tempt an underwriter to change his distribution methods. Competition may force him to reduce his commission; that is, if the underwriter wants your deal badly enough, he may cut his rate from 9 percent to 8 percent; but successful underwriters cannot be tempted into doing deals they do not want, because their customers would not be happy with those deals.

Ordinarily, you are wasting your time, and, instead of trying to make an underwriter accept a deal he does not want by offering him a higher commission rate, you are better off looking for the kind of underwriter who likes your kind of deal.

6

METHODS OF PAYING THE UNDERWRITER WITH STOCK OPTIONS AND "CHEAP STOCK"

First, let's distinguish between stock options and cheap stock, and let's define those terms and see how the devices are used. Then we will look at the effect of stock options and cheap stock, both on the company that is going public (issuer) and upon the underwriter.

Generally speaking, cheap stock is stock offered to the underwriter at less than it is being offered to the public. Typically, cheap stock may be used in a deal such as the following:

John Underwriter begins investigating Joe Company. John Underwriter says to Joe Company: "You are going to go public soon; we are going to sell your stock to the public at $5, however, the book value of your stock is now only $3; that is all the fair market value of your stock is now—just $3."

John Underwriter then says to Joe Company: "Sell me some stock at $3—let's say, 5,000 shares."

If Joe Company agrees to do this, then John Underwriter is being permitted to buy several thousand shares of stock at $2 a share less than than the public is paying for it. Merely by selling his stock to the public, John Underwriter has a built-in profit of $2 per share (if the issue sells out at $5). If he continues to hold that stock and if the stock ultimately goes to $7 or $8, John Underwriter will have a 4 or 5 point profit.

Often, the underwriter points out to the company which is going public that giving the underwriter an opportunity to buy stock at the same price at which the insiders own it (book) is not unfair. "The insiders lose nothing," says the underwriter

There is a certain amount of logic to this argument; but, whether there is logic to it or not, the importance of the matter is that the underwriter, by buying stock at below what it is issued to the public for, has an almost certain built-in profit. The effect of this profit is to cut the underwriter's cost and offer him an additional profit. Cheap stock may make a deal economically sound for the underwriter for a deal he would not take on a straight commission basis.

STOCK OPTIONS AND WARRANTS

What, then, are stock options and warrants? Generally, stock options and warrants give the underwriter an option to buy stock at the same price it is being offered to the public—but the option period may run as long as a couple of years. In other words, let's go back to the last illustration, where John Underwriter sold stock to the public at $5, which stock Joe Company owned at a book value of $3. John Underwriter would be given an option to buy, say, 1,000 shares of Joe Company's stock at $5, such option to be exercisable during a five-year period.

In other words, if Joe Company's stock rose from $5 to $10, John Underwriter would be in a position to exercise his options, buy stock at $5, and sell it at $10.

The theory behind options and warrants (compared to cheap stock) is that options and warrants are more palatable to the public and to the issuing corporation than cheap stock. The reason is that the issuing corporation can see that the underwriter is not getting a break that the outsiders are not being let in on. The underwriter is being permitted to buy stock at the same price as the public. The only advantage he has is that he is able to buy it at the public's price over a long term period.

It is hoped that the underwriter will do everything legally possible to see that the stock moves up. Helping the stock move up is useful not only to the issuing corporation, but also to the public. It is, therefore, felt that stock options and stock warrants (a stock warrant is merely a saleable type of stock option) give the underwriter an incentive to a successful stock offering; they cost the corporation nothing, and, indeed, they may save the corporation money by inducing the underwriter to cut his commission or other expenses in the hope of achieving a profit on the warrants at a later date.

SOME EFFECTS OF WARRANTS
AND CHEAP STOCK

All of the arguments elicited before are valid. Warrants, options, and cheap stock do act as an incentive to the underwriter to take deals he would not otherwise handle, and, to that extent, they help cut the cost of the underwriting both to the public and to the company.

What are the disadvantages? To begin with, cheap stock does raise a psychological objection on the part of many investors. They wonder why the underwriter is being permitted to buy stock at a price less than they are permitted to buy it.

When it comes to warrants and options, even though they are at the same price as the public is paying, if there are enough of them, they may "hang over" the market and depress future stock offerings.

In other words, if a company is going to issue 200,000 shares of stock and it is going to give its underwriter an option to buy 50,000 more shares at the public's price, all sophisticated investors realize that as soon as the stock price rises enough, the underwriter will call on the company to deliver to him his 50,000 shares of optional stock, and that the underwriter will work off that stock by selling to the public, with the result that the equity of every investor will be cut by the newly issued stock and diluted somewhat thereby.

What is more, knowledge that this stock is hanging over the market may depress the rise in stock prices that would otherwise have occurred. These are the theoretical arguments against stock options and warrants.

Nevertheless, stock options and warrants should not be overlooked by the typical new company that is looking forward to going public. Judicious use of this device can make an otherwise uneconomic deal look very good to the underwriter.

Whether you use cheap stock or stock options or warrants in your underwriting will depend on your negotiating position with your underwriter. Do not overlook this useful device; it may save your young, growing company many desperately needed cash dollars and may push a borderline issue out into the open market. Options won't make an underwriter take a deal that he thinks is going to be a "dog," because, obviously, he can't make any money if the stock goes down. However, options may help an underwriter take on a deal that looks otherwise unprofitable to himself, even though he has confidence in the stock.

TAX AND UNDERWRITING PROBLEMS
IN CONNECTION WITH GOING PUBLIC

Restrictions on Underwriters' Compensation

In connection with options and cheap stock for underwriters, one must take into consideration the March 10, 1970 NASD Guidelines and Interpretation. The stated purpose of the release was to point out to members the policy of the Board of Governors in connection with excessive underwriters' compensation.

The Board of Governors insisted that proposed underwritings be filed fifteen days prior to the effective date and that all possible information be disclosed as to present and contingent compensation.

The obligation to disclose to NASD all the facts with reference to compensation is imposed not only on the managing underwriter but on any NASD member who assists or participates in distributing the issue. Substantial penalties, fines, and suspensions were provided for, and NASD members were alerted to the fact that they could not palm off failure to comply with the new stronger disclosure documents on "oversight by our attorney."

Generalized guidelines were set forth in the March 10, 1970 release which provided that overall compensation should be limited to 10 percent of the total number of shares being offered, and that underwriters' stock should be restricted at least one year on transfer.

Included in the definition of underwriters' compensation were securities purchased not only by the underwriter but by "related persons" (officers, directors, and partners of the underwriter as well as the underwriter's attorneys), and the securities to be covered in the 10 percent rule included securities purchased within twelve months prior to the filing of the registration statement.

Other rules covered the position of an underwriter or member of the selling group who owned so much equity in the enterprise that the underwriter might be deemed to be the issuer—which was prohibited.

Similarly, participation in direct offerings was prohibited to NASD members where the issuer hired persons primarily for the purpose of distributing the issue. This was to prevent both the issuer and NASD members from jointly participating in a sales effort, thus dividing responsibility.

SOME OF THE TAX PROBLEMS FACING THE UNDERWRITER IN CONNECTION WITH SECURITIES OFFERINGS

Recent case law, Revenue Service attitudes, and the Tax Act of 1969 have called our attention to a number of problems facing the underwriter who buys stock in issuing companies or gets substantial options or cheap stock as part of his compensation in public offerings. Here are some of the basic rules—some of which will be familiar to you, while others are more subtle:

Obviously, gains produced as a result of the underwriter's performing services are taxed at ordinary income rates, as earned income.

Gains produced by the underwriter's "investing" in property are taxed at capital gains rates.

True, the spread between capital gains rates and earned income is now shrinking to where it may not be more than 15 percent, but, in a substantial deal, even 15 percent is an appreciable amount of money.

Thus, it becomes significant to determine whether the underwriter has bought a stock as part of its investment portfolio or received stock at a bargain price as part of its underwriting compensation. In the latter case, it would be treated as ordinary income.

Section 1236 of the Internal Revenue Code provides that investment property can be segregated on the books of the underwriter as "investment property," but debt securities which were originally received as compensation for personal services cannot be treated as 1236 investments. (See Section 1221[4].)

Obviously, cash underwriting fees are ordinary income to the underwriter (Section 1.61-2, I.R.C. Regulations). Section 1348 of the Tax Reform Act of 1969, however, qualifies those underwriting fees as earned income, which means the fees will be subject to the 50 percent ceiling beginning in 1972.

The registrant—even though the underwriter picks up his fees as ordinary income—must capitalize the underwriting fees if they apply to common stock issues, the underwriter's fees can be amortized, if they are in connection with the debt issue, over the life of the indebtedness. See 1959-2 Cumulative Bulletin 56; Rev. Ruling 59-387.

STOCK UNDERWRITING FEES

What about stock received as an underwriting fee? Section 83 of the Tax Reform Act of 1969 imposes a whole new set of rules on such stock. The tax treatment will depend on whether the stock is restricted when it is issued in such manner as might make it "forfeitable." Under Section 83, stock becomes forfeitable if there is a "substantial risk of forfeiture."

Section 83(c)(1) states that there will be a substantial risk of forfeiture if "full enjoyment of the property" is conditioned upon future services, substantial in nature, to be rendered by the recipient.

In most underwriting cases, this will not be so. Indeed, the House and Senate Finance Committee Reports state that a mere "restriction that stock may not be sold for five years is *not* a substantial risk of forfeiture." Apparently the law intended to reverse Rev. Ruling 68-86 (to be found in 1968-1 Cumulative Bulletin 184) which permitted deferral until the "restraints on alienation" were removed. It would seem that a condition which can be cured by the mere passage of time will not make a stock forfeitable. If the stock is not forfeitable, then Section 83 provides that an income tax is leviable when the stock is received, at its fair market value.

TAX DEFERRAL RULES

On the other hand, if the stock is forfeitable when received, Section 83 defers imposition of a tax until (a) the stock becomes nonforfeitable; (b) the recipient disposes of the stock.

Even in the case of forfeitable stock, the recipient can decide whether he would rather elect to pay a tax when he gets the stock or defer it until he is freed of the forfeitable clause or otherwise disposes of it. The advantage to the recipient of electing to pay a tax on forfeitable stock when it is received is that he will be taxed partly at ordinary income rates (on the fair market value at the time of elected receipt) and partly at capital gains rates—if he continues to hold it until a later date. The theory is that he is taxed at ordinary income rates only on the value received when he gets the stock, and if he continues to hold it, he is presumably holding it as an investor and is entitled to get capital gains rates on the second portion.

The significance of all of these changes in the Tax Act of 1969 is to make compensation by way of cheap stock or free stock much less desirable, particularly when coupled with the new NASD restrictions. Under present law it would seem that most underwriters would be better off paying tax on the fair market value of the stock when they got it, since presumably they are acquiring it at a time when its market value is limited, in the hope of picking up a capital gain on the ultimate appreciation, thus minimizing the ordinary aspects of the transaction at original issue.

OPTION RULES

Options are treated much in the manner of restricted stock. It is impossible for some options to get taxed at capital gains rates and for other options to be taxed at ordinary income rates. Options acquired as an investment are regulated, tax-wise, by Section 1234 of the Internal Revenue Code. In order to avoid having options taxed when they are received, it is important to be able to show either (a) that they did not exceed the price paid therefore as far as market value goes or (b) that they had no "readily ascertainable market value."

Regulations Section 1.421-6 defines "readily ascertainable market value" and points out that if there is an active market for such options, market value will be established thereby. The options, however, would have to be freely transferable, at the time received, and be unrestricted as to any "significant" right.

Options that are received by the underwriter *as compensation* are not governed by Code Section 1234, but, rather, are governed by Code Section 421. Regulations Section 1.421.6 provides that compensation will be taxed at ordinary income rates for any difference between the price paid by the recipient and the fair market value, since such difference is deemed to be compensation for services.

Under Section 421, if the market value of the option is not readily ascertainable at the time it is received, tax will be postponed until there is an arms-length sale, or until the option is exercised, in which case the rules of Section 83 concerning the purchase of "cheap stock" apply, and such questions (discussed above) as whether the stock is nonforfeitable, etc., apply.

WHAT ABOUT OPTIONS ACQUIRED
AS PART OF THE PURCHASE PRICE
OF AN "INVESTMENT PACKAGE"?

Such options are governed by Section 1232 and Regulations Section 1.1232-3(b). The Code and Regulations provide in general that where one acquires an investment package consisting, say, of a warrant and a bond, the allocation is made in terms of cost basis between the fair market value of the two pieces of paper received. The allocation itself gives rise to no tax, but the sale of either piece of paper will cause a tax equal to the difference between the sales price and the allocated basis, and the tax will presumably be at capital gains rates, *if* the package was bought for investment and not received as compensation.

The purchase of convertible debentures, however, is not susceptible of giving a separate value to the option portion, because, presumably, the two rights on a single piece of paper are not severable. See Section 1232 and Regulations 1.1232-3(b)(2).

The acquisition of convertible debentures as part of a reorganization, however, is governed by the reorganization sections, and an interesting ruling may be found in the 1970 Cumulative Bulletin as Rev. Ruling 70-108, where the convertible warrant was deemed to be "boot" and *was* taxed at its separate fair market value.

SOME OTHER OBSERVATIONS ON OPTIONS

In some cases, insiders' stock and underwriters' stock must be "escrowed." That is, it cannot be sold to the general public during a period of one year, but, instead, must be placed in escrow during that period. Such restricted escrow stock is commonly found in Regulation A offerings.

Regulation A escrow is commonly found in the smaller corporate offerings of young developing companies which have not as yet had five years of earnings behind them.

SOME ANGLES FOR THE UNDERWRITER
IN CHEAP STOCK

From the underwriter's viewpoint, stock options and cheap stock have two advantages:

1. They offer a long term speculative profit on the issue which, in many cases, can exceed the underwriting commission to be found in the deal.

2. These long term speculative profits, if handled properly, may be at capital gains rates instead of at ordinary income rates.

Business Week reported on the attractiveness of stock options to the underwriter a few years ago. It pointed out that in an original offering which only involved $300,000 worth of stock, the underwriter was able to get rights and options which ultimately worked out to a potential $870,000 capital gain for the underwriter.

Of course, that capital gain came out of the fact that the stock did very well; the underwriter had selected a fine company, and the public had jumped on the stock. If the stock had been a "dog," the $870,000 gain could never have come about.

Obviously, as long as the possibility exists that underwriters can make such substantial profits on options and warrants, they will be attracted by options and warrants.

Would the stock have gone as high if the underwriter had not had those options? Which came first, the chicken or the egg? This is a question that cannot be answered.

TAX ANGLES IN CHEAP STOCK

This has been repeated over and over again previously: The underwriter will be getting a long term capital gain on his cheap stock or his stock options. Is this necessarily true? If it is true, what does it mean to the underwriter?

Of course, we need not go into too great detail in demonstrating the advantage of a capital gain to the underwriter. The usual underwriting commissions are taxed to the underwriter at ordinary income rates. This means, to a successful underwriter, somewhere between 60 and 80 percent of every dollar he makes goes to the United States Treasury Department and the various city and state taxing authorities.

On the other hand, if the underwriter is able to get his profit out of the deal not in the form of underwriting commissions but in the form of a long term capital gain, then the underwriter has a maximum tax of 35 percent to pay. To an underwriter who might be in the 70 percent tax bracket, $100,000 of underwriting commissions leaves him with only $30,000 after taxes. If the transaction can be labeled a capital gain, to net the same $30,000 after taxes, he need achieve only about $50,000 in capital gains. Obviously, capital gains are twice as attractive to the underwriter as ordinary income.

Whether the underwriter gets capital gains treatment or not is a more complicated question. The Treasury Department says that if the underwriter buys stock at substantially below its fair market value in connection with an underwriting, the underwriter has ordinary income to the extent of the bargain purchase.

For the underwriter to be sure about getting a capital gain, he must hold the stock and acquire it for a substantial amount of time before the public offering. This is not all that easy to do; the seller generally does not want to issue any cheap stock until the underwriting goes through. Furthermore, the underwriter's ability to exact cheap stock (as distinguished from warrants which are discussed later) is more proscribed now. The National Association of Securities Dealers, which regulates underwriters, in 1969 and 1970 issued a number of guidelines regulating the amount of cheap stock and warrants that an underwriter could exact as part of an underwriting.

Since most of you will be issuers and not underwriters, I don't want to take you through all of the details, but, in March of 1970, the National Association of Securities

Dealers issued a number of guidelines for underwriters, telling them what they could and could not do. Indeed, the guidelines proposed various types of ceilings on underwriting commissions which prevent their getting much above 20 percent as a total compensation, which total includes not only the underwriter's commission, but any cheap stock and "reimbursement of expenses." They tend to inhibit transactions with a total compensation package which exceeds 20 percent of the underwriting.

HOW WARRANTS ARE USED

In other words, if the underwriting agreement provides that 10,000 shares of stock are being sold to the public at $5 and 5,000 shares are being sold to the underwriter at $3, the underwriter has practically made out an open and shut case for the tax authorities that he had ordinary income of $2 on each of the shares. Obviously, it would be difficult to argue that the stock was not worth $5, when the public was grabbing it up at that price. The underwriter who gets a bargain purchase at below market value is generally locking himself into an ordinary income position.

When can the underwriter get a long term capital gain? He can in two situations:

(1) Where the underwriter buys cheap stock at a time when there is no public market for the stock and where his purchase price is presumably the fair market value of that stock.

Example: Suppose the corporation owns 100,000 shares of stock with a book value of $500,000; each of the shares of stock is probably $5. The insiders own their stock at $5, and the underwriter asks for the opportunity to buy 10,000 shares at book value. Since there is no public market for the stock at that point, it could be very well argued that the underwriter is not getting a bargain purchase; he is buying at fair market value.

Suppose the company goes public three months or six months after the underwriter has bought his cheap stock: Does the underwriter have ordinary income? Presumably, if the underwriter bought at fair market value at the date of purchase, he should have no ordinary income. You may argue that three months or six months later the public bought the stock at 7 or 8; doesn't the underwriter have ordinary income?

But, if the stock was only worth $5 when the underwriter bought it, the six month waiting period involved the risk that the stock might go down or that the company might never go public, etc.

NO INCOME ON PURCHASE

Purchase of cheap stock at its fair market value does not give rise to any income. If the stock is later resold at a capital gain—as long as it is a long term capital gain (more than six months) and as long as the stock had been held for investment—the underwriter should get a long term capital gain.

The same is true of options. If the underwriter has an option to buy stock at $3 at the same time that the public is buying it at $5, and if he exercises that option at that time, the underwriter presumably will have a gain of $2. He will have that gain merely because he exercises the option whether he resells the stock or not, because the gain comes out of the mere bargain purchase, and it will be at ordinary income rates because it is tied together with the underwriting.

(2) On the other hand, if the public is buying stock at $5 and the underwriter has a five-year option to buy at $5, and if the stock goes to $10 and the underwriter later exercises the option at $5, he will not have had ordinary income merely out of getting options at $5; he will not have any kind of income when he exercises the option at $5, but, if he resells the stock at $15 or at $10 or at some figure higher than his purchase price, he will have a capital gain, provided he holds the stock for six months or more.

SUMMARY

Every stock option or purchase of cheap stock involves two different factors for the underwriter:

(1) Does he realize income out of a bargain purchase, because he buys stock at less than its fair market value at the moment of purchase? If he buys anything at less than fair market value and if that purchase is part of his underwriting compensation, he realizes ordinary income.

(2) If his option is to buy at current fair market value, then the option he gets is presumably worth nothing at the time of issuance, and he cannot be taxed at ordinary income rates. Thereafter, if that option rises in value, the increment presumably arises out of his investment activities (as a result of his holding the option) and, accordingly, should be taxed to him as an investment profit at capital gains rates.

The above is an oversimplification of a much questioned and sure-to-be-litigated area. The only word of warning we can pass along to you, if you are an underwriter, is to make absolutely certain that the legal documents involving any stock rights or options you may be getting are carefully drawn with an eye toward the tax consequences.

The field is changing from day to day and, therefore, you should have all of your options checked each time you draw a contract to see that you are making the best tax deal for yourself at that time. The difference between capital gains rates and ordinary income rates can increase your profits by 100 percent or more.

THE TRUE COST OF WARRANTS

Often we are asked if anybody really has been hurt. The issuing company has not been hurt, and, perhaps without the warrants and options, the underwriter would not have touched the deal. In addition, having those options and warrants must have encouraged the underwriter to help develop a market for the stock. In many cases, when the underwriter has a good issue on which he has options he will do everything he can to educate institutional buyers and the public at large on the growth factor of the company. The underwriter sees to it that full information is given to professional buyers of stock, with the result that mutual funds, insurance companies, pension trusts and the like may step in with their large buying power and zoom the stock upwards.

Because of the underwriter's educational efforts, a market at new highs has been made for the young company's stock, reducing the cost of future financing. From the underwriter's viewpoint, the large rise in the stock has offered to him a long term capital gain of possibly twenty times the amount he could have looked for as an underwriting commission.

Has the company been hurt? On the one hand, you might say it cannot be hurt by a rising market; the overall effect in cutting the cost of the company's secondary offering is such a favorable one that the giving of a nominal amount of options cannot hurt it.

On the other hand, you might argue that if the underwriter was able to unload all of that optioned stock on the public at the higher price, the company could probably have sold that stock for its own account instead of the underwriter selling it. To that extent, the company would have been better off had the underwriter never been given the options.

7

SELECTING YOUR UNDERWRITER
AND DEALING EFFECTIVELY WITH HIM

THE "RIGHT" UNDERWRITER FOR YOU

A recent "census" of underwriters showed more than 800 active in the field. These ranged in size from one-man firms to multibranch, multipartner national organizations. Some of the smaller ones did as little as two or three deals during the year, and all of them were in the under $300,000 class. The larger ones approached the billion-dollar class in good years.

But which underwriter is the best one for you? How do you find him? As in all fields, there are underwriters who will value your account and there are others to whom your issue would be a nuisance. As in all fields, there are underwriters of great imagination; they are few. There are underwriters who are fools; they are also few. There are underwriters with only an average degree of competence and an average degree of imagination; they are the mass—as is the case in every other field of endeavor, including the law.

In the midst of the underwriting field you will find competence and incompetence, geniuses and thieves. It will be your job to find the one best suited to your purpose.

SOME SUGGESTIONS ON FINDING
AN UNDERWRITER

Our first suggestion is to get as many personal recommendations as you can from people in whom you have confidence. Your accountant may recommend a few underwriters, as may your attorney or commercial banker. If you retain an SEC attorney, he will know several underwriters.

Make a list of underwriters and, before you go to see them, find out something about the other deals they have done. Are they large or small? Are they in your type of industry or another type of industry? Have the underwritings been successful (from the company's viewpoint)? Does the underwriter have the time to give you the personal-ized service you need, or will your account be too small for him? Is your deal too big for him? Do you want a national issue of securities, or would you be better off if your securities were sold in a small geographical area adjacent to your plant?

Many of your answers can come from studying your underwriter's past deals. How do you get such a list? Trade publications, such as the *Investment Dealers Digest* and the *Commercial and Financial Chronicle* list each public issue and the name of the underwriter.

If you do not have these publications handy, perhaps your banker can get the information for you. If you have an attorney or an accountant who knows his way around the financial community, he can check out this information. Once you have studied the underwriter's past dealings, you are in a position to talk to him intelligently.

THE UNDERWRITER'S REAL ABILITY

If you are a brass widget manufacturer, must your underwriter have done a brass widget deal before? No. As a matter of fact, if he has done a brass widget deal before, he may be sitting on the board of directors of that manufacturer of brass widgets, and he may feel that doing another brass widget deal will put him in an embarrassing position.

You should check out all of your underwriter's recent past dealings. You will want to know about his failures as well as his successes. Once you find out about the failures, be sure to discuss them with the underwriter when you go to see him. There may be a satisfactory explanation.

After all, no underwriter controls the stock market as a whole, and his deal will fall with the rest of the market, although it may be a better than average deal.

SOME OBSERVATIONS ABOUT
UNDERWRITING COMMISSIONS

We are often asked whether underwriters turn down a deal because the commission offered them is too low. We have not found this to be so. Most underwriters are more interested in whether the stock is the kind they would like to offer to their investor followers than whether their underwriting commission is to be 9 or 10 percent. Reputable underwriters will not take an inferior deal because they are offered a slightly larger commission.

You will find, when you begin negotiating with underwriters, that they will tell you approximately what their average commission spread is. You can check that commission spread against other deals they have done; all these matters are a public record. You need only look at some of the older prospectuses done by the same underwriter.

Do not feel that you will be able to convince the underwriter to take your deal, if he is ordinarily an 8 or 10 percent underwriter, by offering him 25 percent. You will ordinarily find that he is no more interested in the deal at 25 or even 50 percent than he is at 10 percent. Instead, shop around for another underwriter who likes your kind of deal. Don't try to bribe the underwriter by offering him an excess commission. You will be wasting your time and money, in most cases.

Instead of trying to get an underwriter to take a piece of merchandise he considers inferior by offering him a higher discount, we suggest you go over the deal and try to find some stronger sales points to go to a new underwriter with, so that he will consider your deal a superior piece of merchandise. Spend your time and money shaping up your deal; don't spend it on excess underwriting commissions.

When we come to discuss the subject of what is the best price for your stock, we will point out that sometimes you are better off getting a lower price for your first stock issue, provided you can get a higher price for your second stock issue. The fact that an underwriter's stocks have not all gone up should not prevent you from considering him a useful underwriter, from your viewpoint, on your first issue.

THE LOCAL UNDERWRITER

Much fanfare is given to the multibranch national underwriting firms with forty and fifty offices throughout the country who are listed as members of all of the stock exchanges in the United States.

These national firms are looking for securities that can be distributed on a national basis. If you are a small local manufacturer in Rochester, New York, who is looking to market $125,000 worth of securities, these multibranch national firms are not for you. There are many underwritings that just cannot be sold in the New York or Chicago markets because of the high cost of operating in those markets. Legal fees, printing costs, and office overhead is just higher in those areas than in smaller towns.

Many over-the-counter security dealers in these smaller cities would be delighted to handle your offerings on a local basis, and they should not be overlooked. We have seen many issues successfully handled by these smaller firms at a price that could not be managed on Wall Street.

Why? Well, in the first place, the owner of many of these smaller companies is a good securities customer of the underwriter. The underwriter sits on his Board of Directors; the underwriter is familiar with local conditions and is aware that he has a growing company on his hands. The underwriter does not need a market survey team to tell him that the manufacturer has a growth potential; and, being local, he saves those expenses and is able to pass that savings on to the company.

If you are interested in a small local offering, do not overlook the small local house; it may be better for you than the big Wall Street houses. On the other hand, if you are looking to do a large national issue and if you particularly do not want much of your stock held in your own town, bypass the local house and go to New York or Chicago where you can tap the large national organizations.

SUMMARY ON FINDING YOUR UNDERWRITER

Get as many personal recommendations as you can; couple personal recommendations with underwriters whose names and qualifications you have researched independently, by finding out that they handle the kind of security you want sold.

Have someone (either an important corporate officer, your accountant, or your attorney) informally contact each of these underwriters by phone or in person, and sound them out (before getting them too deeply committed in paper work) on whether they would be interested in handling your kind of deal.

Then, having selected the underwriters most likely to be interested, you are ready to go to the next step—giving the underwriter the kind of information he needs.

"SELLING" THE UNDERWRITER

Today is the day of the "growth" stock. More than anything else, the underwriter wants to see that your company has been growing more rapidly than the national economy. With five years' earnings—each year showing an increase over the year before—you are an interesting prospect to almost any underwriter. While it is true that if your company is very small many underwriters will feel that they cannot economically market your securities, if you nevertheless fulfill the growth qualification, you may be able to find a private investor or a group of private investors through the underwriter. If you are one of these growth companies with five years of growth behind you, you are a long way ahead on the road.

SPECIAL FACTORS TO CONSIDER

There are somewhat in excess of 25,000 to 30,000 publicly held corporations in the United States whose securities are traded in the over-the-counter market. Many of them did not have the five-year growth; many of them may be competitors of yours, and when you look at their balance sheets and profit and loss statements, you may feel that yours is an infinitely superior security. What did they have? How did they go public?

In our appendix you will find a detailed checklist compiled by Donald B. Marron, one of Wall Street's more creative underwriters. There, step by step, the underwriters lists the kind of questions he wants answered. If you want to sell an underwriter on marketing your securities and if he wants to sell them to the public, all of you need to see that that questionnaire is answered as thoroughly and as creatively as possible. We have even added our own checklist, in simplified form, which lists what we believe are the seven key points to "selling the underwriter."

If you think about it, the underwriter needs the kind of information that is going to go into a final SEC prospectus. Of course, he won't want to be burdened with all of it on your first trip to see him.

PRESENTING YOUR INFORMATION EFFECTIVELY

You are asking your underwriter to get you a check for several hundred thousand or possibly several million dollars. An alert underwriter once said: "In twenty minutes I can tell you whether a man should have $10,000 or not; but when a prospect wants to raise a couple of hundred thousand dollars, you can spend weeks on it and never really know the answer. It's much harder to decide whether a two-hundred-thousand-dollar investment is going to be more profitable than a $10,000,000 one."

Accordingly, effective presentation is most important. I would suggest that you budget either some time of one of your best executives or of your accountant or attorney to prepare an effective outline or brochure of no more than ten or twelve pages. You can't raise several million dollars with hen scratches on the back of an envelope. The effective presentation which you will show your prospective underwriter should cover the following major items:

1. Financial statements for five years or for the entire corporate existence, if less than five years, together with an explanation of the major balance sheet and profit and loss statement trends, pointing out their significance and accounting for the trends that are not favorable.

2. A cash budget showing what you will do with the money you raise; why you need it; and what will happen when it goes into your till. This cash budget covering the next few years and tied together with your last few years is most important. If done properly, it would demonstrate that your plan is realistic; that your feet are on the ground; and that you will have enough money to accomplish the plan without running for a second offering before the deal is completed.

3. A brief description of the company's history and physical facilities; how the company got started; its major product lines; a discussion of its competitive position; a statement of where it has been, where it is going, how it has done, and proposes to do the job in the future.

If you can cover those points in a brief, well-written outline, you are half-way on the road to going public. If you cannot do it, get somebody to do it for you, and don't hesitate to spend the money to get it done properly. Otherwise you will be wasting time—which can cost you a fortune—and you will be limiting yourself to dealing with underwriters below your stature. Effective presentation is the only way to make sure you get the best underwriting talent available.

A FEW OBSERVATIONS ABOUT YOUR UNDERWRITER

Most corporations seeking to enter the new issue market are very much concerned with how the underwriter distributes their stock. In other words, the new company wants to make sure that the underwriter gets as broad a distribution as possible to as many small stockholders and in as many different cities as possible. By getting broad geographical distribution in the hands of small shareholders, the underwriter avoids putting stock in the hands of people who can bother the management. This avoids putting stock in the hands of large block holders who, should they desire to sell off their stock, can severely depress the market.

Lots of small stockholders are good, from the viewpoint of voting control, from the viewpoint of price stability, and from the viewpoint of providing a nucleus for future issues.

A good underwriter gets you broad geographical distribution via many small stockholders; but, a good underwriter does more than just get you broad distribution—he gets you distribution into the "right" hands.

Example: A good underwriter understands that the public and many brokerage houses follow the leads of the institutional investors and the large mutual funds. If these institutions and funds buy a large position in a new issue, many smaller investors will follow the lead of the institutional investors. As a result, a good underwriter will attempt to place all or a portion of your issue in the hands of these key mutual funds and institutional buyers. By so doing, he may trigger off a response from a large market of investors who "follow the lead" of the funds.

We recently saw an example of a new issue that quickly went from approximately 10 to approximately 70, because the underwriter was foresighted enough to get a number of good funds to buy the stock. The underwriter went to great lengths and spent much time in inducing these funds to buy relatively small portions of the trial issue.

No commission would have been large enough to pay the underwriter for the time he spent in educating these funds to buy as little as one thousand shares, in some cases. However, when the quarterly fund report came out and the public was alerted to the fact that five or six large funds were buying into this small growth company, the stock rose like a rocket. Since the stock was that of a small company and in short supply, and, since many private investors bid against each other in order to follow the lead of the funds, the stock increased sixfold in value in a short period of time. Nothing in the earnings would have warranted such an increase.

Intelligent handling on the part of the underwriter, however, did two things for the company:

1. It gave the stock a spectacular rise, thus making future issues for the company very easy; and

2. It acquainted a large institutional market with the merits of this young, growing company.

The result? Future financings on the part of the company might not even necessarily be public.

This company, whose stock was now held by a large number of institutions, could, in many cases, go directly to these institutions and discuss with them the private placement of debenture loans, etc. The underwriter had taken the time and had shown the foresight to engage in an educational program, and the results paid off handsomely.

WHAT THE UNDERWRITER IS LOOKING FOR

Substantial, capable underwriters want to know that the industry is stable; that you are a stable member of it (have had three, four, or five years records of growth and prospects of continued growth); and that your management is stable and has depth (is not a one-man organization).

They want to know that when they finish the underwriting, there will be between 1,000 and 2,000 separate shareholders, so that there will be a sufficient "after market" which will attract several of the houses that specialize in over-the-counter securities, so that the full burden of supporting the stock does not fall on the underwriter.

An inactive market, where there are too few stockholders, means that each purchase or sale of a couple of hundred shares will make the stock bounce like a rubber ball. Shareholders, also, are unhappy with too thin a market, because their stock is neither stable nor readily liquidatable.

You will recall that there are two kinds of underwriting houses: the majors and the regional or specialized underwriters. While each of them, from time to time, makes exceptions to the general rule, either because the underwriter is looking for "merchandise" or because yours seems to be a particularly interesting situation, generally, each group has certain standards concerning size of issue and stable earnings history, as well as criteria for the size of a particular offering, etc. Here are some guidelines, but they may change from time to time.

In general, the better-known major New York underwriters want a history of earnings over a three or five year period of approximately $1 million per year, and they are reluctant to do an issue of much less than $2,500,000.

The regionals or specialized underwriters may be satisfied with an issue of as little as $1 million and with annual earnings of as little as $250,000.

Bear in mind that if you are looking for 1,000 or 2,000 shareholders and if you want as many of them as possible to be in 100-share lots (both desirable), and if you want to be priced in the $10 to $15 per share area (to avoid the "penny stock" label) you have some other criteria to meet.

SOME SUGGESTIONS ON HOW TO CHECK OUT YOUR PROPOSED UNDERWRITER

We have suggested above that you begin to develop a list of potential underwriters. This list is usually compiled by consulting your proposed SEC attorney (or one selected by your general counsel for his familiarity with SEC procedures, but with various underwriting houses and their strengths and weaknesses), and after consulting with your accountants, commercial bankers, or local acquaintances in the stock brokerage or investment banking industry. Possibly, you might consult with the officers and directors of other companies in your area of similar size who have gone public in recent years.

If you work with each of these sources you will soon develop a list of half a dozen or more underwriters, some of whom will be local or specialized and some of whom may be among the majors. If you are "out there" and the list includes a large number of New York underwriters, you should be prepared to visit New York, Chicago, or Los Angeles, together with your general counsel to do some interviewing and sifting, or you should be represented by local SEC counsel in one of those cities who can help you screen the list.

Before you visit, you should do some homework. For each of the underwriting prospects on your list, you should analyze (or have your controller, accountant, attorney, or whoever is to be in charge of the search do so) not only the recent underwritings of each of the prospective underwriters on your list, but what happened after the underwritings.

In other words, you are not only concerned with the underwriter's ability to sell, but with his ability to support the after market. In each case, you should check out the broadness of the distribution achieved by the underwriter and the strength of the houses supporting his underwriting.

In checking out the underwriter's ability in the after market, not only is the trading history in the stock important, but you should check out with the issuer the underwriter's ability and track record in offering consultation, merger assistance, communications to the financial community, etc., after the underwriting is finished.

It is easy to get an underwriter interested, when he is looking forward to commissions. It is tougher and it speaks much for the underwriter's ability and reputation to see what he has done afterwards, when there are no more fees or the fees are very small.

In your discussions with the underwriter, it is also significant if he asks you to "lay off" a large portion of the stock yourself among insiders, friends, suppliers, etc. It often seems to us, unless there is a particular reason for it, that an underwriter who insists that as part of the underwriting you sell a large portion of the stock yourself, is indicating a certain weakness in his own sales organization.

Certainly, at the very minimum, the stock that you sell should not be commissionable to him. There may, however, be reasons for the underwriter's request, but they would have to be explained.

Another request of underwriters that concerns us is the option to take "all future financings." Generally, where we represent issuers, we resist this. The underwriter's argument usually is that he needs this on new issues, because there is so much work to them that he is only setting up business for someone else and that he "cannot come out" on a single issue. Our own feeling is that the underwriter should earn future issues by his ability and command of the market place, and not by some contractual obligation. Strong underwriters do not need the option; weak ones use it to "hold up" secondary issues.

8

PLANNING THE OFFERING FROM
THE UNDERWRITER'S VIEWPOINT

The underwriter's stock in trade is a satisfied investment public. Without satisfied investors, the underwriter can do nothing for you. The investor is looking for one of two things:

1. Either capital gains in the form of growth;

2. Or current income in the form of interest or dividends.

In some cases, instead of getting exclusively income or exclusively growth, the investor may get a blend of both. If you intend to go public, you must show the underwriter that your stock will offer to the potential investor either income, growth, or both.

Newer companies, coming to the market for the first time, are, since they are newer and less tried, more speculative investments than are the larger, older companies. If the investor is going to buy your stock, he will buy it because it offers the possibility of a larger income or a larger growth factor than he is able to buy in a large, well established company whose stock has been traded for years.

In other words, if you cannot offer the investor a bargain, he just won't take a speculative change on your stock.

"HOT" COMPANIES

Fashions sweep Wall Street just as they sweep other areas of the economy. There was a time when uranium stocks boomed merely if they had the word "uranium" in their name. These were followed in turn by electronic stocks which were followed by publishing stocks, discount houses, computer companies, leasing companies, conglomerates, REITS, the fast food franchisers and many, many more. As each boom came, it was followed by a bust, but some companies survived and grew.

As long as the underwriter sees that every dollar the stockholder puts into the company earns a very high return on the investment, the underwriter and his investor will be attracted thereby. Bear in mind, however, that if yours is one of the smaller companies, the underwriter, in comparing your company with a well established company in a similar industry, will look for a 25 to 30 percent greater return on your more speculative company than he will expect in the older company.

FORECASTING THE FUTURE

Obviously, the investor wants to know that your past growth (as evidenced by your five years earning statement) will continue in the future. The investor, through the underwriter, wonders whether you have developed a strong enough second echelon management team. Many companies grow to the point where they outgrow the one or two skillful men who are now running the corporation. They find, when they become public, that top management is bogged down by an entirely new set of problems and that there is no second management team to handle them.

Once you start expanding a company, you must ask yourself whether it is possible for the present staff (which may have been handling about $5,000,000 worth of sales) to handle $7,000,000, $8,000,000 or $10,000,000. This is the breaking point for many smaller managements. Is the second team heavy enough to handle the sales management; the controllership; the budgeting; the production planning; and the legal and tax ramifications of an $8,000,000 or $10,000,000 business? The boss is just too busy to do it all by himself.

WHAT WILL YOU DO
WITH THE MONEY?

We mentioned the importance of having a realistic cash projection on what use you will make of the funds when they come in and on the earnings the new funds will generate. The ease with which new companies have been able to raise money in the public market during the last few years has left many companies cash rich and earnings poor. Quite a number of small business investment corporations (SBICs) have raised millions of dollars from the public only to find that they cannot put the money to work efficiently, with the result that the stocks have fallen off badly.

In addition to wanting to know your plans for putting the funds to work, the underwriter wants to make sure you are raising enough funds. There is nothing as bad as raising $300,000 for a new plant only to find that a new plant costs $600,000 and that you can only build half a plant. Half a plant can produce nothing but a deficit.

COMPETITIVE STRENGTH

It counts well for a company that it has an exclusive product, a unique sales proposition, a patented product, or a marketing or manufacturing technique with economies demonstratively 20 percent more than competitors. Some sort of uniqueness and exclusivity go a long way toward giving the smaller company a competitive edge in the marketing of its securities just as they give a company a competitive edge in the marketing of its products.

REALISTIC PRICING

The mere fact that your company has grown 20 or 30 percent per year over the past five years will certainly make yours a more readily marketable security, but you should not assume that Wall Street will pay a price that will anticipate your continuing expansion at the rate of 20 or 30 percent over the next five years.

Experience has shown that there comes a leveling off on the rate of growth, particularly as the company begins to climb through the $4,000,000 to $6,000,000 sales barrier.

Return on invested capital is a very significant factor from Wall Street's viewpoint. Presumably, if your company is able to earn 20 percent on the money it now has invested, and if you are able to raise another million (or two million) dollars, the investment is going to be an attractive one.

By the same token, it is absurd to assume that the public is going to fall all over itself and pay you a premium for your stock over and above the price which it will pay for a company that has been listed for years, with a similar growth factor.

Since investors have a present choice between 25,000 and 30,000 public companies, you are telling the public that if they take their money out of those 25,000 to 30,000 public companies and invest it in your company, they will be better off. Your saying so won't make it so; there is only one way to convince them and that way is to price your security right.

In other words, you must offer your securities at a discount over what they can buy listed companies at. You must offer to the public a reason why they should sell their stock in these other 25,000 to 30,000 companies and put their money into your newer company.

What is more, if you want your stock to go up so that your secondary offering will be better, why should you not willfully underprice your stock. After all, the first offering is an offering of stock, the proceeds of which will go into the company, in most cases. It puts nothing into your pocket. If you start out with a low stock price, it will rise, if you move earnings along and have a growth factor.

On the other hand, if you start out by overpricing your stock because your ego tells you you are better than your competitors, the slightest winds of recession may send your stock plummeting to a bottom from which it will never recover. Try to think that one through. We often advise clients that they are better off underpricing their stock on a primary offering rather than overpricing it, if they have their eye on the secondary offering and can demonstrate to the underwriter on the secondary offering that the price went up the first time around.

YOUR SECONDARY OFFERING

Since most of you are going public for the first time and since most of you will find the investment community not willing to let you bail out your investment in your first public issue, you will be selling most of your stock the first time around for the account of your company. In other words, you will be raising funds for the company; you won't be able to raise a penny for yourself and your co-owners.

It is only on your secondary offering (which may come a year or two later) that you will be able to put any money into your own pocket. If you overprice your first issue, the only result will be that the stock will sell at the low issue price. If that happens, and if your stock falls below its original issue price, you will have a difficult time selling any stock for your own account at a later date.

If you are looking at the whole thing from a selfish viewpoint, you are better off underpricing the initial issue (which may be done for the account of the company) so that you will ultimately be able to get the best possible price for your own personal stock on the secondary issue.

Most businessmen are so concerned with getting top dollar for everything they sell that they overlook their ultimate objective. Do not sacrifice the market for your personal stock just to show how hard a deal you can drive with your underwriter in selling stock for the company.

MERGERS AND STOCK OPTIONS

If you intend to go public so that you will be able to use your corporate stock to buy up other companies or so that you will be able to use your stock to keep key employees or to have stock options for yourself and the other insiders, then you must be sure that your public offering is a successful one.

By "successful" we mean you must make sure that your stock climbs above issue price. If your stock falls on its face, you won't be able to use it to buy up other companies; you won't be able to use it to attract or keep management; and you won't be able to use it to work out capital gains for the insiders.

If you are planning to use your stock to buy up other companies, make sure that you think through the deal carefully. I have asked as many as a dozen of my clients who told me they were going public in order to buy up other companies: "Assuming you are public already, what companies would you buy up and what would you pay for them in stock?"

Many businessmen are floating on a cloud when they talk about buying up companies. They have no idea of the techniques involved or the objectives to be followed; they are just inflating their own egos. Make sure that you have thought your acquisition program through, if that is what you want to do with your stock.

It is not necessary that you have an acquisition program in order to go public, but, by the same token, it is a shame to delude yourself and to talk about an acquisition program when you are dealing only in generalities.

THE INSTITUTIONAL MARKET

Ten years ago insurance companies, pension funds, and mutual funds concentrated on "blue chips" with sales in the $50,000,000 to $100,000,000 categories. In their desperate search for higher yields and better growth companies, the institutional investor, too, has begun purchasing the stocks of smaller over-the-counter companies that show growth leadership in their fields. Institutional support can, by itself, drive the market price of a small growing company "right through the roof."

It is a function of a good investment banker to educate the institutional market on the merits of your securities. By getting institutional support for your public offering, your investment banker is almost able to guarantee a successful secondary offering and almost assure ready capital markets for you any time you need the money in the future.

If your banker is going to get you institutional support, you must give him the information discussed before, so that he can educate the institutional buyer, and you must price your offering in such a way that the institutional buyers "get a bargain."

Remember: When the mutual fund reports come out, if half a dozen of them have bought your stock, your future is almost made. Other investors, in the rush to scramble for the limited number of shares that you have made available, will assure your stock of a profitable price rise.

Institutional support also means easy "interim" financing. Once you have the seal of approval of the institutional investor, you should have no trouble getting debenture loans to help you over the growth years ahead. Institutional investors do not dump your stock nervously on the first rumor of a bad market; they hold.

Let me close the discussion of the institutional buyer by pointing out that two important factors are necessary for you to attract that most important of all support—institutional support:

1. A well planned securities offering at a fair price or, better yet, at a low price which can show growth; and

2. A high quality underwriter with a good reputation in the institutional market (high quality need not mean large, but the underwriter must be well-respected).

HOW LONG DOES AN UNDERWRITING TAKE?

Generally, from the time you present the underwriter with the information he needs to the time you get a "letter of intent" (which is the underwriter's preliminary commitment), about six weeks will have elapsed. To do a complete SEC registration, from the time you get your commitment and put your accountants and lawyers to work to the time the SEC clears the registration can take from two to four months.

Once the SEC has been cleared, the company ordinarily gets its money a week or two later.

Under average circumstances, it takes from four to six months from presentation of information to a check. Of course, if your initial presentation is inept and if your financial statements are not properly prepared and if your prospectus is sloppily drawn, your timetable will be slowed down considerably.

9

SUCCESSFULLY NEGOTIATING
WITH THE UNDERWRITER

One of the most important negotiating points in dealing with the underwriter is fixing the best price for your stock, bond, or other security. To begin with, let us note that the best price is not necessarily the highest price. This is a difficult concept for the inexperienced businessman to follow. Ordinarily, experience teaches him to "sell high" and "buy cheap." In securities underwriting, selling high may be the wrong thing to do. We pointed out before that most people, when they go to the stock market seeking public funds for the first time, are interested in getting "top dollar" for their stock or bond. What most of them fail to take into consideration is that successful companies go to Wall Street time and time again. If your first financing is a failure (because your stock falls on its face after issue), future financings will be difficult, if not impossible.

Bear in mind—and we cannot stress this too much—that if you plan first a primary offering to sell some stock (for the company) to the public, to get some working capital, followed by a secondary offering in which you and the insiders are going to sell some stock for yourselves, then, from your own personal and selfish viewpoint, the secondary offering is even more important than the first (primary) offering. Therefore, your initial prospectus, your pricing, and your plans to generate earnings during the first couple of years should all be aimed at the secondary offering—not at the primary one. It is only at the secondary offering that you will make any money for yourself and the other insiders.

GETTING TOP DOLLAR FOR YOUR STOCK

You may say: "I only intend to go to Wall Street once." If this is really so, then perhaps you will want to sell your security at top dollar, regardless of what happens to the stock after it is sold to the public.

If you expect to make money out of selling your stock to the public and don't care what happens to the company's credit reputation afterwards, perhaps you will want to squeeze every last dollar out of the public.

But, as we mentioned before, most businessmen go to Wall Street time and time again. In a simple financing program you might go to Wall Street originally with the intention of raising some equity capital by having the company sell some of its common stock to the public. Then, a year or two later, some of your stockholders might want to sell some of their stock to the public. Visualize the position you will be in if your first offering has fallen apart and the stock went down, down, and down.

Again, you may want to go to Wall Street a third time. Let's assume you have had a first and second offering and that both have been successful. Now, you need expansion funds either to buy other businesses or to move the next rung up the ladder.

There are literally dozens of reasons why you might want additional financings in the future. Investors have a long memory when it comes to failures, and you must take that into consideration. If the price of your initial offering is set too high, you can go nowhere but down. The ultimate cost of a first financial failure may be that your business may never be able to go back to tap the money markets again.

Price your original issue right; let the investor make a couple of dollars, also. You will then be establishing the right relationship for future financings.

PRICE-EARNINGS RATIOS

Of course, you won't want to set your price too low, either. In this connection, many new issuers try to find out how many times earnings their competitors got for their stock when it was first issued. There is nothing wrong in this. You should have some idea of what the appropriate price range for your initial issue should be. Remember, though, that you are comparing your price earnings ratio with the price earnings ratios of other similar companies on original issue. It makes no sense to compare your stock with companies that have been listed for a considerable amount of time and have been tried and tested in the market. Also, in comparing your price earnings multiple with that of other companies you deem appropriate, bear in mind that they may have issued their stocks in an entirely different market than you are facing.

An electronics company that came to the market with an electronics stock at the height of the electronics growth boom would be in a different position in terms of price earnings multiples than you may be if you offer your stock at the bottom of a decline in so-called growth stocks.

WHAT ARE PRICE-EARNINGS RATIOS?

Bear in mind that in many cases it is difficult to compare your price earnings ratio with somebody else's. While it is true that some stocks sell for fifty and 100 times earnings (after taxes), earnings of several companies in the same business are not necessarily the same kind of earnings.

Net earnings after taxes involves, to a certain extent, accounting and taxation concepts. Since good accounting practice involves differences of opinion amongst equally honest and capable accountants, a comparison of the net earnings of two companies in the same line of business may not be a comparison of equal things.

What is more, certain industries have earnings peculiarities all their own. Let me give you an example of some of the difficulties involved in defining earnings. Suppose you have a land development company that sells vacant land in the form of subdivided lots to potential home owners; suppose you have carved out for yourself several thousand acres of desert; and suppose your sales program envisions selling these lots to the public at $10 down and $10 a month until a total of $490 has been paid. It will take four years for the purchaser to own a lot.

DEFINING EARNINGS

Some of the earnings problems you have are these: Suppose you sell a lot to a customer for $10 down and $490 to go. Is it fair to record a $490 sale on the books? How can you be certain that you will collect the remaining $480? The customer is not really at great economic risk; he may never make a second payment. The customer may decide to drop the $10 he gave your high-pressure salesman. Assuming you are able to report a $490 sale based on a $10 deposit, your company will have huge earnings any time it collects many $10 bills.

Of course, your company may not have made a dime; in fact, it may have paid out the entire $10 to the salesman who made the sale. What is more, in our hypothetical illustration, your company may suffer disastrous declines in earnings when it becomes necessary to reverse the income figures, should the customer cancel the order at a later date.

Earnings accruals based on hypothetical sales work both ways. As customer cancellations come in, you will have to write off the $480 balance (having first collected the $10). It is a two-way sword. Your company may suffer in future years, although its earnings may look very glamorous in the initial years.

It is not our purpose to discuss all of the hundreds of accounting concepts that may possibly be involved in defining earnings. However, you can see the position you would be in if you attempted to compare your earnings in an all-cash business with the earnings of a competitor who kept his books on the basis set forth above.

Obviously, your earnings will look pretty sick and your sales will look pretty small, if you are selling land on an all-cash basis compared with your competitor who reports a full $490 sale every time he gets a $10 deposit. By the same token, you should be entitled to a higher earnings multiple because your earnings are more realistic than your competitor's.

Recent American Institute of Certified Public Accountants and SEC rulings, however, are beginning to regulate the question of what constitutes earnings, particularly in land development companies. It is not the purpose of these few paragraphs to tell you how to handle your books, if you own a land development company, but, rather, to show you how selecting a method of accounting can seriously affect your earnings.

If you are planning to go public, an early discussion with the most sophisticated man in your accounting firm on this subject is certainly warranted.

SOME RECENT PRICE-EARNINGS MULTIPLES

First, bear in mind that these price earnings ratios have been computed on stocks which have been on the market for years. Your stock will have to sell on a lower basis because yours is an untried issue.

Furthermore, bear in mind that price earnings ratios change from month to month, and, indeed, from day to day, as the stock market bounces up and down. Obviously, earnings for a particular year remain constant, but prices change from day to day, so that price earnings ratios may change severely.

Nevertheless, because new issuers are always fascinated by the subject of price earnings multiples, we will give you some which we recently computed. Below, we are setting forth a number of recent price earnings ratios, by industry types. These figures are averages, so that there are extremes above and below those set forth. You will want to check out your own industry currently, once you start thinking about going public. The purpose of these figures is not to give you a guideline, but merely to show you how some industries price out better than others in a point of time. Tomorrow all of these figures might be different:

Type of Industry	How Many Times Earnings
Electronic Components	20
Cosmetic Companies	30
Electrical Equipment	12
Machinery (Heavy)	12
Newspaper and Magazine Publishers	15
Medical and Drugs	20
Factoring and Loan	15
Auto and Aircraft Parts	15
Toys	12
Home Appliances	15
Machine Tools	15
Office Equipment	30
Construction and Building	15
Food (Dairy)	12
Retailers (Departments)	10
Retail Drugs	12
Movie Theaters	15
Real Estate	20
Data Processing	60
Plastics	12
Furniture	10
Light Machinery	12
Printing and Engraving	20
Miscellaneous Chemicals	12
Food (Meat)	12
Apparel Manufacturers	15
Electronic Instruments	30
Book Publishers	25
Retail Shoe Shops	12

Retail Groceries	12
Aerospace	15

CRITICAL FACTORS IN TIMING

Is now the best time for you to go to market? Should you wait until next year? It is very important to balance the number of timing factors before you make a decision.

Thus, if an additional year's earnings under your belt will give your company more stability and if those earnings will increase substantially over this year, perhaps the best thing to do is to wait another year or two before going public. This is particularly true when you take price earnings multiples into consideration.

If you are a retailer who has just opened seven new stores and if you expect to sell your stock to the public for ten times earnings, it might be a good idea to wait until those seven new stores develop earnings for you on the books.

This year you may have had large expenses reflected on your record in setting up those stores. Are you not wiser to wait until next year when the earnings can be reflected on your record, too?

You must ask yourself this question before deciding on timing. Of course, when one waits, there is always the risk that the market will go sour. If the stock market declines, your plan to get another year's earnings under your belt may be frittered away by the market fall. By the same token, if you are planning to go to market at a low point and if you expect increased earnings next year, perhaps waiting is the thing to do.

There are other timing problems involved. In some cases, it is better not to go public until you have straightened out your own internal affairs. If your books and records are not now in shape to be audited and certified, perhaps you can get your books and records straightened out in a year or so. The time to start straightening out those records is now—not after you have committed yourself to go public and find that you are incurring a lot of expenses only to have to cancel out later. You must plan for these things in advance.

There is also the problem of whether a closely held corporation should install a pension and stock plan before it goes public. The underwriters usually feel that they should wait to get their public stockholders' consent before committing themselves to pension plans and stock option plans. That is the underwriter's viewpoint.

The viewpoint of the practicing lawyer, on the other hand, is that it is simpler to install pension plans, etc. before going public, instead of going to the stockholders and getting their consent. I would recommend to you that if you plan to go public you should seriously consider whether the slightly lower price you may get (according to the underwriters) as a result of having installed these plans before going public is still not a saving over the heartache that may be necessary to get stockholder consent, afterwards.

I have no definite hard and fast rule except that the problem of stock and pension plans should be thought through, and, if you decide that the sensible thing to do is to install them before going public, you ought to plan on postponing going public at this time.

"INSIDER" PROBLEMS

Here is another timing problem. Suppose—as in most closely held corporations—the company's real estate is now owned by the majority stockholders. Suppose the majority stockholders are leasing the real estate to the company. Suppose the insiders now own some of the sources of supply of the company, and they sell to the company. Suppose the company maintains a private yacht for the personal use of one or two of the insiders. And suppose the company and its majority stockholders are involved in a particularly nasty piece of conspiracy litigation. If any insider problems exist at the present time, they will, of course, have to be revealed in the prospectus. Are you not better off cleaning up the outstanding litigation, divorcing the insiders from the sources of supply, or merging them, or canceling the lease between the insiders and their own corporation?

Before you go public, you should plan in advance to clean up any insider relationships that you feel would give rise to criticism.

LET'S LOOK AT THE UNDERWRITER'S VIEWPOINT

Before getting involved in the mechanics of underwriting, it would be well to understand what the underwriter or investment banker does; how he does it; and how he looks at his role and yours, so that you can understand his strengths and weaknesses in negotiating with you and vice versa.

Generally, the underwriter is an investment banker. That means he commits to buy securities from issuers and to sell them to a group of retail customers of his, as well as to a "syndicate" of other investment bankers or underwriters who will retail to their own customers.

Finding securities to sell, putting together syndicate groups, and selling the securities, however, are only part of his role. If he is to be of use to the companies whose issues he floats, on a continuing basis rather than a "one-shot" deal, he must continue to advise them and continue to help support their securities in the after market, so that he is able to assist them in future securities offerings and to help them make the transition from a private to a public company.

Furthermore, he has a duty to his retail customers and to the other underwriters who comprise his syndicate to support the stock after it comes out and to see that there is a current and active market for it, since many a new stock, when left to seek its own levels, with no one interested in buying it, falls like a lead balloon.

As we have mentioned before, there are two major kinds of underwritings. The first is firm underwriting, in which the underwriter commits himself to buy all of the securities of the issuer, whether he is able to sell them or not. Theoretically, that is the best kind of a commitment to have from the issuer's viewpoint. However, as a matter of practice, it is rare for the underwriter to sign a firm commitment until almost the last day when the SEC declares the prospectus effective; and, even if the commitment is signed, because of the "market out" or "escape" clause (which is discussed in detail in the next chapter), it is entirely possible for an underwriter to walk away from his commitment, even when it appears to be firm, although not many reliable underwriters will do so.

Accordingly, many a successful issuer has selected the less desirable of the two underwriting agreements, the so-called "best efforts" underwriting, in which the underwriter commits himself to do the best he can to sell out the entire issue. Best efforts underwritings, however, are usually qualified on the basis of being a "best efforts, all or none" agreement. In other words, the underwriter is committing himself to sell out either all of the issue or none of it, so that the issuer is not in a position of going to the market seeking $1 million, only to find out that the underwriter has sold only $250,000 worth, so that the poor issuer will get too little money (and in many cases too little is as good as none) and still be locked into a public vehicle.

Thus, without the "all or none" protection, the issuer might be in the embarrassing position of needing $1 million to do some kind of refinancing, finding that only $250,000 is available, and then discovering not only that the $250,000 is worthless to him (because he cannot refinance with less than $1 million), but, also discovering that he is unhappily locked into a public vehicle and cannot do many things he could have done if he were still private.

The difference between a "firm underwriting" and a "best efforts, all or none," from the issuer's viewpoint, because of the "market out" escape clause, is largely theoretical. However, from the underwriter's viewpoint, the difference between a firm underwriting and a best efforts, all or none is significant. A firm underwriting commits the underwriter's balance sheet, and it affects the net worth ratio that the SEC compels the underwriter to have.

In other words, smaller underwriters are prevented from doing very large firm underwritings because they do not have enough net worth. Accordingly, if an underwriter tries to switch you from a firm offering to a best efforts offering, he is most likely telling you that he has not got enough net worth to handle the offering on a firm basis. I suppose there is nothing wrong with this, and many a best efforts underwriting has been very successful. There are some underwriters who are strong financially and weak sales-wise; and there are others who are strong sales-wise and weak financially. From the issuer's viewpoint, you must think the matter through and ask yourself what you are looking for. If you want someone to get you into the market on a primary offering quickly, sometimes the leaner, hungrier underwriter is better for you. If you want someone with stability and prestige and money, you may prefer the larger underwriter, if you can get him.

In either case, when you are switched to a best efforts offering, remember you are doing the underwriter a favor, and you should score some Brownie Points for it.

Underwriters also help with "private placements," which means sales to small groups of insiders or to large insurance companies or pension funds, in which no SEC registration is usually required. In close cases, you may want to make sure that you get an exemption in the form of a no-action letter.

In general, there are two kinds of underwriters:

1. The larger, more prestigeous firms with several generations of experience and capital behind them who are very conservative in their standards concerning the

size of companies they will underwrite and the number of years of earnings history they want those companies to have; and

2. Second in line are a group of underwriters who specialize in taking newer, less established companies to the market.

There is also a small group of "hot shot" sales types who will sell anything to anybody at a price.

Here there are certain specialty houses who may seek out and specialize in the securities of particular fields. These might be houses who specialize in "high technology" stocks or in real estate and building stocks or in service industries, etc.

Usually the underwriter is paid in cash out of the proceeds of the offering. In other words, the underwriter works on a commission basis. Commissions are less on bonds, debentures, and convertibles, generally, than on common stock, and recent common stock commissions have been tabulated in another chapter, with most of them running from 7 percent on the low side to 15 percent on the high side—albeit, there are some aberrations at both ends.

In addition to cash commissions, underwriters seek either warrants, cheap stock, or other opportunities to get a capital gain. As the capital gains rates have gone up, and the earned income tax has gone down, these "goodies" tend to become less attractive.

In addition, there has been increasing regulation in the warrant and cheap stock fields. Because of state securities laws ("blue sky regulations"), underwriters' warrants cannot generally be sold in less than a year or two after the public offering.

Also, the price at which these warrants are exercised is usually restricted either to 20 percent or 25 percent above the public offering price, or on a sliding scale that increases 6 or 7 percent per year, from the initial public offering price.

Warrants generally have a term of about five years and they usually do not run longer.

If the underwriter gets stock at or shortly prior to the public offering, it will be "restricted stock," which cannot be sold to the public without a separate registration, and, as a matter of practice, most of the Blue Sky Commissioners want to keep the underwriters' warrants or restricted stock down to less than 10 percent of the public issue.

Recently the National Association of Securities Dealers (NASD) and the Blue Sky Commissioners have been taking into consideration the cheap stock in limiting the upper level of the underwriters' commissions. The cheap stock and other compensation to the underwriter (fixed fees, representing so-called underwriter's expenses) tend to limit the total compensation to the underwriter at around 15 percent.

Of course, we do not have to tell you that the underwriter's demands on you for reimbursement of "expenses" and for warrants and "cheap stock" will depend on the issuer's bargaining position. If the issuer is in a "hot industry," with a good earnings record and shows substantial asset values and genuine growth, the issuer can make a better deal, particularly if the issuer is realistic about pricing on the initial offering.

10

PITFALLS TO AVOID IN HANDLING
THE UNDERWRITING AGREEMENT

You will find in our forms section, Chapter 17, a copy of an agreement between an issuer and an underwriter. That agreement is a firm commitment underwriting. Obviously, if you are dealing with a best efforts or an all or none agreement, the underwriter's commitment will be weakened. Accordingly, the underwriter, in the best efforts or all or none commitment, does not need as many escape clauses as does the underwriter in the firm commitment.

As a result, we will discuss only the firm commitment in this chapter, because it contains the most troublesome clauses to most new issuers. Many of the representations called for by the firm commitment will also be wanted by underwriters who issue best efforts or all or none commitments. To that extent, this chapter will be a helpful guide.

We will also discuss some of the variations between the firm commitments and the best efforts commitments as we go through the chapter, so that you will see three important distinctions.

THE LETTER OF INTENT

Ordinarily, the underwriting agreement which we are discussing is not signed until the issue has made a fair amount of progress. Sometimes the underwriting agreement is not signed until the SEC has cleared everything but the price amendment.

The letter of intent is an effort to put down on paper the basic understanding between the parties, without involving them in all of the details which are set forth in the full underwriting agreement. You might call the letter of intent a memorandum of what both sides feel the deal will be when the prospectus is completed and the SEC approves.

Since even the firm commitment has its escape clauses, the letter of intent will not be a truly firm document, but an effort to iron out in advance any problems that may occur between the parties.

CONTENTS OF THE LETTER OF INTENT

A typical letter of intent refers to a particular set of financial statements, and the issuer states that he is representing to the underwriter that he believes the statements to be correct; that the accountants who signed the statements are "independent accountants"; and that the common stock which will be issued by the company is presently owned by the people listed in the letter.

The issuer further represents that it knows of nothing which would materially affect its earnings which is not set forth in the annexed financial statements, and the issuer agrees to go to work immediately to prepare a prospectus registration statement.

The letter goes on to state that on the basis of current market conditions it is anticipated by the parties that the shares in question would be offered at a price somewhere in the range of $X and $Y; and that, based on that assumption, the underwriter would receive an underwriting discount of 2 percent.

If there are to be warrants or options, there is a discussion of their features in the letter of intent; then the underwriter and the issuer agree that the issuer will pay all the expenses of the SEC registration and that the issuer will pay such other items as the underwriter's counsel, blue sky registration fees, etc.

Sometimes the letter of intent states that if, for any reason, the underwriter does not accept the issue, the company will be reimbursed for those expenses.

If there has been a finder in the deal, the letter of intent usually mentions what his compensation will be and who will pay it.

THE BEST EFFORTS AGREEMENT

Aside from most of the representations and conditions which you will find discussed below in the firm commitment agreement, the best efforts agreement contains a clause that sets forth the sales relationship between the underwriter (who might better be called an exclusive sales agent, in this case) and the issuer.

A best efforts commitment on the part of the underwriter usually states that the underwriter is relying on the representations, warranties, and agreements set forth in the agreement between the parties; and, subject to the issuer's performing thereunder, the underwriter agrees to act as exclusive sales agent for the issuer, but for the account and risk of the issuer, to sell at the subscription price set forth in the agreement the securities in question.

The underwriter agrees to use his best efforts as such a sales agent to procure purchasers for the shares during the period commencing with a certain date and ending with a certain date. The underwriter is given the power, in his sole discretion, to use the services of other underwriters, brokers, or dealers in connection with making the sales; and the issuer agrees to what the underwriter's compensation will be (so much per share).

The agreement further states what expenses of the underwriter, if any, the issuer will pay. For example, the agreement might go on to state that, in addition to the underwriting discount discussed above, the issuer agrees to pay a certain sum (or a sum not exceeding $X) for the underwriter's counsel fees, and, possibly, to pay a certain additional sum which the underwriter may not have to account for (which represents the underwriter's selling expenses).

If there are to be warrants or options to the underwriter, they are set forth in the agreement.

Sometimes there is a discussion of what expenses the underwriter will bear and what will happen if the underwriter doesn't live up to his commitment.

THE FIRM COMMITMENT AGREEMENT

As we mentioned before, we set forth a full firm commitment agreement in our forms book. Reference will be made to specific clauses in that agreement in the following discussion.

The first paragraph merely describes the stock issue itself as representing a certain number of shares and a grant to the underwriters of certain stock options. Incidentally, the stock options mentioned in this particular underwriting or purchase agreement are not options for the underwriter's benefit, but merely an option to buy up to approximately 10 percent of the stock, so that there will be stock available in case market stabilization operations are required by the underwriter.

We then come to the second paragraph called "The Representations and Warranties of the Company and of the Selling Stockholders."

Subparagraph a merely states that the company warrants that it has valid corporate existence.

Subparagraph b lists the states in which the issuer is authorized to do business.

Subparagraph c warrants that the stock to be sold has been validly and properly issued.

Subparagraph d states that the persons who have signed the agreement on the part of the issuer have been fully authorized to do so.

Subparagraph e states that a registration statement with reference to the proposed stock issue has been prepared by the issuer and that the issuer represents that such registration and the final prospectus will be in accordance with the requirements of the SEC.

Subparagraph f further warrants that the issuer will include no omissions of fact nor any misleading statements in the registration.

Subparagraph g states that the issuer has not entered into nor will the issuer enter into any abnormal transactions between the prospectus date and the sales date.

Subparagraph h and subparagraph i state that issuance of the stock is not a violation of any governmental order or of any agreement the company might have with third parties.

Subparagraph j represents that the accountants are "independent."

FURTHER REPRESENTATIONS

Subparagraph 2b represents that the stock being sold is owned free and clear, etc.

Paragraph 3 comprises the underwriter's representations, and you will note how short it is but that the underwriters do represent that whatever information they have furnished to the issuing company is correct.

Subparagraphs 4a and b provide that the company will do everything it can to prepare and to expedite the registration statement and to keep the underwriters informed of the progress thereof. They further agree, under subparagraph 4c, that if any information comes to their attention, after the filing of the registration, of any material misstatement of fact that they will so inform the appropriate parties.

Subparagraph 4d provides that the issuer will make available to its stockholders financial statements which will qualify under § 11A of the Securities and Exchange Act, and subparagraph 4e states that the company agrees to furnish copies of all of the registration statements and propectuses, etc. to the underwriters.

Subparagraph 4f states that the company will furnish and execute any necessary documents under the state blue sky laws, and subparagraph 4g provides that the company will issue balance sheets and profit and loss statements to the underwriter for the next five years.

Lastly, under subparagraph 4h, the company agrees that it will use the proceeds which come from the stock sale for the purposes stated in the prospectus.

ADDITIONAL REQUIREMENTS

Subparagraph 4c lists the expenses to be borne by the company and the selling stockholders.

Paragraph 5 states the proposed price of the stock and outlines how, when, and where the closing will take place.

Paragraph 6 delineates the terms of the underwriter's stock options, and paragraphs 7 and 8 delineate the conditions precedent to the underwriter's obligations.

Subparagraph 8a provides that the underwriter will not be obligated if there is any stop order issued, nor, under subparagraph 8b, will the underwriter be obligated in case there is any untrue statement in the prospectus.

Subparagraph 8c provides for a number of conditions precedent to the underwriter's obligation, including opinion of counsel, effective registration, due incorporation, proper issuance of the stock, due legal proceedings, good title, certification by the corporation's officers, accountant's certification, etc.

Paragraph 10 contains an important clause known as the "market out" clause. The market out clause permits the underwriter to withdraw from the agreement in the event there has been "a material change in general economic or financial conditions," in the opinion of the underwriter. Frankly, it permits the underwriter to withdraw under very liberal conditions.

HANDLING THE "MARKET OUT" CLAUSE

What do you do about the "market out" clause? You are not likely to get any reputable underwriter to take the market out clause out completely. In some cases it is possible to get the underwriter to modify the clause so that he will not be able to escape merely through his own discretion but only in the case of a major national catastrophe, such as the closing of the New York Stock Exchange, a bank holiday, etc. In most cases, you won't even be able to get the underwriters to do that.

Wall Street is very touchy on the subject of market out clauses, and they justifiably point out that they do millions of dollars worth of business every day on the floor of the exchange merely by waving a hand. It is also true that if an underwriter reneges and invokes the market out clause under ordinary circumstances merely because the deal looked like a money loser to him, his name would be "mud" on the Street.

If you look back over the last few years, you will find that the reputable underwriters have exercised the market out clause only in situations such as the Cuban invasion, a thirty-point drop in the stock market, war, or substantial change in the margin requirements.

Of course, you may argue that you are planning to build a substantial structure and that you are entering into commitments based on your reliance on the underwriter's guarantee. If the underwriter can get out, where will you be?

SOLUTION TO THE "MARKET OUT" PROBLEM

I am afraid that the answer is that while you may be able to get a modification in the language, if you are not reconciled to the market out clause, you will not be able to get a firm commitment.

In some cases, however, if your bargaining power is strong, you will be able to get the underwriter at least to assume many of the legal and printing costs in preparation of the prospectus, if the underwriter is going to exercise the market out clause.

FURTHER PROVISIONS

Paragraph 12 provides for the method by which the principal underwriter will reallocate any shares which any members of the subgroup fail to pick up.

That is all there is to an underwriting agreement. You will find similar clauses in every underwriting agreement you examine. In some cases you will find that the issuer has had a strong bargaining position and has been able to make some changes in the language; in other cases, the underwriter has been very nervous and has made the language even stronger than the sample set forth here, but, whichever type of agreement you examine, the same problems will be covered.

11

SOLVING CRITICAL UNDERWRITING PROBLEMS

There are three types of underwritings:

(1) the firm commitment;

(2) the best efforts underwriting; and

(3) the best efforts, all or none underwriting.

These terms, *firm underwriting, best efforts* and *all or none* are abbreviations for the relationship between the issuing company and the underwriter.

WHAT'S INVOLVED IN FIRM COMMITMENT

From your viewpoint as the issuing company, the firm commitment is the *best deal.* A firm commitment means that the underwriter is contracting as your sales agent in selling the stock and that he is committing himself to buy, at a price fixed in the contract, all of the stocks or bonds which are not sold to the public.

On paper, at least, it means that if you and the underwriter have a contract to issue stock at $5 and if the public does not buy a single share, the underwriter is committing himself to purchase all of the stock being offered at $5.

BEST EFFORTS

On a best efforts basis, the underwriter is merely telling you that he will exercise his best efforts to sell your stock, that he will sell as much as he can, and that if he doesn't sell it all, he is under no further obligation.

The best efforts underwriting leaves the issuer in the difficult position (unless more is said) of not knowing in advance exactly how much stock will be sold. Thus, the issuer will be put to the expense of preparing the SEC registration, etc., and yet the issuer will face the possibility that the underwriter, either through his own fault or through no fault of the underwriter, will be unable to sell any stock except a small number of shares. If that happens, you will find yourself in the position of having public stockholders with all of the nuisances thereof, and having had to pay all the expenses of an underwriting, such as printing, legal, and accounting fees, only to discover that the underwriter has sold but a few hundred shares—with the result that you have a net loss on the underwriting and are now faced with a hybrid organization, part public and part private.

ALL OR NONE

The best efforts, all or none basis involves the underwriter's undertaking to sell either all of the stock or none of the stock within a certain prefixed time limit. If all the stock is sold, then the underwriter gets his commissions and the stock is issued to the public.

If the entire issue is not sold within the time limit, then the public gets its money back and no stock is issued. The underwriter may or may not receive some sort of compensation (depending upon the deal which is bargained out).

Obviously, the firm commitment is the best deal from the issuer's viewpoint, because it assures him that by a date certain he will have a sum certain.

The next most desirable deal would be the best efforts, all or none, which puts the risk of sale on the issuer, but at least assures the issuer that unless all of the stock is sold, the issuer will not be a part public, part private corporation.

The least desirable is the best efforts, although much stock has been sold this way.

There are some underwriters who feel that if the deal is not worth a firm commitment, it is not worth doing at all. There are other underwriters who do not have a large enough capitalization to commit themselves to firm commitments, but they do a creditable job in the other two fields.

CHOOSING THE BETTER OPTION

There are some underwriters who offer you a choice, but they adjust the price according to the risk they take. You must evaluate all of the possibilities, and this is the reason why it is very often advisable to sound out the underwriters before getting yourself and the underwriter too deeply involved.

In other words, it is a good idea to know in advance whether the underwriter you are contacting would consider doing a best efforts, an all or none, or a firm commitment for a company such as yours in size, type of earnings, etc. The fact that one underwriter may not do your kind of deal does not mean that no underwriter will.

In Chapter 17, you will find a form of firm commitment underwriting contract and further on in this volume you will find a discussion of some of the clauses therein.

WHO PAYS FOR WHAT?

One of the negotiating problems is the question of who pays for the underwriter's attorney; who pays for your attorney; who pays for the accounting expenses; who pays for the sales costs the underwriter has expended; and who pays the other expenses in case the underwriting is unsuccessful? This discussion is particularly important in the best efforts and the all or none deals.

A discussion about those expenses is also pertinent even in a firm commitment. In some cases, although there has been a firm commitment, the underwriter may seek to escape through the market out clause which permits the underwriter to be released in the event the underwriter, in his sole discretion, finds stock market conditions such that he does not think it makes sense to take down the stock.

If that happens; if the underwriter relieves himself of his obligation as a result of a catastrophic fall in the stock market, should the underwriter not pay his own legal expenses? Should he not also reimburse you for the printing bills in connection with printing the prospectus? Should he pay for your lawyer, also? These are items to be negotiated.

It will not be the purpose of this chapter to take you clause by clause through a firm underwriting agreement; that will be your attorney's function, but you will find a form of such agreement later. By going over that form, you can decide in advance which clauses you think will be troublesome, which clauses you would want to negotiate with the underwriter, and which clauses you would be willing to give in on.

WHAT KIND OF SEC REGISTRATION?

There are two major kinds of SEC registrations: full registrations and offering circulars. Sometimes the full registration is called an "S" registration, and the offering circulars are called "Regulation A Offerings."

Let's say a few words about each of the two types. The so-called Regulation A offering generally involves sales of stocks or bonds totaling less than $500,000. It is possible to have a full or "S" registration in the under $500,000 area, but since the Regulation A offering circular is simpler to prepare and, in theory, involves less legal and accounting problems than the full "S" registration, generally people in the under $500,000 range use the Regulation A exemption.

Before going on, we would like to point out that some of the advantages of the Regulation A offering are theoretical. However, they are not practical; in many district offices of the Securities and Exchange Commission, it takes as long, if not longer, to clear an "A" registration as it does to clear an "S" registration.

While it is true that all the "S" registrations have to clear through Washington, and the "A" registration may clear locally, because the "A" registrations have involved so much trouble to the SEC and because many of them are prepared in such an amateurish or fradulent manner, it may actually take you longer to clear through an "A" registration than an "S" registration. Of course, the timetable will differ from local office to local office.

BENEFITS OF REGULATION "A" ILLUSORY

It is also true that the financial statements in an "A" registration do not have to be certified, while they must be certified in a full "S" registration. However, this, too, is an illusory advantage in many cases. In the first place, while the figures do not have to be certified, the unofficial position of the SEC has been that the financial statements must be in accordance with good accounting practice.

Thus, in most cases, the financials will have to be recast in accordance with standard SEC practice, which means, in many cases, hiring a good accounting firm to put the statements together.

In some cases, however, a substantial amount of time may be saved by not requiring statements to be certified. The time involved in confirmations, special audit work, etc.—particularly if you are in a rush to get to market by a certain date—can be a substantial drag. We do not feel, however, that the saving of time ordinarily warrants the use of "A" versus "S," since the other problems of the "A" offering discussed above tend to more than offset the few weeks of audit time saved by using Regulation "A."

FORMATION BY THE UNDERWRITER OF A SYNDICATION GROUP

It is important for you to know the underwriter's past track record and current performance in the setting up of underwriting syndicates. The quality of the people the underwriter has worked with before tells you a lot about his reputation in the field. Your SEC counsel should be able to find out a lot about that for you.

In times of active new issue markets, the underwriter begins to feel enormous pressure in his syndication section. If he is short-handed back there, you can clear your SEC registration only to find that the underwriter is not ready for you. It is wise to find out what is going on in the syndication section, how well it is staffed, and how much they are on top of their job at the time you get ready to sign up with a particular underwriter.

For those of you who are unfamiliar with syndication, bear in mind that typically, the underwriter does not sell all of the stock himself at retail. He puts together a group of other underwriters, each of whom buys the stock at his price and attempts to make the retail mark-up, and each of whom is committed to sell a certain number of shares. You should understand that your selection of the lead underwriter is going to dictate, to a certain extent, the strengths, weaknesses, and prestige of the subunderwriters who comprise the syndicate.

In general, high prestige houses with many years of reputation behind them are most reluctant to take smaller pieces of deals put together by lead underwriters for whom they have no respect.

The subunderwriters commit themselves to pick up a specific portion of the commitment; the obligation of each subunderwriter is specific, and no one theoretically is obligated to pick up any more than his pro rata portion. As a practical matter, the lead underwriter may help his subunderwriters if they get into trouble, so that they can do business once again. These behind-the-scenes deals do not, however, affect the issuer—at least not directly.

In addition to underwriters, there may be a group of brokers behind the scenes who have been allotted or who have agreed to pick up certain portions of the stock, and who are selected because they have good retail distribution. They may not typically be a part of the underwriting agreement, however.

The underwriting agreement itself (as distinguished from the letter of intent) is almost always signed on the very day of the public offering, after clearance of the final SEC prospectus. The agreement usually calls for delivery of the securities against payment therefor in cash (the closing) approximately a week after the first day of the public offering.

As a condition precedent to the closing, the issuer warrants that as of the closing date, all of the representations and warranties in the underwriting agreement are still in full force and effect and are updated. At the closing, opinions of counsel, updated letters from the auditors, representations that there have been no material adverse changes in the company's business, etc. are given in exchange for the check.

12

WORKING EFFECTIVELY WITH FINDERS

First, what is a finder? Generally, a finder is an individual who brings to the underwriter a prospective underwriting. For this service, the finder gets the equivalent of a commission which may be payable as a fee out of the underwriting, or may involve the finder's sharing in stock options, etc.

PROS AND CONS ON FINDERS

A good finder can be of great assistance to you. He knows the underwriting field and is able to place your issue with one or more underwriters who would be interested in it, thus saving you time and, in many cases, money, by going to an underwriter who evinces the maximum interest in your issue.

The finder, if he is to be of use to you, should know the underwriting market and be able to present your issue effectively. The underwriter's role is to translate your company into the kind of terms that underwriters like to hear and understand. As all good brokers, the finder knows how to present your strong points, how to explain your weak points, and he knows who are the likeliest prospects for you; and the good finder knows how to avoid wasting time with underwriting houses that would not be suitable for your kind of deal. The good finder can save you time and money.

There are bad finders, also. These are people seeking to edge themselves into a deal where they have no function. In many cases, they don't know what they are doing and, by ineffectively presenting your material, they may ruin an opportunity you would otherwise have to make an effective presentation to a good underwriter. Once the underwriter has rejected the deal, he is not likely to revise his opinion in the event someone other than the original finder presents it to him again. Your finder may be irrevocably ruining your name among the underwriting houses.

WHAT KIND OF PEOPLE ARE FINDERS?

Sometimes the finders are people familiar with the underwriting markets who devote their full time to locating suitable underwriting prospects and to presenting their proposed underwritings to suitable underwriting houses. Such finders act as the eyes and ears of underwriting organizations who do not have the time or the staff to send men out into the field.

There are also a large number of part-time finders, and some of them are quite good. These may include accountants, lawyers, commercial bankers, trade association executives, and other people who are constantly on the lookout for deals suitable for an underwriting. These secondary types of finders usually engage in this activity on a part-time basis and very often their sole function is to make an introduction, whereupon they leave all further negotiations directly to the underwriter and the company itself.

If these part-time finders know where to go and if they put your interests ahead of their own, they, too, can perform an effective function.

CHECK THE FINDER'S REFERENCES

When a finder comes to you, it is most important that you find out something about him—what deals has he done; what commission arrangements did he make in those other deals; what are the names of some of the underwriters and firms he has dealt with; how long he has been doing finding and for whom, etc. Concrete pieces of information such as this, subject to checking, are the kind of information you want to know about your prospective finder.

Bear in mind that if the finder is going to represent you, the underwriters will judge your reputation by him. They will judge your know-how by his. If you are not satisfied with your finder, by all means get rid of him before you ruin your own reputation or get yourself committed in such a way that you are subject to a lawsuit.

WHO PAYS THE FINDER?

Ordinarily, the finder is paid by the underwriter out of the underwriter's commission. However, it is possible for the finder to be paid by the prospective issuer, and, indeed, if the finder reveals the facts to all of the parties, the finder may be paid by both sides.

Since there is nothing definite on who is legally obligated to pay the finder and each deal depends on its own set of circumstances, if you are a prospective issuer you should have an immediate understanding with the finder when he first comes into your office. Are you going to be expected to pay him? If not, who will pay him should be ironed out in the first conference and this should be reduced to writing to avoid further lawsuits.

Some of the other things that should be ironed out with the prospective finder are: Will you be able to negotiate on your own with underwriters not being contacted by the finder; if not, are you going to give the finder an "exclusive"; and, if you are going to give him an exclusive, for how long a period will he have it?

Problems like these are best ironed out by a written agreement between the finder and the issuer and between the finder and the underwriter, as early as possible. Much grief has come to finders, to issuers, and to underwriters when the problems of each were not delineated in a letter early enough in the negotiations.

If you are a finder, you would not want to be deprived of a commission that might run into several hundred thousand dollars because you failed to put it in writing.

If you are an issuer, you would not want to discover—after you signed an underwriting agreement—that you were expected to pay the finder several hundred thousand dollars.

If you are an underwriter, you certainly do not want the finder to make a claim on you for a large commission if, for some reason or other, the underwriting falls apart and the SEC throws out the registration, through no fault of the finder, but through no fault of yours either.

All parties should "get it in writing"; ordinarily, you are working with large figures and messy lawsuits.

WHAT SHOULD THE FINDER'S LETTER COVER?

A simple finder's agreement will be drawn between the finder and the issuer or between the finder and the underwriter, and it will state that the finder is authorized to act on behalf of the underwriter; that he is recognized by the underwriter as the finder of a particular deal; and that the finder will receive compensation either by way of a portion of the underwriter's fee or by the issuance of some of the warrants or stock rights being granted to the underwriter.

The finder also agrees that in the event any other finder claims a portion of the commission, he (the finder) will hold the underwriter harmless from such a claim and that under no circumstances is the underwriter to be liable to the finder unless and until the deal is consummated and the stock sold to the public.

If the finder represents an issuer, a time limit should be set on the finder's rights. The prospective issuer should reserve for himself the right to act as his own agent and without obligation to the finder, if the issuer is the one who locates an underwriter through his own efforts. Of course, the amount of the finder's compensation should be spelled out in the agreement.

If the finder is paid by the underwriter, his compensation may typically represent anywhere from 5 to 15 percent of the underwriter's net fee. If he is to be paid by the issuer (I suppose, realistically, he is always paid by the issuer, even if the underwriter gives the finder his check), he might conceivably be working on the so-called 5:4:3:2:1 sliding scale. There is really no standardization of these fees. In some cases, the 5:4:3:2:1 figure represents a percentage of the first $1 million, the second $1 million, the third $1 million, etc. through the first $5 million and up. In other cases, the sliding scale will run in half-million dollar gaps.

For example, if you are using the 5:4:3:2:1 scale and are applying it to the raising of $5 million of common stock, and if you are using the million dollar gaps, the finder would get 5 percent of the first $1 million (or $50,000), 4 percent of the second $1 million (or $40,000), 3 percent of the third $1 million (or $30,000), 2 percent of the fourth $1 million (or $20,000) and 1 percent of the fifth $1 million (or $10,000), for a total of $150,000 on $5 million.

As mentioned, there is no hard and fast rule and, in some cases, finders have gotten as much as a straight 5 percent across the board, or $250,000 on $5 million.

CONFLICTS OF INTEREST

It is important to note that an independent public accountant who is counting on certifying the financial statements of a particular underwriting is in no position to be a finder. That is, he may not claim a portion of the underwriter's commission; the SEC will disqualify him as the independent certified public accountant if he has an interest in the offering. One cannot be independent and, at the same time, seek a part of the underwriting commission.

One comes to a more delicate question in dealing with the functions of attorneys as finders. While an attorney who represents an underwriter could very well be a finder, it is more difficult to see how an attorney who represents an issuer can also be paid by the underwriter. Technically speaking, if all of the parties know that the attorney is representing both sides and if all consent in writing, I imagine it would be possible for the attorney to represent the issuer and at the same time collect a commission from the underwriter.

I, myself, do not think that the attorney would be particularly comfortable representing both sides, but this is a matter for personal judgment and involves practical and legal, as well as ethical considerations. The most sensible thing to do is to decide which side you want to be on and have that side pay you.

Employees, too, are in an unusual position. The case law of certain states has held that an employee ordinarily owes a fiduciary duty to his employer and cannot claim a commission from somebody with whom he deals on behalf of that employer. However, I imagine it might be possible in certain circumstances to get the employer to consent to the employee's collection of a commission from the underwriter. If that be the case, may I suggest that if you are such an employee that you get it in writing. Otherwise you may find great difficulty in collecting your commission at a later date if the employer claims surprise.

Whoever the finder may be—whether he is an employee, an accountant, an attorney, a banker, or a financial adviser—the finder must be prepared to see his name imprinted on the SEC prospectus. The SEC requires that finders who share in the underwriting proceeds must be named in the prospectus and the amount of their compensation stated thereon.

As a result, if you intend to be a finder, bear in mind early in the game that you cannot have a secret relationship to the deal. Your relationship will have to be disclosed; no reputable underwriter would pay you an under-the-table finder's fee.

13

DETERMINING WHICH SECURITIES OFFER THE GREATEST REWARD

All corporate securities break down into two simple types, although there are many minor variations. The two major kinds of corporate securities are:

Bonds—which represent a noncontingent, fixed obligation of the corporation to pay a definite sum of money together with a definite interest rate thereon. Bonds are noncontingent because they do not depend on whether the corporation has good earnings or bad ones. If the company fails to meet its bond obligation, it must go into bankruptcy.

Stocks—which represent equity participations; the corporation is obligated to pay nothing on them unless the board of directors finds that there are earnings and unless the board declares dividends.

VARIATIONS ON THE STOCK AND BOND THEMES

Even within the bond field you have various grades or types of bonds. There are bonds which are collateralized, such as mortgage bonds, in which prime real estate or plant or equipment is pledged as collateral for the security of the bonds. Thus, you get not only the guarantee of the company's credit status but, also, you are in a position (through a trustee) to foreclose on a valuable asset, if payments are not met.

Then there are debentures, which are simply promises to pay and are usually backed only by the corporation's credit. In other words, if the corporation doesn't have sufficient earnings to pay the interest and principal, the bond holders, acting through their trustee, can put the company into bankruptcy; but that is not as good as having some kind of collateral pledged to secure your obligation.

Of course, even collateralized bonds are sometimes deceptive. The strength of those obligations will depend on how marketable the collateral is. Thus, a first mortgage bond whose collateral depends on the resaleability of an old, dilapidated plant in a poor location is not a very good bond.

111

On the other hand, bonds which are collateralized with something as marketable as modern rolling stock of a railroad are so good that, even though the railroad may itself be in bankruptcy, the bonds may be sold at a premium because the equipment is so readily marketable.

If you are going to be a bond buyer, you must ask yourself whether your collateral is any good or not; and, if you are talking about a noncollateral bond or simply a debenture, then you must ask yourself whether the corporation has sufficient earnings so that you can be sure of getting your interest and principal, come what may.

If there is only a small earnings cushion, the debentures are probably not very good; but if the corporation has six or eight times enough earnings to make good on the bonds, then you probably have a very fine security.

STOCKS vs. BONDS, FROM THE ISSUER'S VIEWPOINT

Bonds are a fixed commitment. Companies that issue them in good times learn to rue them in bad times. Those corporations that issued large bond commitments during the '20s were among the first companies to go bankrupt during the '30s.

On the other hand, those companies with largely equity or stock financing have great flexibility. Earnings may rise and earnings may fall; the stock itself may rise and fall, but the company is not affected thereby. If there are no earnings, the directors just pay no dividends.

Of course, corporations with large bond financings and little common stock financing have a very volatile common stock. Since bonds represent a fixed commitment with, generally, a relatively low interest rate, as earnings rise, the entire earnings over and above the interest are left for the common stockholders.

Corporations with large bond issues and small common stock issues have a very attractive common stock in a rising economy. Every dollar over and above the bond requirements winds up in the hands of the common stockholders.

By the same token, as earnings fall in a declining market, the common stock which stands behind a large bond issue rapidly sees its entire earnings wiped out by the large fixed charges involved in paying off the bonds and the interest thereon.

An intelligent decision on how much bonds and how much stock to issue depends on a number of important factors: First, what is the best for the company (as against the company's past earnings history and its future projections); next, will a stock or a bond bring top dollar in a particular market.

Sometimes you have no choice. There have been periods when the common stock market has lagged and only bonds could be issued. There have also been periods when bonds showed little market acceptance and only common stock could be issued. What is more, you are planning not only for today, but for a long time to come. To plan and decide on how much bonds, how much stock, and what kinds of each is a key function of the best financial brains you can get within your own organization, coupled with the best underwriting advice you can get.

It is this kind of decision that requires your getting the best possible underwriter for your company instead of looking for the underwriter who may be cheapest at a particular time or who may offer the best price for your issue.

Remember: there is more to underwriting than selling stock; you need topnotch financial advice from your underwriter.

HYBRID SECURITIES: THE PLUSES AND MINUSES

In the preceding paragraphs we have discussed common stocks and bonds. Bonds are firm commitments on the part of the issuer to pay interest and principal on definite dates. The promise to pay is not conditioned upon earnings, and it is a prior claim on the company's assets.

Stock gives you a right to vote on the management of the company, and it is a secondary claim behind the bond holders, available to you only if there are earnings. No earnings, no dividends. Indeed, even if there be earnings, the corporation is not obligated to pay dividends, ordinarily.

Nonetheless, as we illustrated above, the common stock is the more volatile, the more speculative, and the larger participant in the future of a growing company.

Of course, it is difficult to find securities that are completely black or completely white. To satisfy market demands, underwriters and issuers have developed a number of hybrid securities which offer variations on stocks and bonds. Investors who are looking for securities that have the prior claim of a bond and yet who want a chance at the speculative future of the company may buy a convertible bond. That is, a bond which is convertible into common stock of the corporation over a certain period of time.

The investor has the guaranteed security of a bond, and, if the common stock increases in value, he may exercise his option, thus coupling his security with the speculative advantages of being a stockholder.

Of course, any time you blend something together you get certain new strengths (such as the speculative advantages of the convertible bond) but you also get some weaknesses, too.

There are also "preferred stocks"; that is, stocks which are entitled to receive dividends on either an accumulative basis or in preference to dividends which will be paid to the common stockholders. Such securities are more conservative than common stocks because they have a preferential lien on earnings, but they are not as good as bonds because they are not a claim on the company's assets. No earnings, still no dividends.

There are also other hybrids such as income bonds. These are bonds which depend on their interest upon the corporation's having earnings. No income (net), no interest. These bonds are inferior in security aspects to other common noncontingent bonds.

CONVERTIBLE BONDS: IMPORTANT ASPECTS TO CONSIDER

It is interesting to note that from 1930 to 1952 approximately 20 percent of all the bond issues contained certain opportunities to convert the bonds into common stock. During the 1950s and 1960s, almost 60 percent of the bond issues contained convertible features. Convertibles were used by such giants as the American Telephone & Telegraph and such smaller companies as Vornado.

The convertible debentures typically offered the bond investor an opportunity to convert his bonds into common stock at varying fixed prices over the life of the conversion feature. In some cases, the conversion feature is separated from the bond (a separately tradable warrant), and in other cases, they are locked together with the bond.

Corporations which issue convertible bonds use them to help raise money at a time when funds are scarce, and the premium which the investor is willing to pay for the conversion feature permits the company to raise funds at a lower interest cost than it would otherwise have to pay out.

The convertible feature defers to the company the cost of the financing by offering to the investor, in exchange for a lower current interest rate, the opportunity to buy stock at below its market value at a later date.

In addition, the convertible feature is attractive to such institutional investors as insurance companies which must put a specific portion of their portfolio into bonds and which find in convertibles an opportunity to legally invest in bonds at the same time they can participate in the company's growth, as if they had purchased equities.

The conversion feature offers to the company another benefit. It permits the company to sell its common stock at a higher price in the future than today's market and to receive the capital which would go into it immediately in the form of the bond purchase.

For example, if you sell a $1,000 debenture today, convertible into common stock in five years at $35 per share, when the common stock is selling at $30 per share at the time you issue the debentures, the investor who purchases debentures is in effect paying the higher price for the common stock at the time he purchases the debenture. At the time of conversion, the debenture will be worth a specific number of shares, and the company will be paying off the debenture with those shares. Since the company receives the money at the time it sells the debentures, it pays the investor interest on that amount until the conversion takes place.

When a company issues convertible debentures, it is assuming that the stock will reach the conversion price, so that the conversion will actually take place by the time the option to the investor expires. Obviously, if the stock does not reach the predetermined level or higher, the investor will not exercise his option and will continue to own a debenture—but a debenture at an inordinately low interest amount.

Theoretically, convertibles avoid diluting per-share earnings because they are not presently common stock. Of course, they hand over the market and ultimately will be converted. Accounting rules require that this be recognized in the balance sheet, one way or another, and the Accounting Principles Board, under Opinion No. 14, has dealt with the subject recently and the situation, balance-sheet-wise and earnings-per-share-wise, is still in a state of flux, so that you will want to check out the matter at the time you issue the securities.

As mentioned before, sophisticated securities analysts take a look at the conversion features hanging over the market and tend to discount the earnings per share, if there are substantial convertible issues in the corporation. The contrary argument offered by many companies issuing convertibles is that if the conversion feature is ever to be exercised, it will be exercised because the price of the stock has risen, and the price of the stock will rise only if earnings per share go up, so that the two should cancel each other out.

Very few lay investors are capable of this sophisticated analysis and convertible issues continue to be popular in periods where equity financing is difficult to get for particular companies or in periods where interest rates for debt securities have a tendency to be ceiling-high.

Other factors to be considered in connection with convertibles are their advantages in retiring debt. If the convertible works, there is no need to set up a sinking fund to pay off the bond issue. Furthermore, if the company needs financing at a time when it cannot market common stock, the convertible offers an opportunity to raise capital on the basis of a long term debt security, deferring both the overhanging common stock and the payment of the debt into the future.

Convertibles are also useful because, in many cases, their bond characteristics permit them to be financed outside of stock margin requirements and permit them to be financed when the company's common stock, because it is unlisted or otherwise, would not qualify for margin.

Convertibles, since they partake of the nature of a bond, generally get the benefits of the lower underwriting discounts of the bond business rather than the higher fee schedules applicable to common stocks; and, if the choice is between issuing a plain debenture and a convertible debenture, the opportunity to convert to common stock permits the underwriters to market a security which has less restrictions than an ordinary bond.

Thus, restrictions which would be found in ordinary bonds such as subordination, restrictions on dividends, acts of default, etc. tend to get watered out in convertible securities when compared with simple senior debt.

Those who criticize the use of convertible financing point out that the biggest problem which arises in a convertible is what happens when it is not converted. Thus, if the stock "does not make it" because something is wrong with the business, the bond feature of the security may fall in on the company at the worst possible time. In other words, if the company is doing too poorly to warrant a conversion into stock, what on earth will the company do to refinance the debenture?

Furthermore, convertible critics point out, the use of the convertible tends to depress common stock prices, and, even if the conversion is successful, the conversion into common stock may come at a time which is inconvenient to the company. Thus, if a common stock issue has to be floated when conversion is imminent or when conversion has just taken place, the market price of the stock may be depressed by the flooding or potential flooding of new common stock on the market.

There are those who say that the issuance of a convertible security is an indication that the company is too weak to go to the senior securities market without the feature. This is not necessarily so; A.T.&T. cannot have used convertible bonds so frequently because it is weak credit-wise; it is apparent that "Ma Bell" is utilizing the convertible because it considers the convertible good business, and not out of a sense of weakness.

Several sophisticated decisions have to be made by management at the time they issue a convertible:

They must decide on the conversion ratio. How many shares of common stock will be exchanged for the bond and what will the timing be? If you guess it wrong (if you miscalculate future values of your own stock) the conversion will never take place. The conversion ratio, if the conversion is to take place successfully, is just as important as the pricing of the debenture at the time of original issue and a certain amount of crystal-balling is required.

WHICH KIND OF SECURITY FOR YOUR COMPANY?

Now that we have delineated the different kinds of securities and, since we are not looking at them from the investor's viewpoint, but from the issuing company's viewpoint, let us see the advantages and disadvantages each type of security has for you as an issuer.

Common stocks impose the least obligation on the company over the long run. The issuance of common stock does not tie the company down to a repayment date nor to an interest commitment. Companies that had large common stock financings weathered the depression very well, even though many of the investors lost their money when the stocks fell badly. From the company's viewpoint, a common stock financing offers maximum flexibility for the future.

On the other hand, it means that you are giving away a major portion of your future earnings to the new investors. If you, yourself, are now a large common stockholder and if you issue nothing but common stock, while you are not committing the company to any definite payment in the future, bear in mind that the issuance of more common stock dilutes your share of the corporation's future earnings.

If you expect business to continue on the up-grade, from your own selfish viewpoint, if you are now a 100 percent common stockholder, you might be better off issuing bonds; you would retain for yourself the lion's share of the future earnings of the corporation. In addition, the issuance of nonstock securities does not dilute voting control. Again, bonds or preferred stocks ordinarily have little voice in the management (except if there has been a default in payment).

By the same token, common stocks are ordinarily divided into two categories: voting and nonvoting (also called "A" stock and "B" stock); or, even though you may have two kinds of voting common, one class of common may have better voting rights than another class of common.

There are occasions when you issue an "A" stock and a "B" stock where the "A" stock (which may be held by the management) is always permitted to elect ten directors out of a total of fifteen. This means that if all the "B" stock is issued to the public and if the public can only elect five directors, the public will never be able to get majority voting control.

Bonds, as we have stated above, are a firm commitment to pay interest and principal. Bonds have a substantial tax advantage from the corporation's viewpoint, also. Bond interest is deductible to the corporation. Dividend payments on common or preferred stock are not deductible. Code Section 249 of the Revenue Act of 1969 affects the deductibility of some interest charges on convertible bonds and it clearly affects any premium paid as a cost of redeeming the bonds, should they not be converted. The section should be checked out carefully for its applicability to any convertible security you intend to issue.

If your corporation is in the 50 percent tax bracket, you only have to earn $100,000 before taxes to pay $100,000 of bond interest to your investors. However, to pay that same $100,000 down to the investors in the form of dividends, if the corporation were in the 50 percent tax bracket, you would have to earn $200,000 (before taxes). That is because the pretax earnings are cut 50 percent by the Federal government's slice. If you are looking at the question of whether to use bonds or stock in financing, from the viewpoint of cost to the corporation bonds are cheaper than stocks because bond interest is deductible; stock dividends are not.

SOME OTHER PROBLEMS

There are no open and shut answers as to what kind of financing is best for your corporation. Let's look at some of the possible variations. Suppose you do a bond issue because you decide you would like to deduct the interest and because you feel that you would have to allocate less earnings to interest payments which are deductible than you would have to allocate to common stock. The decision is a sound one.

In five years, however, earnings drop off to practically nothing and the corporation is faced with bankruptcy if it does not pay its bond holders.

Let's now look at another situation, to show you that corporate financing involves delicate considerations that have to be planned for carefully. Suppose you issue convertible bonds. You do this because your underwriter tells you that convertible bonds are very popular now because they give investors the feeling of security, while the investor gets a "play" on the future of the stock.

You follow your underwriter's suggestion and you issue convertible bonds. The bond interest is deductible as long as the bonds are not converted into stock. You set aside $100,000 a year to pay your bond interest; that $100,000 is deductible and passes through to your investors, giving the corporation a deduction therefor.

However, because you are an excellent corporate manager, the common stock goes up quite a bit. As a result, the convertible debentures begin to get converted into common stock. Every stockholder who converts a bond into a share of stock automatically deprives you of an interest deduction. The moment the stockholder gets a common stock certificate, he eliminates your interest payments. At the same time, however, he hopes to get the dividends equal to the old interest rate.

The result is that you now have to get $200,000 of earnings, pay approximately $100,000 of earnings to the tax collector, and then you will be able to pass through $100,000 of earnings to the stockholder. Because you have been so successful and run up the stock, your company will be penalized by losing the interest deduction.

In addition, convertible bonds have a tendency to hang over the market. That is, since everybody knows they are available and ultimately will be converted, they depress the market for the common stock by having a tendency to put a ceiling on that stock and also by acting as a warning to the stockholders that conversion is imminent any time the common rises.

If you, yourself, are a common stockholder and are hoping to keep a major share of the earnings for yourself by remaining a common stockholder, the issuance of convertible bonds may dilute your equity in the future and may prevent the common from rising to its full height.

Of course, the use of convertible bonds has the advantage of giving you interest deductions in the early years and may have the further advantage of being the only kind of certificate you can go to the public with. In that case, you don't really have much choice; you will have to use a convertible bond whether you like it or not. However, we are asking you to think through carefully the kind of security you are going to issue and to ask yourself:

1. What is the immediate cost of issuing such a security?
2. Is that security the cheapest way of raising money in the current market?
3. What effect will that security have on the future securities issued?
4. What tax effect will the issuance of a particular kind of security have on the corporate structure, both now and in the future?
5. After looking at the proposed security from the corporate viewpoint, how about looking at it from a selfish viewpoint? What will the issuance of this new kind of security do to your stock in the future?

VOTING RIGHTS

We touched lightly on the subject of having two classes of stock before—"A" and "B" stock. We mentioned that there are two ways of loading the voting rights. One is by having insider stock get two or three votes for each share as compared to only a single vote for each share of outsider stock. Another way to accomplish the same result (sometimes deemed a more palatable way) is to have each class of stock elect a certain number of directors with the insiders electing two or three times as many directors as the outsiders.

One word of warning about loaded voting devices. Underwriters and the public ordinarily do not like them, and if you decide you want to do an "A" stock and a "B" stock deal, you must reconcile yourself to finding greater difficulty in dealing with the underwriters and to the probability that you may have to give up something else in your issue in exchange for the more complicated voting structure.

We don't say that an "A" and a "B" stock cannot be done in a small new issue; we have seen many where it has been done. You must ask yourself whether you are not giving up something to get that voting protection. As long as you know what you are buying for the voting protection, it is all right.

On the other hand, if you are only going to do a small issue of perhaps 30 or 40 percent of the company's total stock, why involve yourself in a complicated voting structure; why penalize yourself in terms of the money you could get for the issue when you don't need the complicated dual voting rights anyhow.

14

PROFESSIONAL HANDLING OF SEC REGISTRATION REQUIREMENTS

To begin with, you must ask yourself whether the SEC has jurisdiction over your offering. The SEC's jurisdiction is very broad, and you should start out by assuming that the SEC does have jurisdiction over your offering. Thus, any time you use an instrumentality of interstate commerce (such as the mails or the phones or you cut across state lines), the SEC has jurisdiction. There are certain exemptions, and this chapter will outline the major ones, but you should start out by assuming that the SEC does have jurisdiction, and, before you assume it does not have it, make very sure you are right. In doubtful cases, it is best to have the SEC give you a written opinion (a no-action letter) to protect you against the possible charge of willful violation of the statutes or falling within the ambit of an SEC "stop order," or "fraud order," which may do you and your company irreparable harm.

THE MAJOR EXEMPTIONS FROM REGISTRATION BY THE SEC

There are three important major exemptions from full SEC registration, and they are:

1. The private placement exemption (known technically as the §4(2) exemption).

2. The single state offering (known as the §3(a)(11) intrastate exemption).

3. The so-called Regulation A exemption which permits you to dispense with a full prospectus and file a much more simplified form, if your securities issue involves an offering of less than $500,000 (this used to be a $300,000 exemption).

PRIVATE PLACEMENTS EXEMPTIONS

The SEC itself has issued, for the general guidance of interested parties, a release dated November of 1962 (Release No. 4552) relating to the so-called private offering exemption. The SEC points out that generally the private offering exemption is intended to cover the private placement of securities with such institutions as banks and insurance companies.

Release No. 4552 points out that whether a transaction is a private offering which does not have to be registered or a public one, which does, unless it comes in under one of the other exemptions, depends upon all of the facts. Some of the factors in determining whether it is public (and therefore registerable) or private (in which case registration is not required) include the relationship between the person making the offering and the prospective investor and the nature, scope, size, type, and manner of the offering.

It has generally been said that if there are less than twenty-five offerees, there is no requirement to register with the SEC. This is not strictly true, and it is more important who the offerees are than how many of them there are. In other words, what the registration statutes intend is to protect the unsophisticated investor. Who is an unsophisticated investor? That depends: Some of the criteria that have helped the courts and the SEC to determine whether the investor is sophisticated or not deals with the relationship of the parties. Thus, an offering by a customer to his supplier, where the supplier knows the business and the customer, would probably be a private offering. On the other hand, as the courts decided in SEC v. Ralston Purina (346 U.S. 119) where the offerees were a group of employees, sophistication did not automatically follow.

In the Ralston Purina case, where the offerees were a number of relatively low level employees who did not have the entire business picture before them, the SEC felt that the proposed investors were entitled to the protection of a prospectus.

Some of the tests seem to be the sophistication of the offerees (their knowledge of a particular business issuing the securities and of the industry itself); the net worth of the offerees (the theory is that wealthy men are able to protect themselves better than little old ladies); the access to information equivalent to or better than registration would afford on the part of the prospective investor (such as the underlying documents and the books and records); the size of the offering; the method of offering (whether it is broadcast about by a number of broker-dealers or offered directly by the principal to the presidents of investor corporations); whether the offerees are buying for their own account or are actually acting as distribution agents or conduits; and, finally, the subject of integration. "Integration" means putting together (or integrating) a whole series of separate offerings, each of which, standing alone, would not require registration, but when the total of the offerings is integrated, registration becomes imperative.

Thus, one might escape registration requirements by offering three sophisticated investors interests of one-third each in a particular piece of real estate or in an oil deal. When those three investors are added to five other investors in another real estate deal and ten in still another, and five more in the following year, one could logically argue (and the SEC has so argued) that all of the offerings ought to be added together, and, when they are added together, the sum total, integrated, results in a public offering, even though a single issue might stand alone as a private offering.

What do you do to protect yourself, if you really have a private offering? Well, if you use third parties to solicit customers, you make certain that you know everyone to whom the third parties have offered the issue, and you ask your broker to represent to you in writing not only to whom he has made the offer but have him get from each of the employees information as to the net worth and sophistication of each such offeree, as well as a statement of whether the underlying documents have been offered to the accountants and attorneys of the offeree.

The issuer (the corporation distributing the securities) should find out and is responsible for what the broker does in soliciting customers. If the broker uses a private placement memorandum, look at it and make sure he is not misrepresenting your deal, or it may come back to haunt you.

In general, to avoid the problem of selling to people who intend to chop up the unit and retail it to other people; one should get a so-called investment letter from each offeree. The investment letter usually states that the buyer is purchasing the security for his own account and not with a view toward distribution or resale, and that the buyer agrees to indemnify the security seller from any loss which results from a breach of this agreement by the buyer's retailing his unit. Stock sold subject to this investment letter is called "investment letter stock," and generally the stock certificates bear a legend to the effect that the stock certificates have been "acquired for investment and have not been registered under the Securities Act of 1933" and that "the underlying shares may not be sold or transferred in the absence of registration, unless in the opinion of the attorney for the issuing company, such registration is not required."

Another important factor to bear in mind, if you intend to seek the private placement exemption under §4(2), is the number of offerees. (Note the word "offerees" and not "investors.")

You may insert an advertisement in the *Wall Street Journal* or *New York Times* which says: "Seeking twenty-five investors." Perhaps you think that by seeking only twenty-five investors you have escaped the need for SEC registration because you have twenty-five or less "offerees." Not so. Actually, everyone who sees the advertisement in the newspaper is a potential offeree, even though he may not become an investor. It is the number of people you have offered the issue to and not the number of investors that counts.

Thus, if the *New York Times* has a five million circulation, you have five million offerees and not twenty-five, even though only twenty-five people ultimately become investors. The same is true if you use the mails. If you send out 5,000 letters seeking twenty-five investors, you have 5,000 offerees and not twenty-five.

Indeed, if you wind up with twenty-five investors, it will be pretty hard to convince anyone that you have twenty-five or less offerees, because if there are twenty-five investors and if you argue there are that many offerees you will have to prove that every offeree accepted and no one turned you down. In other words, if you have twenty-five investors and if two people turned you down, you must have had twenty-seven offerees.

EVEN ASSUMING A PRIVATE PLACEMENT, WHAT MUST YOU DISCLOSE?

Many issuers feel that just because you have a private placement, you need tell the investors nothing. This is not so. For example, Rule 10(b)(5) of the Securities Act of

1934 makes it unlawful to make an untrue statement of a material fact or to omit to state a material fact which, in the light of the circumstances, is misleading.

In other words, even if you don't have to register, if you fail to state a material fact, by suppressing it, or if you willfully make an untrue statement, investors may be able to sue for their money back, and, in addition, the SEC, of course, has broad jurisdiction.

Note that the rule is applicable if a security is being sold and if the mails or an instrumentality of interstate commerce (the long distance telephone) is used in the transaction. There are other civil rights available to investors who feel they have been defrauded, primarily under §17(a) of the 1933 Securities Act, and §12(2) of the 1933 Securities Act.

Furthermore, there are various state blue sky laws protecting investors, and we usually urge clients, even where there is a private placement, to prepare a document in the form of a prospectus, setting forth all the material facts, so that an investor cannot complain later that he was not apprised of the realities of the situation. Such a document, if properly prepared, protects issuers from the dangers of subsequent suits by disgruntled investors, when the market for the particular type of securities changes.

The document used to effectuate this disclosure is sometimes called the "private placement memorandum," and you must be careful to whom you show it, because too broad a distribution of private placement memoranda may give rise to a public offering. (See the preceding discussion concerning offerees.)

It is generally wise to number the private placement memoranda and to keep track of what happens to each copy, and this is true whether you distribute them yourself or whether you distribute them through agents or brokers.

THE ONE-STATE (INTRASTATE OFFERING)

This is the so-called §3(a)(11) exemption which provides that registration and preparation of a formal prospectus are not required for "any security which is part of an issue offered and sold only to persons resident within a single state or territory, where the issuer of such security is a person resident and doing business within; or, if a corporation, incorporated by and doing business within, such state or territory."

Note, therefore, as a beginning, that both the company and the investor must be within a single state.

In other words, if I have my plant in New York State and if I offer only to New York investors and if my main office is in New York, I will have a one-state offering within the SEC's regulations.

But, if I make my offer in New York State, but if my place of business is in New Jersey, then, under the SEC's administrative rulings, I have a two-state offering, and, unless I keep the number of offerees down and unless I can comply with the private placement exemption just discussed, I must register.

Note, then, that if I restrict myself to a single state offering and if the company and the offerees are located within that state, I may have as many offerees as I want and still need not register with the SEC. But, the moment I cross state lines and make an offer outside of the state or have a place of business outside of the state of the offer, I must comply with the private placement exemption, and this generally requires a limited number of offerees.

But as long as I stay within a single state, I may have as many as several thousand offerees and still not be compelled to register.

A WORD OF WARNING

The SEC law provides substantial civil and criminal penalties for failure to register where registration was required. If you expect to use an underwriter, you will find that registration is going to be required. No underwriter wants to take the chance that all of the offerees will be limited to a single state, nor will the underwriter be content to offer the deal to only twenty-five people.

As a result, professional underwriters in all fields (except real estate syndication) will require registration under one section of the law or the other.

Failure to register when required, aside from the criminal penalties, puts you in a very difficult position civilly. Under the SEC law, if you should have registered but didn't, investors are in a position to demand their money back. Imagine the position you might put your corporation in if you made an offering to fifty investors in several states and should have registered but didn't. Suppose, furthermore, that your fifty offerees put up a total of $250,000 with which you built the plant. As a result, the whole $250,000 has been spent. Now, business gets difficult and you are not able to pay regular dividends to your investors. A number of them demand their money back, starting suit under the SEC statutes, claiming that you should have registered but did not and that they want their money back.

Where will you get the $250,000 to refund to them? To protect yourself against disenchanted stockholders and against professional trouble makers, we suggest you follow the SEC's requirements rigidly.

REGULATION A OFFERINGS (UNDER $500,000)

There are two major kinds of SEC registrations: The full, long form registration used for public offerings exceeing $500,000 (known as "S" registrations) and the purportedly simpler Regulation A offerings which involve less than $500,000 of securities.

The major practical difference between an "A" offering and an "S" offering lies in the saving you may possibly make in being able to file an "A" offering without certified financial statements. Conceivably, this could save you $5,000 to $10,000 in accounting fees.

In addition, since an "A" registration does not require centralized clearance through Washington, there may be some saving in time and legal fees as a result of your being able to file at the local office.

You will recall that when we discussed underwriting fees we pointed out that many of the better underwriters refuse to handle "A" registrations, since they themselves lack the protection of certified financial statements. With many of the major underwriters refusing "A" registrations, you may discover that the savings in accounting and legal fees on the simpler form is offset by higher underwriting charges and that the saving in time of an "A" registration compared to an "S" registration is only a matter of days, on paper, and actually may take longer because "A" registrations get more careful scrutiny. Nevertheless, let us assume that you have decided to do an "A" registration.

You will note that I have referred above to the Regulation A registration. Technically, Regulation A is not a registration at all, but an exemption from full registration. For years the Regulation A exemption was referred to as the "$300,000" offering, but under Securities Act Release No. 5125, the $300,000 figure became a victim of inflation and was increased to $500,000.

There are some problems with the Regulation A offering that you should be aware of. To begin with, as mentioned above, the better underwriters refuse to handle Regulation A offerings, and their use generally puts a stigma on your security from which it may never recover. In general, it seems unwise to save the accounting fees and take on the other additional costs mentioned above, as well as the larger risks which come from not being able to rely on certified statements, in case the investors challenge the figures at some later date.

Remember that a properly prepared, full registration protects the issuer and its officers and directors, whereas the weakened Regulation A exemption may not protect them.

Furthermore, remember that the $500,000 figure includes all securities sold by affiliates of the issuer within the past two years. You may recall the discussion about integrating all securities, when we discussed private placements. In other words, if you issue $100,000 worth of stock this year, $100,00 worth of stock next year, $500,000 worth in the third year, you really have an integrated offering of $700,000—not $500,000—and the Regulation A exemption probably will not be available to you.

Also, if any director, officer, affiliate, principal security holder, or predecessor of the issuing company or any promoter of the issuing company or any underwriter, partner, director, or officer of any underwriter has ever been involved in certain types of criminal, injunctive, or other unfavorable SEC proceedings in connection with securities, the Regulation A exemption is not available under Rule 252(c).

Furthermore, in some cases, because of the weaker type of security generally issued under a Regulation A offering, the SEC may hold up your formal filing longer under a Regulation A exemption than under a full "S" registration, although, in general, clearance can be faster than in the case of a full "S" registration.

SOME "A" REGISTRATION PROBLEMS

To begin with, there is a $500,000 limitation. The $500,000 figure refers to the price at which the stock is offered to the public and not to the par value of the stock, nor the price at which it is being offered to the underwriter.

You must also subtract from the $500,000 limitation any securities which should have been issued in the past and which you inadvertently or willfully omitted registering. The effect is that any time you do an "A" registration you open up a question about past violations.

Also included in the $500,000 limitation are promoter's and underwriter's stock (unless the stock is escrowed, i.e., made unmarketable by depositing the same with an escrow agent).

The effect of the practical and legal limitations on "A" offerings is to make them inadvisable in any situation where an "S" offering can be put together at anywhere near the cost of the "A" offering. Don't forget to include in the cost of an "A" offering the higher price you are going to have to pay the underwriter to sell the stock.

Also, you might include the fact that stocks issued under an "A" offering often sell at a greater discount than stocks issued under an "S" offering.

THE FULL OR "S" REGISTRATION

Included as part of the appendix to this volume is a step-by-step analysis of an "S" offering, with the requirements of the SEC set forth, paragraph by paragraph, followed by illustrative clauses which have been taken from actual SEC filings.

We would urge anyone about to prepare a prospectus to read that section of the book carefully and then to go through the forms and look at half a dozen additional offerings to get an idea of what kind of language the SEC considers "presentable." Always keep in the back of your mind that the purpose of an SEC registration is disclosure, disclosure, and more disclosure.

In order to protect yourself and the underwriters, you must set forth every fact which an investor might be interested in knowing concerning each of the items outlined by the SEC.

There are, of course, two different philosophies on the preparation of an SEC prospectus. Everyone agrees that all of the negative statements must be included in the SEC prospectus if everyone is to be protected. That is, the inauspicious side must be fully revealed.

There are those who draw prospectuses who state that if you set forth all of the facts, particularly the negative facts, you cannot be criticized. This is true. We have no argument with it; however, we like to feel that something affirmative can be done in the SEC registration, also. We urge issuers to call to their attorney's attention the positive facts, also. If the company has been making progress in a certain area, that fact should be called to the attorney's attention. As far as the attorney and the underwriter are concerned, they should make an effort to state the affirmative facts, also.

There is no need to make the prospectus read as a death warrant. The bad can be combined with the good so that the investor gets a fair presentation not only of the negative but also of the positive.

SOME ADDITIONAL TIPS

If you are interested in preparing an SEC prospectus, aside from the information to be found in this volume and the companion forms volume, we suggest that you contact any one of the professional printing companies (such as Pankick Press or Sorg, of New York City) and ask them to mail you their descriptive pamphlets outlining the requirements of the SEC prospectus. Also, the looseleaf services, such as CCH and Prentice-Hall, Inc., have loads of material that can be of assistance to you in preparing the prospectus.

SOME PRACTICAL PROBLEMS IN PROSPECTUS PRESENTATION

Among the troublesome areas of the registration statement are these:

Use of Proceeds. The purpose of this item is to show to the investor the purpose to which you expect to put the funds raised from the public. You should be able to demonstrate that the proceeds will be sufficient to accomplish the program you intend to undertake, and you must state, in case there might be any change in the program because the funds should be insufficient, to what other use you would put the funds.

If you are planning an expansion program, it is important that you demonstrate the necessity for the expansion program. If you intend to raise the funds for additional working capital, it is important that you show to what particular areas you intend to delegate the funds and why you deem them necessary.

In other words, if you expect to use the funds for acquisition of additional inventory, explain why, and demonstrate the necessity wherever possible.

If you are not careful, you will have to file additional amendments, and this will slow up the whole registration process and may be very costly.

A registrant who began by stating in his first registration that he intended to "use the proceeds to reduce loans" was compelled to amend by stating to whom the loans were payable; to show why the total was required; to indicate that a portion of the funds being raised was being used to retire certain preferred shares and to redeem certain officers' loans; and, lastly, to demonstrate that a portion of the requirement, instead of going for loans, was going to pay off taxes in arrears.

Exchange Offers. These are also called sales for other than cash. A detailed discussion of the purpose of the exchange offer must be set forth, as well as the details. Thus, the prospectus must state that a certain number of shares of one company's stock are being exchanged for a certain number of shares of the other company's stock. An explanation must be made of what the status of the two companies will be after the exchange; a discussion should follow, stating how the exchange ratio was determined by the board of directors of the various companies after consideration of the market values of their stock, past histories, etc., and the facts such as who will pay the expenses of the exchange, including legal fees, etc., and what those expenses are. You must also include a discussion of the Federal income tax status of the exchange.

Description of Business. The kind of business done by the registrant must be discussed, and the history of the past five years' development must be covered. If several kinds of products are manufactured, each must be discussed separately— particularly those products which contributed 15 percent or more of the gross volume of the company's business.

In addition, general competitive conditions in the industry must be set forth, and the registrant's position in the industry, if known or determinable, must be discussed.

Where appropriate, registrants have stated that the company believes that it is presently one of the largest manufacturers of the product, but that several of its competitors have larger net worths and larger capacities, etc.

Smaller companies have often been compelled to insert a caveat reading similar to the following: "The company is a small unit in a highly competitive industry. As indicated under the caption method of the operation, the company must compete with much larger organizations in its industry. Certain of the company's competitors, in addition to having far greater resources and facilities and a far wider geographical distribution, also own, operate, or control their own processing plants and warehouses. This company owns neither processing plants nor warehouses."

Financial Statements. The registrant must file a balance sheet as of a date within ninety days prior to the filing of the registration. That balance sheet need not be certified. If the balance sheet is not certified, a certified balance sheet as of a date within one year must be filed.

Profit and loss statements for each of the past three fiscal years preceding the date of the latest balance sheet filed must be part of the registration statement, and these past three years profit and loss statements must be certified up to the date of the latest certified balance sheet.

The importance of these timely certified balance sheets and profit and loss statements cannot be overestimated. If you expect to go public, you must alert your accountant for the required certification in ample time. You cannot go to an accountant on December 31st and tell him: "I expect you to certify my statements as of December 31st."

If you give the accountant ample time, he can arrange for interim tests of your records; he can prepare for an economical verification of accounts receivable, accounts payable, and he can test your inventory and accounting procedures, your internal control, etc. If you spring all of this on him at the last minute, he can still do it, but the expense may be prohibitive because of the burden of overtime work and duplication of effort which comes from not having enough time to prepare intelligently.

If you plan with your accountant early enough, you may be able to select a period for certification in which you will have either a full year's figures or a representative sample, so that your earnings will show a favorable pattern. There is no point in running statements as of a point in your fiscal year where earnings look very bad in comparison with prior years' earnings.

No amount of explanation will convince a potential investor that the actual facts set forth in your financial statements which are certified to by your accountant really should be rosier than the figures set forth. If you are going public on the basis of getting some kind of an earnings multiple for your stock, every dollar saved through efficient operation and every increase in earnings developed through cutting expenses may bring you $10 or $20 at capital gains rates, when you sell your stock at ten and twenty times earnings.

Accordingly, preplanning is one of the most useful devices in going public, and preplanning can be of maximum assistance to you in preparing for proper financial statements. Your earnings will look better if you have planned for them in advance, and accounting fees will be lower if you give your accountant half a break and let him plan for your closing properly.

Also, planning and timing can help you avoid the March/April rush. As you know, March and April are the months during which your accountant is the busiest because of tax returns and annual closings. If you add to your accountant's already heavy work load the necessity of certifying financial statements for you for an SEC registration, you are bound to pay for the inefficiencies inherent in such overtime work. This will slow down your registration clearance, because the SEC gets so many registrations at the end of March and early April (to fill the ninety-day requirement for calendar years ended December 31st). If you can time yourself for another part of the year, it may be well to do so.

WHAT CANNOT BE INCLUDED IN THE REGISTRATION

Forecasts and hypothetical increases in earnings in future years, budgetary projections, and appraised values cannot ordinarily be inserted in SEC registrations. The SEC wants you to give the investor the facts; the SEC does not want you to pass along opinions. The SEC will not permit you to tell the public what you think your earnings will be five years from now.

There are some exceptions on earnings projections which lie mainly in the real estate field. Thus, if you file a Form S11 (which is used for certain types of real estate corporations), the SEC will permit you to set forth an income projection based on signed, enforceable leasing contracts, because the assumption is that the leasing contracts are enforceable and the income is determinable.

Certain equipment leasing corporations may be able to get a similar dispensation, but ordinarily, the SEC is not interested in your hopes; they want facts, and they will not permit you to put your sales forecasts in an SEC prospectus.

SOME PROBLEM AREAS IN PREPARING REGISTRATION STATEMENTS

Since 1969, under Securities Act Release No. 4988, it is important that the registration statement determine the specific "lines of business" in which the issuer is engaged and to break down the information, line by line, not only as to the percentage of gross sales which are in a particular area, but, also, as to the profitability of each sales area. The question of what constitutes a "line of business" is a troublesome one, not only because management must make that decision and be prepared to explain it to the SEC, but because the accounting records of the corporation may not be in form necessary to make allocations in accordance with good accounting practice.

If your corporation is engaged in a number of different lines, this problem should be taken on early, before you get too deeply involved in the registration problems.

Great care should be given to the "use of proceeds" section of the registration statement, so that you disclose other contingent plans in the event you fail to realize the goals set forth in the registration statement. If you raise the money for one disclosed purpose and use it for another, because business circumstances change, you may find yourself sued by disgruntled stockholders, if the stock does not do well in the market place.

Caution: Throughout this book you will find sample forms, statements of accounting principles, and resumes of SEC regulations. This material is constantly being updated. This book is not intended as a substitute for a full looseleaf service on SEC regulations.

This book is intended to simplify and guide you in the techniques of putting together a public offering. It is not a substitute for up-to-the-minute legal and accounting advice; nor can any printed work replace checking out the latest changes with the governmental regulatory agency involved. This *caveat* is particularly pertinent in dealing with "The Forms Appendix," wherein SEC filings are listed as examples to show you how they are put together and what a complete set of forms looks like. They are not inserted for you to copy.

DISTRIBUTION OF PROSPECTUS

Once there has been an initial filing of the prospectus with the SEC, enough prospectuses are printed up to commence initial distribution through channels via the underwriters of copies of the prospectus to dealers, salesmen, a few selected prospective buyers, and to organizations such as Moody's. These prospectuses are imprinted in red with a warning that they are a preliminary registration statement not yet become effective with the SEC. The red imprint prospectus has been nicknamed a "red herring."

The SEC, under current practice, encourages reasonable distribution of these red herring prospectuses so that the investment public has an opportunity to review the preliminary information and think through whether it wants to make an investment prior to the time the final prospectus is approved. As a result, the SEC now wants evidence that the preliminary prospectus has received reasonably broad distribution.

Of course, if the original prospectus requires extensive alteration, the SEC may require that a memorandum of the changes or a redistribution of the revised prospectus go to each person who received the preliminary red herring prospectus in the first place.

In April of 1969, the Commission established the policy that a copy of the preliminary prospectus, together with its last amendment, be distributed to each person to whom a sale is anticipated, at least forty-eight hours prior to the confirmation of the sale.

Since broad distribution of the initial prospectus is encouraged, it is most important that the initial prospectus be carefully drawn so that extensive changes are not required between the first and final drafts. Otherwise, purchasers will become disenchanted by the changes, and there is the possibility that someone will sue you later on the grounds that the initial prospectus contained too much "baloney" which had been absorbed by the prospective buyer who did not spot the changes in the subsequent draft.

THE BAR CHRIS CASE: A WARNING TO DIRECTORS
AND PROFESSIONALS

The *Bar Chris* case (*Escott* v. *Bar Chris Construction Corp.*, 283 F. Supp. 643 [1968]) shook up the financial community and the professionals who worked on it, not so much by propounding new law, but by applying well known law to a number of people who felt it was somebody else's responsibility to watch what was going into the registration prospectus.

In *Bar Chris*, the Court found there was inadequate protection for the investors by the officers, directors, accountants, and attorneys who signed a prospectus, each of whom felt it was somebody else's job to check out the facts.

Bar Chris was a construction company that collapsed in the deluge which followed the shake-out in the bowling alley boom in the early '60s. When the company went into Chapter 11, five officer-directors, four outside directors, one nondirector officer, eight underwriters, and the certified public accountants were sued by purchasers of subordinated debentures of the company for signing a prospectus in which sales were overstated 8 percent, operating income 15 percent and contingent liabilities understated by one-third.

The sales and income were overstated by including sales of equipment to bowling alleys in which the customers had defaulted. The liabilities were understated by miscomputing Bar Chris's liability under a factoring agreement in which the factor had recourse for endorsed paper he had to take back.

There was a 180 percent overstatement of an alleged backlog of orders for which there really were no valid, enforceable sales contracts. There was a failure to disclose that officers' loans had been outstanding and were unpaid and a failure to disclose that, of the proceeds sought in the registration, over 60 percent would be used to pay outstanding debts.

Furthermore, there was no disclosure of the fact that the factor had threatened to require that Bar Chris repurchase the notes of its delinquent customers, and a failure to disclose that customer delinquencies were becoming more substantial (so that 38 percent of the public offering funds were used to repurchase delinquent notes).

THE "INSIDERS'" DEFENSES TO BAR CHRIS

The officers and directors defended themselves from the security buyers' charges by claiming that they were relying on the accountants; and the accountants sought to escape liability by claiming that they were relying on management; and management passed the responsibility to the attorneys. This "buck-passing" was made short shrift of by the Court. Recent charges by the SEC in an entirely separate matter involving allegedly inadequate prospectuses indicate that attorneys, also, are required to avoid preparing prospectuses which they either know do not comply or which they could reasonably have discovered do not comply as true disclosure documents.

EFFECT OF BAR CHRIS ON TODAY'S PRACTICE

What does one make of *Bar Chris*? *Bar Chris* means that any securities purchaser has the right to sue if his prospectus contains an untrue statement of a material fact or if his prospectus omits material facts which are relevant.

Among the potential defendants in cases involving dissatisfied securities holders is everyone who signed the registration, including the issuer, every director who had offices at the time the registration statement was filed (whether he signed or not), as well as every director designate who was named in the registration (if your name is used, be careful), and every accountant, attorney, and other expert who was involved in the preparation or certification of the prospectus, and each and every underwriter.

While it is true that officers, directors, and underwriters are not liable if they rely on experts in "expertised" fields (i.e., directors can rely on the statements of certified public accountants), it is also true that there is a duty on everyone to "reasonably investigate" the facts set forth in a prospectus before signing the same "in blank."

While the Court stated that it is "impossible to lay down a rigid rule suitable for every case which defines the extent to which verification must go," experts such as lawyers and accountants are expected to go beyond merely asking company officials what the facts are; they are, instead, expected to examine the underlying documents themselves and make independent verification thereof.

Thus, if an accountant or lawyer is told that the company has signed contracts, he should examine copies of them, so that he can tell that they exist; that they have been signed; and then, by looking at them, he can tell whether they are in effect.

The Court pointed out a number of "hard-nosed" facts. Officers who were also directors were presumed to have knowledge of what was going on in the company. Thus, if substantial numbers of contracts were in default and in arrears, it would do little good for the treasurer to say he did not know about it, unless he could show that somehow or other the facts were hidden from him.

Similarly, inside directors who knew that the company had substantial contracts in default were not entitled to pass the buck to the accountants by saying that they had received financial statements which showed substantial accounts receivable.

Outside directors who had no knowledge of the inside facts were, on the other hand, entitled to rely on the certified financial statements of the independent accountants.

The independent accountants, on the other hand, were not permitted to rely on the naked statements of the management that there were signed contracts and that they were not in default. They were expected to examine the documents.

The mere fact that a "cold comfort" letter had been given to the accountants and a "due diligence" meeting held was not considered to be significant. The mere holding of the meeting is not a substitute for doing the underlying work.

SOME SUGGESTIONS TO PREVENT TROUBLE

All directors, insiders, attorneys, and accountants who are going to sign the prospectus should keep in mind the necessity of an independent investigation. Underwriters, lawyers, officers, directors, and accountants should get copies not only of the proposed financial statements but of the drafts of the prospectus as early as possible, so that each can be alerted to problems within his own area of expertise, thus avoiding a last minute hurried signing by a bunch of people who have done no investigating.

Each professional should ask himself whether he has independently verified the fields within his own expertise; thus, lawyers should look at legal documents and accountants at such evidence as liability documents, canceled checks and signed contracts.

In addition, very early in the game, a questionnaire should be sent out to all the officers, directors, and experts, asking them for specific answers to matters required in the prospectus, in writing; and they should be alerted to review the drafts going past them very carefully.

Among the information to be put together in a package by the attorney drafting the prospectus (with a view towards alerting everybody to trouble spots) might be the following:

THE INFORMATION NEEDED AS A CHECKLIST
OF PROBLEMS IN CONNECTION WITH THE
PREPARATION OF AN SEC REGISTRATION

1. Procure copies of all legal instruments such as deeds, mortgages, loan agreements, and promisory notes.

2. Copies of all mortgages, notes, and indentures.

3. Minute books.

4. Certificate of incorporation, by-laws, and any amendments thereto.

5. Copies of articles and speeches appearing in the press with reference to the company.

6. Copies of any "tout sheets" put out by brokerage houses concerning the company.

7. Copies of all annual interim reports to stockholders, including proxy statements and any and all annual reports made to Federal or state regulatory agencies.

8. Copies of any previous registration statements and any reports filed with the SEC in the past, such as 10-Ks, etc.

9. Names and addresses of all officers, directors, and experts.

10. History of any pending litigation.

11. Copies of any employee benefit plans, accident and health plans, options, or warrants.

12. Copies of recent financial statements, special audit reports on which the registration is to be based, and Dun & Bradstreet and other trade information in connection with the client.

BY WAY OF SUMMARY

In truth, *Bar Chris* tells us nothing new. Lawyers should be lawyers and accountants, accountants. If they do not do their jobs as one might reasonably expect, they can be sued, even though they are not the issuers themselves. The public is entitled to rely on their name and letterhead when they see it in a registration statement.

If a high professional standard of work is kept, there will be no problem. Otherwise—disaster!

Similarly, concerning officers and directors: Outside directors are expected to ask questions, and they are permitted to rely on professional advice. Inside directors carry on their backs the burden of knowing what is going on in the company, and they cannot pass that burden off to the professionals, unless they, in turn, have been kept in the dark by their subordinates.

HOW TO GO ABOUT DRAFTING THE PROSPECTUS

When your lawyers get ready to draft your registration statement they will have before them many sources of material. First, they will have the letter of intent between yourself and your underwriters. Second, they will have other sample prospectuses in your industry which have recently cleared, the outline forms prepared by various prospectus printers, their own files of similar registrations, plus a number of suggested forms given to them by the underwriter.

Your lawyers will prepare a tentative job assignment sheet and timetable laying out who does what and "when" in a format, and covering the details discussed elsewhere in this book.

Your lawyers will have before them such exhibits as those which go in the "back of the book" (see Part 2 of the Full Registration Statement included in the Appendix of this book).

Your lawyers will have contacted your accountants to find out whether all the financial statement information will be available, and how long it will take to compile it, and your lawyers and your accountants together will estimate the approximate deadline for audit reports and discuss whether any problems exist which were unknown to your draftsmen at the time you started to work on the prospectus.

Your lawyers will start by drafting the "front of the book" (Part 1 of the Registration Statement) which is the prospectus portion usually distributed to the public. Part 2 consists of various exhibits.

A typical registration, as you will see later, consists of a description of the company, of any unusual risk factors, of the use to which the proceeds of the offering will be put when the money is raised, a history of the company's prior earnings, its capitalization and dividend history and intentions; the company's prior stock or bond pricing range, wherever applicable; and a description of the company's business, its competition, and its management.

There will also be in the prospectus a description of employees and employees' benefits, stock options, and compensation; a description of the common stock and the underwriting agreements, as well as a description of any unusual transactions between the company and insiders, together with the necessary legal opinions, expert opinions, and accounting reports.

Having laid out a "who does what," your lawyers are ready to get to work drafting your prospectus.

15

ACCOUNTING AND FINANCIAL ASPECTS OF GOING PUBLIC

THE "INDEPENDENT" ACCOUNTANT

The SEC requires that your financial statement be certified by an independent public accountant. The most common question we receive from accountants is "How do you define an 'independent' accountant?"

You may read volumes of literature on this subject, go through dozens of cases and hundreds of opinions, and nowhere will you find a satisfactory definition of what an independent accountant is. You will find dozens of examples of things an accountant can do to invalidate his independence, and you will have to settle for that.

The SEC has found it easier to rule out the kind of situations it does not like and to exclude accountants who fall into those areas as not being independent. In other words, you can find out quickly enough what an independent accountant is not, but you will have great difficulty in finding a definition of what an independent accountant is.

If you, as the issuer, are in doubt as to whether your accountant is independent or not; or if you, as an accountant, are in doubt as to whether you may be independent as to a particular client, the most sensible thing to do is to go down to Washington and talk your problem over with the SEC, and, if the matter is doubtful, get a ruling.

If you are an accountant who hopes to certify his client's statements and if you have been with the client for many years, you will want to know whether you are considered independent or not. If you are an issuer and are planning to use a particular accountant, you will want to know as early as possible whether his earlier statements are useful to you or whether you are going to have to get somebody else to come in to do the job.

Here are a number of important things which destroy the independence of an accountant, if he is involved in any of them:

An independent accountant cannot be an officer, director, or employee of the corporation.

An independent accountant cannot have "written up" the books, because if he has written them up, he is not in a position to independently pass on their accuracy.

An independent accountant cannot be a "substantial" investor in the issuer. What is substantial? You will find in the Accounting Series Releases published by the SEC an example in which it was held that an accountant who had approximately 1 percent of his net worth invested in a client could not be independent because his investment was substantial.

An accountant who is also a trustee and who votes substantial amounts of stock cannot be independent.

An accountant could not be considered independent if the company whose financial statements he certified agreed to indemnify him against all losses, claims, and damages arising out of the certification.

An accountant cannot be considered independent if he "consistently submerges his professional convictions as to correct accounting principles to the wishes of his client." In other words, if you have a record of "yessing" the client and aiding him by changing financial statements at his whim, your independence is destroyed.

An accountant who had loaned $5,000 to a registrant and whose son was an officer of the registrant could not be held independent.

An accountant who took stock in the registrant instead of cash for his services and who held an option to purchase stock at market could not be considered independent.

A few years ago, a partner in an accounting firm was serving as a member of the board of directors of the registrant. Another partner in the same accounting firm conducted the audit of the registrant and certified the financial statement in his own name—not in the firm name. The SEC held that the certifying accountant could not be considered independent because his partner was serving on the board.

Conclusion: If there is any doubt about your independence, be careful to read all of the Accounting Series Releases published by the SEC and be certain to check out the problem in Washington. Do not put yourself in a position of having the registration held up when the facts turn up, and to not put yourself in the position of being disbarred from practice before the SEC because you overlooked something important.

Lastly, you will be twice dammed if you make an honest mistake, and it turns out you were not independent all the while. Imagine how it will look, either to the SEC or to a jury, if you have made a mistake and have withheld the facts as to your nonindependence. It will certainly look like a willful fraud.

THE INVENTORY AND TAX PROBLEM

Most closely held corporations value their inventory very conservatively. By using extremely conservative methods of inventory valuation, they cut current income tax payments to the bone. The practice has been so common that the Internal Revenue Service has warned the public that it intends to look into the matter of understatement of inventories in closely held businesses.

However, when the closely held corporation decides to go public and has its financial statements certified and suddenly discovers the necessity of having its inventory count and valuation checked by independent accountants, inventory values rise steeply.

What is the effect of having very low valuations on inventory while you were private, and increasing inventory valuations sharply in the year in which you go public? The answer is simple: Understatement in the early years coupled with actual inventory in the current year results in a sharp jump in earnings in the year of registration. Actually, if you think about it, a good portion of the increased earnings is due to the sudden appearance of the previously hidden inventory.

Often, in examining registration statements of companies that have newly changed over from private to public, one can detect the sharp inventory rise, the sharp earnings rise, and the concomitant increase in gross profits percentage.

The most important problems flow from the pattern of closely held businesses which suppress their earnings in private years and bring them all out at once in the year in which they go public. These are:

1. The income tax problem.
2. The SEC prospectus problem.

THE TAX PROBLEM OF HIDDEN INVENTORY

Many closely held businesses worry about the fact that they may be faced with an income tax fraud case if they reveal their hidden inventory by going public. Of course, no two sets of circumstances are the same, and it is impossible to generalize whether or not an inventory valuation problem will give rise to a charge of tax fraud, except if one has all the facts before him.

To begin with, you always have the question of degree. If the hidden inventory represents a minor percentage of the company's total profits and if a current tax is paid on the inventory when the mistake is discovered, and if that tax comes in at the 50 percent rate, it is hard to see how the government has been deprived of any tax revenues, and it is even more difficult to see how a tax fraud case could be made.

True, there may have been a tax deferral, but, if the inventory undervaluation was an honest one—a mere difference of opinion—we do not think a fraud case could be made.

On the other hand, if you have an inventory distortion of 50 or 75 percent and if that inventory distortion is coupled with half a dozen other fraudulent practices and if an effort is made to spread that inventory over 30 percent years instead of 50 percent years, it is entirely possible to make out a relatively strong fraud case.

We feel, however, that the worry about the fraud is overstated. In most cases, the filing of an accurate current return with the full revelation of the inventory and payment of the 50 percent tax thereon, if such filing and payment is made before there is any investigation by the Internal Revenue Service, should clear the company of any possible fraud.

It is difficult to see how the government could enrage a jury enough to get a conviction against a taxpayer who pays his bill in full at the top tax rate and who claims that the only difference between the current year and the earlier years is an honest difference in calculating market values or in estimating quantities lying on the shelves.

On the other hand, if you feel some grave misgivings in this area, certainly the time to check the problem out and to consult a tax attorney is before you file your SEC registration statement and before you throw the fat into the fire. If the area is a sensitive one for you, get competent advice so that you may do what has to be done to properly clear yourself with the appropriate authorities.

SOME ADDITIONAL TAX PROBLEMS IN CONNECTION WITH "GOING PUBLIC"

If the old, privately held company is going to reconstitute itself to go public, tax problems arise. Thus, if an old single proprietorship or partnership is going to convert itself into a corporation, or if the old business is going to split itself into multiple corporations, or if multiple corporations are going to consolidate themselves into a single corporation, you have to ask yourself what the tax consequences will be.

Each of the preceding changes can result in a serious ordinary income tax falling on someone, and, in each case, the tax ramifications should be considered in advance, and, if necessary, the opinion of tax counsel, or a ruling, should be obtained.

While Section 351, which provides ordinarily for tax-free incorporation, is usually available, there are certain strings attached to the use of it.

Thus, in order to obtain a tax-free incorporation of the new entity, it is important that "immediately after" the exchange of the assets of the old entity for stock of the new corporation, the old stockholders must be "in control" of the new entity.

Under Section 368(c), the old stockholder transferors must own at least 80 percent of the total combined voting power of the voting stock of the new entity, as well as at least 80 percent of the total number of nonvoting shares.

In some cases a strict compliance with Section 351 will not be sufficient, if it is part of an over-all scheme or "dependent step" in going public in which the transferors will not wind up with the necessary 80 percent control.

A number of interesting questions arise. Does the mere entering into by the old stockholders of an underwriting agreement cause loss of control under Section 351, and, if so, is there some way to work around it? Is there another way to get a tax-free "reorganization" which will not result in the imposition of a tax? (See such cases as *American Bantam,* at 11 T.C. 397 (1948), and *Overland,* 42 T.C. 26.)

TAX PROBLEMS INVOLVED IN MERGING AND CONSOLIDATING:

Usually related brother and sister corporations, affiliates, or independently owned corporations may be put together under a single corporate umbrella for a suitable public offering. This is typically accomplished by a tax-free reorganization as set forth in Section 368(a)(1), so that a tax-free exchange of stock may be procured under Section 354. Some of the tests and complications are these:

Regulations § 1.368-1(b) requires that the acquiring entity offer a "continuity of interest" to the old shareholders. If there are some "selling shareholders" who are getting out, there may be a failure to meet the continuity requirement.

Sometimes a consolidation into a single vehicle of commonly-owned affiliated brother and sister corporations is required; the result is accomplished by a statutory merger or consolidation. Technically, this meets the requirements of an "A" Reorganization; but sometimes it is better to utilize an "F." (See *Stauffer,* 404 F. 2d 611, and *Associated Machines,* 403 F. 2d 622.)

Section 351 is used to put together combinations of single proprietorships, partnerships, and existing corporations through the formation of a new corporation. Sometimes the technique of using a "C" reorganization is used to transfer corporate assets into the new vehicle, (Rev. Ruling 68-357). Be careful of Rev. Ruling 68-349, where the Service held there was not a business purpose but simply a tax avoidance purpose.

Tax-free mergers of parents and subsidiaries are governed by Section 332; however, occasionally Section 332 will not be applied where a merger is simply a single step in and part of a transaction which results in the transfer of the old subsidiary's assets into a new corporation. A tax may fall on a transaction where less than 80 percent of the subsidiary is owned by the parent and a liquidation follows.

Furthermore, intercorporate sales of appreciable assets between controlled corporations may give rise to an ordinary income tax under Section 1245 or 1250.

TAX PROBLEMS INVOLVED IN DISPOSING OF ASSETS

As mentioned above, a closely held corporation often acquires assets or corporate entities which must be disposed of prior to going public. A number of tax problems arise. If the purchaser controls the seller, there may be an ordinary income tax imposed by Section 1239.

If the stock of an unwanted subsidiary is to be disposed of, Section 355 must be scrutinized, to make sure that the distribution is tax-free. But, if the distribution is followed by a merger, you can have trouble under Section 355.

Thus, in *Curtis,* 336 F. 2d 714, a split-off followed by a merger where the old company disappeared was held to be taxable.

In *Morris,* 367 F. 2d, 794, and in Rev. Ruling 68-603, a similar split-off was held to be nontaxable because the transferor continued to exist after the merger.

Sometimes a "C" reorganization is used as a substitute but you have to be careful to comply with the "substantially all of the assets" rule. For a discussion of this problem, see *Elkhorn*, 95 F. 2d 732.

TAX PROBLEMS ARISING OUT OF SHAREHOLDER LOANS

In many cases, the most desirable thing that can happen is that old shareholder loans be replaced by stock certificates or be paid off. They do not look so good on public balance sheets. In some cases, Section 118 is utilized to have a shareholder forgive the indebtedness. In other cases a Section 351 exchange of debt for stock is utilized. In some situations, the reorganization provisions are used to simplify the corporate capital structure. In other situations, problems arise where there has been a forgiveness of dividends by the insiders.

Take a look at Section 305 to see whether such forgiveness results in tax to the forgiving shareholders under the constructive receipt concept.

The revamping of pension and profit-sharing plans and stock options may be required prior to going public, but, before going ahead, you should consider the possibility that plans which were O.K. at inception may now no longer be acceptable to the Internal Revenue Service either as a result of case law or changed Service policy. Modification may require the giving up of substantial benefits which would continue to accrue under the old "grandfather" type of treatment, if modification were not required by underwriting and going public considerations.

The tax and benefit cost to insiders giving up these rights is something to be taken into consideration in deciding the cost of going public and whether to go ahead or not.

THE TAX PROBLEMS IMPLICIT IN "KEEPING TWO SETS OF BOOKS"

The closely held corporation may do everything possible to maximize tax shelter and minimize earnings. The underwriter wants to reverse the entire transaction. Accelerated methods of depreciation, the fast write-off of otherwise capitalizable expenses, and the change from cash to accrual accounting all involve conflicts between minimizing income taxation and maximizing acceptance of the security by the public.

The cost to insiders of the giving up of tax shelter and the imposition of new and higher income taxes must be considered, as must be the problem of whether it is permissible or logical to take one position for income tax purposes and another for financial reporting purposes. In some cases, the decision will be made to continue the tax shelter practices even after going public; but the accountants have to be consulted so that they can tell you how this differential will be treated in financial statements sent to stockholders and what the impact on earnings will be as far as the securities analysts go, who are constantly multiplying your "earnings per share" in comparing the price of your stock with that of one of your competitors.

Here is one place where the tax impact cannot be considered alone, but a team effort must be made to evaluate the conflicts between

1. minimizing taxes;
2. reporting earnings;
3. maximizing cash flow, after taxes;
4. simplifying financial reporting to financial analysts;
5. putting the whole thing down in a prospective form which will meet SEC disclosure requirements.

THE SEC PROBLEMS INVOLVED IN INVENTORY VALUATION

The hidden inventory problem concerns not only the tax impact, but the SEC impact. Since most investors examine earnings histories carefully to see whether there is a growth pattern present, any jump in earnings interests potential investors, and, if it interests investors, it interests in the SEC.

If you have understated your inventory in earlier years and overstated your inventory in this year, you have made this year's earnings look very good compared with earlier years. In other words, it can be argued that the effect of your hiding inventory in earlier years has been to overstate this year's earnings.

The SEC argues that if you overstate this year's earnings and if you are selling your stock at a multiple of earnings, you are preventing the investor from intelligently determining whether the stock is worth the money he pays for it.

As a result, the SEC recently has insisted on more vigorous inventory procedures by certified public accountants. For a while and as a result of temporary wartime conditions, the SEC permitted accountants who were not present at the physical inventory takings of earlier years to state in their certificate that although they had not examined the company's inventories in those earlier years, there had been a test for clerical accuracy of the old worksheets, and the accountants had reviewed the gross profit ratios, with the result that they did not believe the earlier years' inventories to be unreasonable.

Note that language: The accountants did not believe the earlier years' earnings to be unreasonable. Of course, that is not the same thing as saying that the accountants believed that the inventories were reasonable. In discussing this matter with an accountant, I teasingly pointed out that the distinction between saying that the inventories did not look unreasonable and a statement that the inventories had been tested and looked reasonable was the kind of hair splitting distinction of which I and my brethren at the bar are usually accused. The subtle difference between stating that the inventory was not unreasonable and stating that it was reasonable became an annoying one to the SEC, in view of the pattern of hidden earnings.

As a result, you will find in the appendix a number of certifications by accountants. Most of those certifications are the "old form" in which accountants were permitted to state that they did not find the inventories to be unreasonable.

Finally, you will find an abstract from an Accounting Series Release No. 90 in which the SEC says, in so many words, that the accountants must do enough work to satisfy themselves that the inventory in all of the years which they are certifying is reasonable. The SEC warns accountants that if they cannot do sufficient work to certify that the inventories look reasonable in each of the years, the accountants will not be permitted to double-talk the subject by stating that they do not look unreasonable.

The SEC is saying: Accountants, verify the inventory by good auditing practice, and, if you find it acceptable, certify the statement. If you cannot check out the inventories by good auditing practice, do not certify the statements at all. Under no circumstances will you be permitted to certify the statement and to take an exception by using the old double-talk that "the inventories do not look unreasonable." If you cannot certify properly, you cannot certify at all.

This leads to the question of what can be done. The answer: if there is no human way to verify the earlier inventories (because the inventory sheets are lost or because they cannot be checked out properly), then the issuer may have to wait until he has accumulated enough certifiable earnings so that he can go to the SEC.

If you have an inventory problem, be certain to check out both the tax and SEC aspects of it early enough to come to an intelligent decision on what should be done about both the tax and the SEC problems. If you are an accountant and are being asked to certify, be certain that you check with other accountants who have gone through a number of such registrations, and, if there are any problems, call in outside expert advice, or go down to Washington and thrash the problem out with the SEC yourself.

WHAT GOES INTO THE ACCOUNTANT'S FINANCIAL STATEMENTS?

Assuming that we have an independent auditor, what must he disclose in his financial statement? To begin with, every accountant and anyone new to the SEC registration practice who wants to understand the details should look at Regulation S-X which deals in great detail with what goes into the financial statements. The Regulation will be discussed later in a separate section, in abbreviated form.

In general, the standards of the profession as to "good accounting practice" necessary to "fairly" disclose the financial condition of registrant governs. The rule has been stated largely in that form in the famous case of *Escott* v. *Bar Chris,* 283 F. Supp. 643.

All information essential to a fair presentation must be disclosed on the financial statements, and anything which, if omitted, would be misleading, must be set forth therein. There is no specific bulletin or listing concerning what constitutes "fair presentation," nor has the American Institute of Certified Public Accountants ever attempted to do so for the simple reason that in most cases the test of relevancy and essentiality depends on all the facts and circumstances.

There are in many areas specific rules; thus, inventory is typically stated at "cost" or "market," whichever is lower. But, in many areas, you are dealing with the matter of professional opinion. For example, what is a "reasonable" allowance for bad debts is a subject as to which many fair-minded accountants might differ. The trouble is that the question of whether the presentation was "fair" usually comes up in the case of a financial disaster, bankruptcy, fraud, or unsuccessful marketing of securities. In those cases, disgruntled stockholders who sue corporate officers, underwriters, and accountants have the benefit of 20/20 hindsight. The company has gone broke, and, at that stage of the game, it is much easier to point out what information should have been put in the financial statement and what information should have been omitted, and what is misleading, than at the time the registration was filed.

For true "disclosure," the accountant must sift the relevant from the irrelevant. If he stated every single fact to protect himself, disclosure would become obscured by an unwieldy mass of details and trivia. It is important to bear in mind that for a financial statement to be a true disclosure document, it must essentially be a "summary" of relevant financial facts.

There are a lot of touchy questions in the financial disclosure area. It is the purpose of this chapter only to briefly touch on them, since this is not a work on accounting. However, we shall try to be selective here, also, and try to pick up the questions that cause the most trouble. Let us next deal with a few of them.

"QUALIFIED" AND "UNQUALIFIED" OPINIONS BY THE ACCOUNTANTS

Every certified accounting statement found in an SEC prospectus contains in it the accountant's opinion. In general, an unqualified opinion states that the auditor has determined that the financial statements present fairly the financial position of the company on the basis of an examination made in accordance with generally accepted auditing standards, and the presentation conforms with generally accepted accounting principles applied on a consistent basis and includes all the information necessary to make the statements not misleading. That is what an "unqualified" statement says.

Let's break it down into pieces. Note that the accountant starts out by saying that in his opinion the financial statements fairly present the financial position of the company. Second, they state that the accountant has made an examination in accordance with generally accepted auditing standards; that means no short cuts and no skipping of standardized procedures.

Then, the statement goes on to say that the presentation conforms with generally accepted accounting principles, *and* that they are consistently applied from year to year (because, if they were inconsistently applied, the results would be meaningless).

Finally, there is the statement that all the information is disclosed which is necessary to make the financial statement not misleading.

If that is an "unqualified" opinion, what is a "qualified" opinion? Well, a "qualified" opinion might have to state that some of the audit work was short-cut; thus, that because of the unavailability of certain records, they were not verified. Of course, if too much of the standard audit program is omitted, then the accountant must honestly state that he has not done enough work to render an opinion because he had not "made an examination in accordance with generally accepted auditing standards."

In other words, if you have to qualify your opinion to death, you should not render an opinion.

Another problem which requires qualification might be the fact that the accounting principles of the corporation were not consistently applied. Thus, for some part of the period under audit, a different accounting technique of valuing inventory or of reserving for bad debts or for depreciation might have been used. If so, the different technique should be explained, and an effort should be made to point out the significance of the inconsistent application.

All of these "qualifications" set off alarm bells at the SEC and may require further amplification. Furthermore, they upset underwriters and investors, and most clients as well as most accountants prefer a clean, unqualified opinion.

Certain unusual uncertainties concerning future developments may cause substantial qualification of the accountant's certificate. Thus, pending litigation of a substantial nature; doubtful collectibility of certain accounts receivable; and important tax examinations and disputes may all bulk so large as to hang over the financial statement like a cloud and make the issuance of an unqualified opinion impossible.

In general, if the auditor has such great uncertainty about substantial portions of the financial statement or has been so limited in his audit work that the financial statements cannot be verified or made "fairly," the accountant may not be able to certify to the statement at all.

WHAT KIND OF FINANCIAL STATEMENTS ARE REQUIRED?

In general, the full "S" registration requires a balance sheet within ninety days to six months of the filing date, profit and loss and surplus statements for three years, plus a short or "stub" period, depending on the date of the most recent balance sheet filed, and a summary of earnings for five years, plus the current stub period, together with the comparable stub period for the preceding year.

As a minimum, certification is required of a balance sheet within one year of the filing date, together with profit and loss and surplus statements for three years. Furthermore, separate financial statements are required for unconsolidated subsidiaries 50 percent owned or more, and statements are required of any affiliates which secure or guarantee the issue being registered.

Also, it may become necessary to submit financial statements on businesses which will shortly be acquired or which have recently been acquired.

The preceding discussion relates to S-1 type of filing generally used for industrial companies. Real estate companies take specialized forms (S-11) and different financial reporting requirements exist for each of the other different types of registration statements.

FINANCIAL STATEMENT REQUIREMENTS

It is important to note that in such areas as inventory reporting, conglomerate accounting, multiple business lines, tax reserves, inventories, business combinations and good will, pooling of interests, and consolidated and unconsolidated companies, the accounting profession is by no means unanimous as to what constitutes "good accounting principles."

As mentioned previously, it is not the purpose of this chapter to make an accounting expert out of you, particularly in a field in which there is now a state of flux. It is important, however, to note that because there are differences of opinion, different accounting firms have been known to look differently at identical problems. If yours is a field in which one of these controversies arises, you should carefully discuss the matter with your accountant, find out what his position is, what the alternatives are, and then seek to determine for yourself what the significance of the various alternative ways of presenting the financial material in the statements can be.

This is not to state that we are suggesting "shopping" for the "best" accountant, because both the accounting profession and the SEC take a dim view of this practice. You should assume that the accountant you select to prepare your financial material will do the best he can to fairly present it in the most favorable light consistent with accounting practice. In selecting your accountant, it is advisable to know what the problem areas are so that they may be discussed in advance and so that you may know the firm's attitude thereon.

Generally speaking, because of the independent accounting requirements and the necessity in most cases for the use of nationally known firms, it may very well be that your SEC registration will require the use of an accountant new and strange to you, and not your corporation's regular accountant. If this be so, you should be forearmed and forewarned, so that you may discuss the problem areas intelligently.

MEETING REGULATION Sx REQUIREMENTS

Article I of Regulation Sx, as we just mentioned, is mainly a definitional discussion of such items as what constitutes an affiliate, what constitutes a 50 percent owned person, and what constitutes a significant subsidiary, while Article II deals with the subject of who is an "independent accountant" and the form of the "accountant's certificate" and how it is to be qualified or unqualified.

Article 3 contains some twenty-plus rules defining "disclosure" and dealing with the kind of material that goes in the footnotes of balance sheets and profit and loss statements.

Article 4 deals mainly with consolidated and combined financial statements and is highly technical in nature, while Article 5 delineates the technical requirements unique to SEC filings, dealing in detail with such items as inventory classification, and the form of presentation of current assets and current liabilities, in an effort to get uniformity to the greatest extent possible in SEC registration financial reporting.

Details are laid out concerning what must be set forth in some seventeen supporting schedules to the balance sheet and profit and loss statement. Each of the forms, ranging from S-1 to S-11, has its own particular requirements.

GOING PUBLIC FROM THE AUDITOR'S VIEWPOINT

Up to the present, we have discussed a number of technical rules governing the accounting practice which covers an SEC registration. Many of the substantive rules we have discussed above are presently undergoing intense scrutiny not only by the accounting and legal professions, but by the SEC and the financial community. Everyone agrees on the objective: clearer information for the securities analyst and the public, procurable in a rapid and economical manner.

Thus, no one argues that the public should get, and, indeed, requires clearer financial statements. The arguments are about what constitutes a clearer financial statement and how to get the information before the public while it is timely and meaningful. As of this writing, not only has the Accounting Principles Board (a quasi-official CPA organization) but also the SEC has been giving careful scrutiny to such subjects as what constitutes a proper consolidation for financial statement purposes; what shall be done about good will; when are particular methods of accounting (such as the completed contract method, the installment method, etc.) appropriate and when they are misleading; and under what circumstances should a client be permitted to "shop" auditors to find someone who will give him the most favorable financial report.

The pot is boiling; day by day new pronouncements come out and they will be constantly debated until they receive general acceptance, at which time they will become "generally accepted accounting principles." In the meantime, controversy and turmoil are necessary prior to general acceptance, lest one group or the other feels it is becoming merely a rubber stamp "yes man."

SOLVING IMPORTANT PROCEDURAL PROBLEMS

One of the key questions in determining whether a company should go public is whether its financial statements are such that they can be put into a prospectus and what the cost of putting those financial statements together is. The question is not as simple to answer as one might expect. The closely held corporation rarely is concerned with whether its financial statements are understandable to the public or not. In many cases, since the only people who are interested in the financial statements are management plus possibly the corporation's bank, closely held corporations abstain from the additional expense of careful auditing.

Detailed accounts receivable and accounts payable confirmations and even an annual inventory account by the auditors are frequently waived by closely held corporations which feel secure in the knowledge that the insider-officer-director-stockholders know what is going on. They feel that the expense of the audit may be prohibitive when contrasted with the benefits obtainable by the closely held corporation.

Similarly, closely held groups which involve themselves in operations such as real estate or building are often more concerned with presenting a favorable tax picture than presenting a favorable earnings statement, so that for many years the books and records of closely held corporations may be kept to impress the tax collector and not the underwriter.

THE ACCOUNTING CHALLENGES OF GOING PUBLIC

But unless the corporation's books and records have been audited or can be audited retroactively for the period required by the SEC, the company just may not be able to go public because it cannot prepare a prospectus.

As outlined above, three years, in most cases, and, in many cases, as many as five years of consistently applied financial statements may be required. In some cases, not only the books and records of the registrant must be certified, but in some cases, those of subsidiaries and affiliates.

If consolidated statements are required, the subsidiaries may have to be audited, as well as the parent. Furthermore, the Accounting Principles Board has been discussing the requirement that consolidation and audit may be required in companies in which the registrant has an interest of 20 percent or more, if the minority interest is "material" to the consolidated financial statements of the registrant.

Finally, if the registrant has acquired "significant" businesses during the last three years, the underlying records of the acquired business may also need audit (see SEC release 33-4950).

The accountant and the registrant must both ask themselves very early in the game what records are available; what must be audited; is audit possible; and what will audit cost?

If subsidiaries or affiliates are involved, do we have access to their records for the periods required; or can we get such access?

THE PRELIMINARY STUDY

Very early in the game, the client should approach the accountant to study whether certified financial statements in accordance with SEC requirements can be obtained, and what they will cost. Sometimes it is advisable to plan substantially in advance of going public. Thus, many a client has retained a national public accounting firm several years in advance of going public with instructions that the accounting firm should bear in mind that the client intends to go public in due course.

Preplanning for going public results in books and records being kept in accordance with "generally accepted accounting principles" and results in annual audits being made, while the information is current, so that the extra audit fees which result from a rush job to meet an SEC deadline several years past closing dates can be saved. Also saved is the expense of trying to recast in accordance with generally accepted accounting principles a set of books and records that has been kept on a pure tax saving basis with no regard to generally accepted accounting principles.

CURRENT vs. RETROACTIVE AUDITS

It is always easier to do audits currently than to try to do them under the pressure of a printer's deadline during registration, and it is always easier to audit records shortly after the close of the fiscal year rather than to try to figure out what happened two and three years ago when audit confirmation is almost impossible to get.

The advantages of preplanning are that the client and the entire staff of the client begin to learn in advance what is going to be required of them when they go public and they start to "think public." Then, when the time comes, the initial shock is not too great and the client and his staff have benefited from the slower but deeper educational process instead of being forced into a crash program under the glare of the public spotlight.

You will recall when we previously discussed "Independent Accountants" we pointed out that the accountants who "wrote up" the books, accountants who had financial interests in the registrant, and accountants who are substantial stockholders, officers, or directors of the registrant were disqualified from preparing certified financial statements pursuant to Regulation Sx (see rule 201 thereof).

Preplanning permits you to avoid this problem at the last minute. If you want to keep an accountant who has a specialized knowledge of the industry and with whom you have a very close relationship, there is no reason why this cannot be done, even though the accountant would be disqualified by reason of financial interest or stockholdings or otherwise. What needs to be done is simply to have two sets of accountants: one who is the disqualified "friend of the family" accountant, and the other, the outside, independent auditor who will ultimately certify the statements.

Indeed, a working relationship between these two accounting teams can best be worked out if planned several years in advance since less friction results and a clearer definition of job duties develops which avoid expensive overlaps.

SOME BASIC PROCEDURAL REQUIREMENTS

As previously mentioned, the key document governing accounting statements has been promulgated by the SEC as Regulation Sx. While the complete regulations may be obtained either from the SEC or from the Superintendent of Documents, it is best for one's own accounting personnel to read Regulation Sx as early as possible in updated form, preferably in one of the standard looseleaf reporting services (such as Prentice-Hall, Inc.'s SEC Service) so that the accounting personnel are familiar not only with the latest draft of the Regulation, but can also see the latest Accounting Series Releases issued by the SEC. These give the SEC's opinion on various matters and the accounting personnel can understand how the SEC's Accounting Series Releases reconcile with statements of the Accounting Principles Board and with the other compilers and commentators on "generally accepted accounting principles."

Typically, Form S-1, the registration form used for most SEC initial offerings, requires the following information:

BALANCE SHEET REQUIREMENTS

There must be a balance sheet within ninety (90) days of the filing which does *not* have to be certified. However, if the most recent balance sheet is unaudited, then there must also be included the latest audited balance sheet. Typically, the latest audited balance sheet is as of the end of the last fiscal year.

INCOME STATEMENTS

Income statements and application of funds statements (if required) must be given for the three most recent fiscal years, and all of them must be audited. Also, there will have to be short period or interim statements from the end of the fiscal year to the most recent balance sheet date. The interim statements may be unaudited, unless the most recent balance sheet is audited.

SUPPORTING SCHEDULES

Regulation Sx generally requires a number of schedules supporting the financial statements which appear in the filed part of the registration statement under Part II.

Also, there is required an analysis of any changes in stockholders' equity which would support or explain the financial statements otherwise required.

SOME SPECIFIC PROBLEMS

"Generally accepted accounting principles" are required throughout, and if there is any interrelationship between the registrant and other companies, the statements must be prepared in such a manner as to clearly present the picture of that interrelationship.

In many cases the separate statements of affiliates and subsidiaries are required, particularly if they "significantly" affect the registrant.

In addition, there are a whole batch of *pro forma* requirements, particularly where the registration involves the proposed acquisition or merger of a new business. In this latter case, the financial statements must show the effect of the acquisition; sufficient details on the acquired company must be set forth as if it, too, were being registered; and a *pro forma* balance sheet must be prepared showing what would happen if the two businesses were combined, the full nature of which will depend on whether a "purchase" or "pooling of interest" accounting technique is being used.

If a pooling of interest is planned, a *pro forma* statement combining the operations of the acquired company and the registrant will be needed to cover the past five years, together with any interim periods.

If a purchase method of accounting is planned, the statements must give effect to any adjustments which would affect the good will account, asset depreciation values, etc.

PREPARING THE EARNINGS SUMMARY

Financial analysts and underwriters, as well as sophisticated investors, consider the summary of earnings part of the prospectus a key document because it shows the "key" tends and, hopefully, enables one to predict the future, to the extent that past performance is important.

The earnings summary has to cover each of the last five fiscal years together with interim periods from the end of the last fiscal year to the date of the most recent balance sheet, and must compare that interim period (the so-called "stub") with the corresponding period for the preceding fiscal year.

The summary of earnings need not be audited, but, generally, three years will be certifiable, since, generally, there will be at least three years of income statements which are certified.

Form S-1 plus Regulation Sx specifies the detail required in the summary of earnings. It also imposes the burden on the registrant and his accountants that, if there are material factors which the investor should know and which are of significance in the earnings summary, those significant factors should be set forth in the audit report at the appropriate place.

SOME SEC ACCOUNTING RELEASES

Under SEC Release 33-5133, the method of calculating earnings per share is outlined, and the details of how the computations are made can either be set forth in a footnote to the audit report or as a separate registration statement exhibit.

The subject of "dilution" as a result of "overhanging options" or complicated financial structures must also be referred to if the earnings statement is to be meaningful.

Nonrecurring items which fall into the earnings section have to be explained; erratic, seasonal patterns which affect iterim "stub" periods should be referred to; and the effect of acquisitions during the earnings summary period should also be referred to.

Substantial deficits, important litigation, and the debilitating cumulative effect of losses year after year may even give rise to the question of whether the registrant's financial statements can be prepared on a "going concern" basis.

The SEC's Accounting Series Release No. 115 warns both accountants and registrants that a sick company which looks like it may go out of business *cannot* prepare financial statements which assume that a going concern valuation exists. This means that if the company looks too sick to last much past the registration, both the accountants and the registrant had better be pretty careful not only about the possibility of future stockholder suits, but even about the cost of going through a registration procedure, since the SEC may either refuse to accept the financial statements or, even worse, may insist on a rescission offer after distribution has taken place.

WHAT ABOUT OTHER REGISTRATION FORMS ASIDE FROM FORM S-1?

Basically, S-2, since it deals with "new" companies in the "developmental" stage, does not call for three years of audited statements. Instead, statement of "assets and unrecovered development costs" and details of liabilities and proposed capital structure are required, together with a statement of whether or not all shares in the hands of the promoters have been issued for cash or for other considerations (such as services).

Cash receipts and disbursements for the past three years or for the life of the "new" registrant (if less than three years) will be required; and all statements must be certified.

Form S-3 (which relates to mining companies) is similar to Form S-2, except that it requires some specific geological information.

Form S-11, which deals mainly with the securities of real estate companies, requires specific information, aside from the financial statement information set forth in Form S-1, concerning leasing, mortgages, etc. This latter information is usually required on a property by property basis. Details of the conversion of earnings into "cash flow" after taking into consideration depreciation and mortgage amortization are also required in S-11.

SOME GENERALLY ACCEPTED ACCOUNTING PRINCIPLES

What is a "generally accepted accounting principle"? Even the definition is not generally accepted, for the simple reason that "accounting principles" are no more generally accepted than are other principles. There are honest differences of opinion—some bitterly fought out—within all professions, and the accounting profession is not exempt therefrom.

However, some of the more generally accepted accounting principles can be found codified in such documents as the opinions of the "Accounting Principles Board" of the American Institute of CPA's, the releases of the Securities and Exchange Commission, and the findings of various regulatory agencies and the recommendations of various trade associations propounding uniform accounting practices.

In 1965, the American Institute of Certified Public Accountants published a bulletin entitled "Accounting Research Study No. 7," which itemized some of the more generally accepted accounting principles, but you should know that the Accounting Principles Board ("APB") has been grappling with some serious problems and that the only way to be up to date on this subject is to get the latest bulletins from the American Institute of CPAs.

Some of the more generally accepted accounting principles to be found in Accounting Research Study No. 7 published by the American Institute of CPAs are these:

SALES REVENUES AND INCOME

These should neither be anticipated, overstated, nor understated. The important concept is to make sure that inventories have been properly taken into consideration and that there has been proper "cut-off" accounting both at the beginning and at the end of the period being audited.

Similarly, liabilities for cost and expenses at both the beginning and end of the period must be checked out with appropriate charges being made for depreciation and amortization, and appropriate contingency reserves set up, with the particular caveat that contingency provisions and reserves must *not* be used as a means of arbitrarily shifting nor reducing income in one period at the expense of another.

Similarly, proper cost distribution must be made to avoid unfair shifting or build-up.

To avoid overstatement or understatement, nonrecurring or extraordinary gains and losses should be recognized when they occur, but separately stated from ordinary and usual income, to avoid giving an unfair inference.

ACCOUNTING FOR EQUITY CAPITAL

If there are two or more classes of stock, each should be shown separately, and the rights and preferences concerning dividends and liquidation should be shown in the statements.

Impairments of capital which result from losses or operating deficits or from distributions in excess of earnings or from treasury stock purchases should be accounted for in the statements both currently and cumulatively, so that the investors can see what is causing the erosion or improvement of their capital position.

However, the capital surplus account should not be used to disguise current or future charges, thereby preventing them from falling into the current income account where they would be more readily spotted by investors.

Retained earnings should represent the cumulative balance of past earnings, less dividend distributions in cash, property or stock, plus or minus the extraordinary items which could not be included in current operations in the past. Unless something specifically is stated to the contrary in the financial statements, one should be able to assume that the entire balance in the capital surplus account would be available for future dividend distributions, unless restrictions thereon are specifically stated (in the financial statements). Stock options and revaluation credits should be specifically itemized in the capital surplus account, to call attention to them.

ACCOUNTING FOR ASSETS

Current assets should be items which one expects to be realized within a year, and cash must be segregated between restricted and unrestricted cash.

Similarly, accounts receivable should have allocated to them their debt allowances; while receivables from officers, stockholders, employees, or affiliated companies should be shown separately.

Inventories should be carried at cost or market—whichever is lower; and costs should consist of direct costs plus factory overhead; while the basis of valuation (i.e., last in, first out; first in, first out; or average) should be set forth.

Fixed assets should generally be carried at cost except for items no longer in service which should be charged to the depreciation reserve, and situations where cost is no longer meaningful.

Long term investments and securities should ordinarily be carried at cost, but, if market quotations are available, they should be disclosed.

ACCOUNTING FOR LIABILITIES

All known liabilities should be set forth, regardless of whether a definite amount can be fixed thereon at the time of preparation of the balance sheet.

Items which cannot be reasonably approximated should be disclosed on the face of the financial statement in the form of a footnote.

Current liabilities will consist of items payable within a year, and the accounts should be broken down separately to show notes payable to banks; to others; to trade accounts payable; to Federal income taxes accrued; to accounts and notes payable to officers; and to accounts and notes payable to affiliates.

Concerning specific liabilities which are liens against assets, the assets should be earmarked so that one can tell how much liability there is to offset what specific asset.

Important contingent liabilities (such as litigation) should be disclosed.

SEPARATE BUSINESS LINES

SEC Release 33-4988 requires that separate lines of business and separate classes of products or services of the registrant and any subsidiaries for the past five years, beginning with years January 1, 1967, be revealed. For each line or class, it is necessary to state the approximate percentage of each specific line or class when compared with the total sales and revenues, in order to separate income or loss and extraordinary items, if such separate lines of business or classes of products accounted for 10 percent or more of the total sales and revenues.

If the registrant's entire sales and revenues did not exceed $50 million during either of the last two fiscal years, instead of a 10 percent rule, 15 percent will be the testing point, so that smaller businessmen will not be compelled to break down their figures, line by line, until they reach the 15 percent test for any particular line.

WHAT HAPPENS AFTER THE FINANCIAL STATEMENTS ARE PREPARED AND GO INTO THE REGISTRATION STATEMENT?

The accountant's job is not finished with the filing of the registration statement. Typically, the underwriters require a "cold comfort" conference and letter covering the short period from the filing of the registration to the date that the underwriting becomes effective. What the underwriters want to know is: Did anything of significance happen which would make the financial statements less meaningful than they were when they were originally issued?

The cold comfort conference becomes even more important in light of the *Texas Gulf Sulphur* and *Bar Chris* cases discussed elsewhere in this book, since the accountants must show that they have tried to "update" their reports in the interim and must be prepared to explain away at a later date why they did not discover things which, in retrospect, look perfectly obvious.

Generally speaking, the cold comfort letter states that the auditors are "independent," within the meaning of SEC regulations; that the subsequent audit did not reveal that any of the "stub" registrations were incorrect; and the accountants have not discovered any important "changes in financial position" which would destroy the "going concern" value of the financial statements submitted.

SOME KEY TIPS ON "COLD COMFORT" LETTERS

The extent to which a cold comfort letter can really be useful either to the registrant or to his underwriters is a matter of current dispute. If you are an accountant asked to give a cold comfort letter, or a director or officer of a corporation who is relying on one, you should familiarize yourself with Auditing Procedure Bulletin No. 35, which states that accountants are generally limiting their ability to financial data or matters which can be found specifically in the accounting records of the registrant.

It is wise for accountants, lawyers, and registrants to discuss the potentialities of the cold comfort letter long before it has to be signed, so that both the accountant and the attorneys for the registrant will know exactly what is going into the letter and so that no one is surprised when a letter is needed in twenty-four hours in order for the issue to become effective.

If the letter is discussed in advance, almost all of the problems can be solved by inserting appropriate auditing procedures. Disaster occurs only when accountants have not worked with particular lawyers before and are faced with sudden cold comfort demands, for which they are not prepared at a moment in time when sale of the entire issue is imminent. No one likes to be under that kind of gun, especially if the problem can be avoided by preplanning.

ACCOUNTING PROBLEMS AFTER REGISTRATION IS COMPLETE

There are, in general, continual financial reporting forms required of public companies. First, there is the annual 10-K report, which is due ninety days after the end of the company's fiscal year, and which must include audited financial statements and schedules which are comparative in nature for each of the last two fiscal years, and which must be prepared pursuant to the requirements of Regulation Sx.

Whether consolidated financial statements with subsidiaries will be required, or whether separate statements of the subsidiaries are needed will depend on their percentage "significance." The "lines of business" tests to determine significance are similar to those required under S-1.

There is a quarterly financial report on Form 10-Q (not required of real estate companies) which is due forty-five days after the end of each of the first three fiscal quarters of the year plus quarterly analysis of stockholder equities and capitalization, unaudited, but similar in form to that required on the annual 10-K.

Real estate companies use Form 7-Q instead of 10-Q, since this latter form requires information more meaningful on real estate companies, including statements of application of funds generated and disbursed, and statements analyzing funds generated for distributions, after gains or losses on investments have been taken into consideration.

FUTURE CHANGES

As mentioned previously and as has been publicized in the trade press, in *Fortune* magazine, and in the "Wheat" report, financial statement reporting by accountants is now a rapidly boiling pot, and, in examining any of the forms in this book and any of the comments set forth herein, you should be aware that large changes are imminent and expected. Nonetheless, if we can leave one thought with you, we will have accomplished much: Always bear in mind that financial statements are matters of opinion in which two well-principled, well-respected accounting firms may differ. It is your duty as a prospective issuer to understand whether or not you are in a controversial area, what the controversy is all about, and what effect such a controversy will have on the preparation of your financial statements—not only in the original prospectus, but in future years, also, in your annual reporting.

If you are going to be an earning conscious company, you had better understand in advance not only what your SEC prospectus will look like, but what your quarterly and annual reports will look like, when placed alongside of the prospectus as a measure of your company's progress.

It is important to note that many trouble spots disappear as a result of consistency. In other words, a conservative method of valuing inventory need not depress earnings, if consistently applied, because the shortage which you feel may depress one year is likely to be made up by an overage next year.

One of the things to watch out for in preparing your prospectus and your financial statements is the techniques being used by competitive stocks. In other words, if you are a member of the boating industry and if you use a different accounting technique than anybody else in the industry, this may be puzzling to securities analysts, especially when they compare your stock with a competitor's stock. If you are going to be different, understand what that difference is and bear in mind what the effect will be when your stock and its assets, liabilities, and earnings are measured against the so-called industry "norm."

16

GOING THROUGH AN ACTUAL REGISTRATION-- STEP BY STEP

Let us take you through an actual registration so that you will see some of the practical problems involved. Let us assume that an underwriter has been selected; you have gotten a letter of intent; you have decided on the kind of stock you are going to issue; how much; and now you are ready to go ahead and draw up an SEC registration—what happens next?

THE FIRST PLANNING CONFERENCE

This first conference should take place the moment the deal has been decided on. The earlier you get started, the fewer hysterical last-minute crises you will have to face as you go along. The purpose of the first planning conference is to assign job duties; to plan a timetable; and to try to think through in advance all of the problems that will arise.

Accordingly, the following key people should be present at such a planning conference: the account executive from the underwriter; the certified public accountant who is going to do the registration; the president and treasurer of the issuer; the attorneys for the issuer and the underwriter; as well as the issuer's general counsel (if the issuer is going to use a specialist in SEC work, in addition to his general counsel).

ASSIGNING TASKS

The purpose of the first planning meeting is to assign personnel to the various job duties, to lay out a realistic timetable, and to discover hidden problems and traps that may come up if not discussed in advance.

Generally, a long agenda is prepared for the meeting before anyone arrives. Such an agenda is the result of either the underwriter's lawyer, the issuer's lawyer, or both of them together preparing a list of the proposed problems that might come up.

The longer the list, the less likely it will be that surprises will arise. As stated before, the list is only the opening gun. Once the meeting is started, each of the participants will be expected to raise new problems.

WHAT KIND OF PROBLEMS COME UP ON A REGISTRATION?

Let us examine a typical agenda:

1. Problems of corporate law

What must be done by the shareholders, directors, and officers prior to the registration? Who must ratify what? Must anything be cleared with the State Corporation Commission?

2. Real Estate Problems

Is title clear to all the properties owned by the issuer? Will it be necessary to get abstracts or certificates of title in various states? If so, how much time should be allowed?

3. Use of proceeds

Bear in mind that your prospectus is going to have to go into a fair amount of detail on the company's future plans. For example, if you intend to relocate your plant and you haven't told anybody about it, bear in mind that your present employees and the union may discover it from your prospectus.

Other "secret business plans" may have to be revealed in the prospectus. Plan for this in advance; discuss such items at the first meeting as they come up, and then you can break the news gently (or perhaps postpone the issue). The time to find out about this is at the very beginning.

4. Consent problems

Do any existing agreements prohibit the new issue? What about current debentures with insurance companies, stockholder agreements, commercial banking arrangements, etc.? What will be their status and how will they be affected?

5. SEC and blue sky law problems

Will the underwriting arrangement and the "insider" options be permissible under the various state blue sky laws?

As to the SEC—what accounting problems will arise; what timetable should be set up for the certification of the statements; what work can be begun immediately?

A *pro forma* questionnaire suitable for digging up the required information for the prospectus should be read to the group so that each one can appreciate the information required of his specialty. Often, going over such a *pro forma* questionnaire raises specific problems not otherwise worked out.

6. Are there any *accounting or SEC problems* which should be discussed with the SEC or other governmental body in advance?

7. Are there any *contracts or insider deals* which should be terminated now or dropped rather than inserted in the prospectus?

8. In *bond offerings*, what problems will arise under the Trust Indenture Act? Who will be trustee, registrar, etc.?

9. Printing problems

Now is the time to start shopping around for a printer, decide who will be the registrar, and whether the stock certificates are going to be printed or engraved. If engraved, be sure to find out how long it will take to get out of the engraver's shop. Engravers cannot be rushed.

10. Job assignments

It is advisable generally to break up each individual job into as many small pieces as possible. In other words, instead of listing as a job assignment that John Lawyer will prepare the prospectus (which is ridiculous because everything about a registration is teamwork), your job breakdown should state that John Lawyer will draft the answers to Items #1, #7 and #16, while Louis Controller will do Items #13, #17 and #22.

11. *Deadlines and regular meetings* are vital if everyone is to keep on top of the job. The more "in-between" meetings you hold, the more likely you are to move along those people who are falling behind and to fill in the gaps. Preparing registrations is not a science; it is an art. Discretion is vital, and there comes a point where you can hold too many meetings (so that you spend more time meeting than working).

SOME PROBLEMS CONNECTED WITH "CLEANING UP" THE CLOSELY HELD CORPORATION

The most important problem in converting a closely held corporation to a public one—and a problem which concerns not only the lawyers and accountants but their client, the proposed public corporation, is the "clean up" or conversion of the old closely held corporation stock into "new" securities suitable for sale to the public.

In that connection, not only must the capitalization of the old corporation be restructured to meet the new public needs, but all of the underlying documents evidencing the corporation's assets, liabilities, and contracts must be reviewed and cleaned up to put them in format suitable for sale to the public.

THE IMPORTANCE OF STARTING EARLY

Timing is a key factor. The emphasis on preparing the registration documents is such that very often, not until the issue is ready to go public, it is discovered that someone has overlooked getting a corporate charter in a particular state or revising a particular document, until it is too late to do so without disrupting the timetable of the public issue and postponing the underwriting, with resultant embarrassment and expense, just at the wrong time. Here are some of the trouble spots:

1. Cleaning Up The Corporation Itself:

Sometimes the old closely held entity consists of a number of separate corporations that have to be consolidated under a single corporate umbrella. Thus, the plant may be owned by a subsidiary corporation which has a minority stockholder. The stockholder may have to be bought out or one corporation dissolved into another, so that all the assets are under a single umbrella.

Sometimes, while the corporation was closely held, it acquired assets that are not needed for the new public vehicle or may hinder its growth. In connection with these consolidations and dissolutions, someone has to consider the income tax aspects of these transactions, as well as the accounting effect of them, and enough time must be allowed, where pertinent, to do buy-outs, legal mergers, transfers of title, transfers of leases, consents of regulatory bodies (such as the ICC, the FCC, the FTC, etc.) or the obtaining of tax rulings.

If the closely held vehicle has to be recapitalized, enough time must be allowed to effectuate the necessary changes at a secretary of state level, and, in some cases, it may even be necessary to consider reincorporating in an entirely different state where the corporation law is more lenient, and, therefore, more suitable for a public vehicle.

By-law and charter changes may be necessary, and such provisions as the requirements that directors own stock, that they reside in a particular state, that cumulative voting is available, that officers and directors can be indemnified against suit, and that pre-emptive rights to subscribe to new securities be eliminated, must be considered. Again, there is a lead time and there are tax consequences to these various changes.

If the corporate name has to be changed, it may have to be searched, and, in some cases, the SEC may have to be consulted (see Release No. 5005, Guide No. 54) where the SEC might feel that the new corporate name was confusing.

Thus, if you wanted to change your name to "American Telephone and Telegraph Company," or if you intend to include in your corporate name an industry designation which gives the stock a "hot" connotation, and if someone might feel that the new name is misleading, you had better check that out in advance, also.

In many instances, a closely held corporation can operate with informal, oral understandings. These may have to be reduced to writing or signed contracts. Typical areas in which closely held corporations can work on an informal basis but where signed, written documents are necessary for public corporations might be oral bonus and employment agreements with key stockholder employees, oral leases or plant and equipment from major stockholders, loans to and from important shareholders, oral understandings concerning bank lines and exclusive franchises.

Stock options and fringe benefit plans should be reduced to writing for public corporations; and, if stockholder consent is necessary, that, too, should be documented.

The whole subject of by-laws, corporate minutes, and ratification of important previous acts must be reviewed by counsel for the issuing corporation, and the necessary paper work tightened up, even though, in the past, the only way important agreements were ratified was by the two major stockholders talking to each other and shaking hands.

Perhaps a rule of thumb might be "If it says something in the prospectus, do I have something in writing to back it up?"

THE DEFICIENCY LETTER

Assuming that you have prepared what you deem a final registration statement, what do you do when the inevitable deficiency letter comes which points out some shortcomings and asks that certain portions of the prospectus be reworked?

Of course, the first thing to do is to call the whole team together again and begin to work immediately on redrafting the objectionable parts. One hopes that there will be very few comments in the efficiency letter, and if you have carefully prepared your registration and have looked at it through the eyes of the SEC, even more thoroughly than the SEC, you will be rewarded by having to make very few changes.

One of the decisions to be made is whether to file an "interim amendment" or to include the corrected material as part of the final price amendment. Obviously, if there are many items to be cleared up in the deficiency letter, you would probably be better off filing an interim amendment, so that you can clear up matters in dispute instead of gambling on last-minute hysteria when the price amendment is ready.

Since time is always important and everybody is on edge when the price amendment comes through it is best to give the SEC a chance to look at your material at leisure and to leave as little new material as possible for the price amendment.

Of course, filing an interim amendment adds to the printing bill and may delay the final price amendment, but, in most cases, the interim amendment will be the safer course.

DELAYING AMENDMENTS

What happens if the SEC is ready but your financial market is not ready? It happens occasionally that there is to be a delay in the securities offering, in which case you will want to file some delaying amendment to avoid the necessity of withdrawing and starting all over again.

Of course, if you delay long enough, you will be faced with the problem that the financial statements will be obsolete and you will have the expense of going through another certification by the accountants.

As you know, every time an amendment is filed, the twenty-day waiting period starts running all over again, so that if you wish and provided you bring your financials up to date, you can postpone your final offering for quite a time. This is not a desirable thing to do, but sometimes you just have no choice.

Acceleration. Once everything is cleaned up and the SEC has accepted your registration, after the price amendment has been filed, it is often advisable to ask the SEC for permission to accelerate the effectiveness of the registration so that the full twenty days need not elapse.

Where the SEC has been on top of a situation from the beginning and you have drawn a careful prospectus, the SEC will often grant such acceleration. The SEC usually requires, however, whether there has already been a broad distribution of the "red herrings" so that the registration statement has been in the hands of various dealers for a reasonable amount of time before they are asked to make an investment decision.

If you would like to know when the SEC will accelerate and when it won't accelerate, we suggest you read Rule 460 propounded by the SEC and the Securities Act Releases interpreting it (including SAR No. 3672).

WHICH FORM DO YOU USE?

Most of this work has involved a discussion of the S-1 registration statement which is the full registration for the ordinary industrial company or financial enterprise.

In passing, however, we should call your attention to the fact that there are, of course, the A Form for the Regulation A offerings (you will find abstracts from an A offering in our forms appendix on how to prepare a prospectus and you will find A offering forms in the forms appendix).

Real estate companies require a special type of form known as S-11, and you will find a filled-out sample in the forms appendix (Real Estate Investment Trust).

There is one other form slightly different from those we have discussed; that is the S-2 form which is used for new "promotional" companies (which have not had substantial gross sales or substantial income for any fiscal year ended during the past five years). The S-2 prospectus is similar to the S-1 except that it probes in greater detail what the promoters are getting out of it and pushes for more detailed information concerning the use of the proceeds of the registration.

SUMMARY

This volume and the included forms are the outgrowth of a transcript we made of one of our "Going Public" Workshops. The topics covered in it are the result of speaking to hundreds of people at all stages of the going public process.

We spoke to underwriters and we asked them what kind of advice they had for new companies about to enter the public market. We spoke to other attorneys experienced in SEC matters. We called accountants and discussed with them on an off-the-record basis the problems in a typical registration.

We answered questions of accountants, attorneys, controllers, businessmen, and underwriters who attended our workshops, and, by answering questions and asking some ourselves, we accumulated an insight into the kind of thing that bothers the particular going public prospect.

The results of accumulating the opinions and reviewing the problems of the persons mentioned above, together with our own experience have been anlayzed for you in this volume.

The forms appendix assembles for you at one place a number of sets of actual prospectuses as filed or filled in by various issuers and their attorneys. (See Chapter 17)

The purpose of the forms appendix is simple: It will help you analyze your own situation and compel you to start putting your own deal down on paper. By reviewing other prospectuses, even though in dissimilar industries, you will begin to find out what kind of information is going to be required of you. Each of the prospectuses in the forms appendix has been selected to illustrate a particular point or kind of deal. You may use the appendix in two ways: You may take any one or more prospectuses and try to read them in conjunction with your own business and see how yours would stack up. The other way would be to read typical clauses of many prospectuses, regardless of industry or type in areas in which you expect trouble.

Thus, if you believe that "insider dealings" will create disclosure problems for your company, if you read "certain transactions with management" in a few prospectuses, you will see how others have treated similarly difficult situations.

PROCEDURE—STEP BY STEP

The first four chapters of this book force you once again to ask yourself whether you are certain you want to go public. Many have decided to go public merely because competitors have done so, and others have decided to go public solely out of ego satisfaction. The results of making illogical decisions can be more disastrous in the switch from private to public corporations than in almost any other field. We urge every reader to go over the first four chapters very carefully.

Chapter 5 will help you compute the cost of going public. Subtracting that cost from your proposed issue will tell you whether the results are worth the effort.

Chapters 6, 7, and 8 deal with finding the right underwriter for your company; checking out his strengths and weaknesses; recognizing the underwriter's viewpoint and what he needs; selling the underwriter; negotiating with the underwriter; and using stock options and cheap stock in connection with your issue.

Chapters 10 and 11 deal with the underwriting agreement itself and the typical clauses thereof (the form of underwriting agreement may be found in the forms appendix).

A discussion of the function of finders, the ways of protecting yourself if you are a finder or if you use finders may be found in Chapter 12.

Chapter 13 points out a very important consideration for the new issuer. The underwriter may want you to issue the kind of securities that are "stylish." There are times when convertible debentures are the thing; there are other times when only common stock can be sold, and still other times when nothing but bonds are marketable.

You must read that chapter carefully because you must decide whether, for the long-run future of your company and yourself as an individual stockholder, you want to be tied down to a particular type of financing. Often, what is saleable is not tolerable.

Thus, by the time you get to Chapter 14, we have assumed you decided on an underwriter, the type of stock to be issued, and the fact that you are going public.

The remaining chapters of the book show you how to do the important paper work. There is a discussion of SEC procedures at Chapter 14 (together with an important discussion of when you do not have to register with the SEC).

Chapter 15 points out the typical problems involved in the financial statements of a new issuer.

Chapter 16 takes you through typical registration problems.

Going public is a logical procedure. If you follow through it step by step, you should have no trouble. Thirty thousand other American companies ranging from the very small to such giants as the various New York City banks have gone public and offered their stock.

With the assistance of capable professional help who have had experience in the field and by following a logical step-by-step analysis, your company can put the public behind its business, as many others have.

17

FORMS APPENDIX

FORM OF CORPORATE QUESTIONNAIRE FOR
MERGING OR GOING PUBLIC

Introduction

Please bear in mind that the following questionnaire was written to cover a broad segment of industry classifications and that some of the questions will not apply to your company.

When making forecasts or projections called for in this questionnaire, you should assume that your financial requirements can be fully satisfied by our firm.

I. *GENERAL*

A. Name of company, address, when it was started and by whom.

B. Description of corporate activity and industry.

1. Position in the industry.
2. Corporate philosophy.

C. Name of subsidiaries, if any; amount of ownership.

II. *MANAGEMENT*

A. Officers and directors.

1. Principal duties.
2. Other affiliations.
3. Resume of qualifications.

B. Top and key middle management (other than officers and directors).

1. Principal duties.
2. Resume of qualifications.

III. *MARKETING*

A. Organization—describe the organization of the marketing function.

      1. Sales.

      2. Advertising and promotion.

      3. Dealer and distribution organization.

  B. Products.

      1. Describe outlets for products and method of distribution used.

      2. Patented or licensed products.

      3. Principal competitors.

      4. Provide available product brochures and price lists.

  C. Sales.

      1. If dollar volume of any one product is significantly relative to total sales, furnish breakdown of sales by product.

      2. Names of principal customers and proportion (if significant) of total sales taken by each during the past year.

      3. Geographical distribution of sales.

      4. Terms of sales. Proportion of credit and cash sales.

      5. What is backlog of unfilled orders now on books and the relation of such backlog to current rate of deliveries, and comparison with like periods of previous years.

  D. Pricing.

      1. Comparison of company's and competitors' prices.

      2. What is monthly sales level necessary to break-even.

      3. In the event of an increase in direct costs (materials and labor), can the company increase prices for its products without materially decreasing sales volume?

      4. How many times per annum are inventories turned over (ratio of sales at cost to average inventories)?

IV. ENGINEERING

Describe the engineering function and state activities in the following:

  A. Product engineering.

  B. Research and development.

V. MANUFACTURING

  A. Plants and warehouses.

      1. Size, type, and location of buildings.

      2. Owned or leased—terms of lease.

  B. Condition of machinery.

  C. Manufacturing process and time required from raw material to finished product.

  D. Raw materials and purchased parts used and principal source of supply.

  E. Transportation facilities for freight-in, freight-out, etc.

VI. PERSONNEL

  A. Production employees.

      1. Total number in this category.
      2. Labor union representation.

  B. Sales, general, and administrative personnel.

      1. Total number in this category.
      2. Number by type:
        a. Administrative.
        b. Sales.
        c. Technical and scientific.
        d. Semitechnical (draftsmen, engineering assistants, and technicians).
        e. Maintenance and security.

VII. FINANCIAL

  A. Assets and liabilities.

      1. Furnish a comparative statement of assets and liabilities for each of the past five years.
      2. On what basis are inventories valued on books?
      3. On what basis are plant and other fixed assets carried on books?
      4. If any of the receivables are overdue, state the amount thereof and supply age schedule (1-30 days, 31-60 days, 61-90 days overdue).
      5. What proportion of inventories are normally represented by:
        a. Raw materials and purchased parts.
        b. Work in process.
        c. Finished goods.
      6. Supply details as to security, interest rate, maturities, etc. of any loans or debts outstanding.
      7. Has any change occurred affecting materially the value of character of assets or liabilities since the date of the latest financial statement to be supplied to us in connection with proposed financing?

  B. Profit and Loss Statements.

      1. Furnish comparative statements of profit and loss for each of the past five years.
      2. Furnish breakdown of cost of sales.
      3. Furnish breakdown of selling and advertising expenses.
      4. Submit monthly sales for the past twenty-four months.

  C. Accounting.

      1. Audits.
        a. Name and address of outside certifying auditors.
        b. Date of latest audit.
      2. Credit.
        a. Name of bank(s).
        b. Names of principal suppliers and percentage of sales volume represented by each.

VIII. PLANNING

A. Sales forecast for the next two years. Explain basis of this forecast.

B. What are the long-range estimates of potential markets and on what facts are they based?

C. Present organization plans to cope with forecasts.
1. Marketing and sales.
2. Manufacturing.
3. Personnel (including management).
4. Engineering (including research and development).

D. Details as to the purpose of proposed financing, showing amounts intended to be used for each purpose.

GOING PUBLIC - STEP-BY-STEP

Check List of Major Items to be Considered

I. 1. Should you go public? Some substitutes?
    a. Insurance company debenture loans.
    b. Small Business Investment Corp. loan.
    c. Inside or family funds.
    d. Inventory or accounts receivable financing.
    e. Mortgage money.
    f. The investment banker and "interim" financing.
    g. Equity financing: sell the stock yourself (to customers, suppliers, employees, etc.).

II. 2. Advantages of going public.
    a. Increases net worth and value of "insider" stock.
    b. Working capital and credit improved.
    c. Merger ability.
    d. Estate tax liquidity.
    e. Incentives to top management.
    f. Stock options.
    g. Diversification of insider holdings.

    3. Disadvantages of going public.
    a. Insiders give up "privileged" company yacht, lump sum entertainment expenses, etc.
    b. Tighter accounting controls on sales and inventory.
    c. Public airing of confidential information (insider dealings - large contracts - financing statements, etc.).
    d. Representation on board by public or banker.
    e. Stockholder meetings.
    f. Stockholders' rights to information and arms-length dealing.

    4. What does it cost?
    a. Underwriting commissions and options.
    b. Professional fees (legal, accounting, engineering, etc.).
    c. Printing bills.
    d. Imprinting stock certificates.
    e. Registrar and transfer agent's fees.
    f. Tax liability on "accumulated" inventories.
    g. Registration and "blue sky" fees.
    h. Recurring expenditures: accounting, legal, public relations and annual reporting fees.

5. Which underwriter?
    a. Does he do deals of your size - type - and industry?
    b. Aside from immediate sales benefits - will the underwriter
       offer useful financial guidance in the future?
    c. Will our connection with the underwriter help us or hinder
       us in the future (depending on his reputation)?
    d. Will the underwriter help make an "after market" or will the
       stock "fall on its face"?
    e. What will the underwriter cost - in commissions - other
       expenses - stock options or warrants?
    f. To whom does the underwriter ordinarily distribute (geo-
       graphically - investor type, etc.)?

6. Dealing with the underwriter.
    a. Effective presentation to the underwriter (see separate
       outline - how to "sell" the underwriter) with emphasis
       on 5 years financial statements - cash flow analysis, etc.
    b. What is the "best" price for your issue - bearing the future
       in mind.
    c. Will stock be sold only for the corporate issuer - or will
       insiders be bailing out also.
    d. Timing - go to the market now? (Will next year's earnings
       be better?) Wait? (Will there still be a market for the
       stock?)
    e. What kind of underwriting? Best efforts, all or none, firm
       commitment?
    f. Full "S" registration - Regulation A registration? Note that
       savings on experts fees may be offset by higher underwriting
       cost of "A" registrations.
    g. Discussion of typical underwriting agreement clauses: option
       on future financings, representation on board, "market out"
       escape clause (broad or narrow), liability on default by
       underwriter - issuer - representations and warranties by
       both parties.

7. Registration problems.
    a. Can I keep the entire offering in my own state?
    b. Can I limit myself to less than 25 offerees?
    c. Will I be able to use Regulation A (less than $300,000) - other
       Regulation A requirements.
    d. Problems of full registration (S)
    e. Specialized real estate forms (S11)
    f. Blue sky law registration - New York State - other states.

8. What type of securities should be offered?
    a. Bonds - mortgage or debentures? Tax and financial problems
       of both.
    b. Preferred stock.
    c. Common stock.
    d. Hybrids:
            i.   Bonds with warrants.
            ii. Convertible debentures vs. preferred.
            iii. Packages of bonds plus stock.
    e. What percentage of outstanding stock should be sold to public?
    f. Who shall sell - the corporation or the insiders?
    g. Retaining control.
            i.   Sell less than 51%.
            ii. Disproportionate voting rights for insider stock.
            iii. Effective control is less than 51%.
    h. Will projected financing inhibit future growth?

9. Finders.
    a. A "good" finder can be an effective negotiator - helpful guide.
    b. A "bad" finder - a disaster.
    c. Checking out the finder: what are his qualifications - refer-
       ences - other deals - reputation - know-how?
    d. Who will pay him and what will the cost be? (5-15% of under-
       writer's net).
    e. Will you be free to place your deal elsewhere without the
       finder?

f. For mutual protection - both the finder and the issuer should have a written letter.
g. Can lawyers and independent accountants be finders (conflic*t* of interest)?

10. Financial statement and accounting problems.
    a. Qualifications of the accountant - staff-wise, experience-wise.
    b. Is he "independent" (A.S.R. No. 81 - December 1958)?
        i. Directly or indirectly interested in the company?
        ii. Did he "write up" the books?
        iii. Is he part of the "management"?
        iv. Previous or current "subservience" to management?
    c. Disciplinary proceedings - accountant's liability for false statements to underwriter - the public, etc.
    d. Original work on accounting records (write-ups).
    e. Placing of staff members on client's personnel.
    f. Connection with lender or factor.
    g. Some particular accounting problems.
        i. Inventory verification (A.S.R. No. 90).
        ii. Projections of income.
        iii. Good will and appraisals.
        iv. Recasting past earnings.
        v. Duty to bring statement "up-to-date" (due diligence letter)

11. Legal problems.
    a. Verification of title - review of contracts.
    b. Revision of by-laws, certificate of incorporation, stock certificates and bonds.
    c. Review of minutes - holding of necessary meetings - covering appropriate action by board of directors and stockholders.
    d. Review with underwriter's counsel or special SEC counsel of stock provisions, trust indentures, stock option plans, etc.
    e. Negotiation and preparation of underwriting and indemnity agreements.
    f. Compilation of material required to prepare prospectus and preparation of the same.
    g. Coordination with underwriting counsel or special SEC counsel.

12. Income tax problems.
    a. The "accumulated" inventory "reserve" problem.
    b. Tax rulings - tax free exchanges and recapitalizations.
    c. Cheap stock and "options" taxable as capital gain or ordinary income? When taxable?

"Sell" the Underwriter with Facts

1. Financial statements: 5 years profit and loss statements - balance sheets and surplus information with explanations of significant changes therein.

2. Explanation of purpose: Why do you want the money and what will you use it for (budgeted in reasonable detail).

3. The cash flow statement: Projection of the next few years budget tied together with your new financial plan. Will the new funds increase earnings and provide for their retirement or value protection?

4. Describing the company: A short history and description of its major product lines by sales percentages. Discussion of company's competitive position in the industry - analysis of profit by product lines for reasonable period.

5. Brief description of plants and production equipment.

6. Brief biographical sketch of officers and directors.

7. Brief discussion of company's future plans and explanation of its weaknesses - backed with factual data wherever possible.

FINDER'S LETTER

Mr. Joe Finder
123 B Street
Scarsdale, N.Y. 10583

Dear Mr. Finder:

This letter will set forth our agreement that you act as finder in connection with your locating for us a proposed underwriter in connection with our contemplated offering of common stock.

In the event you procure an underwriter acceptable to us, and a public offering actually takes place, and we receive the proceeds thereof as set forth in an SEC registration statement, then you shall receive as a finder's fee in full payment for your services in an amount equal to 5 percent of the first $1 million, 4 percent of the second $1 million, 3 percent of the third $1 million, 2 percent of the fourth $1 million, and 1 percent of any amounts over $4 million.

It is to be specifically understood that under no circumstances are you to disclose the information being given to you herewith, nor are you to contact any proposed underwriter without getting our permission in writing first, as to the specific underwriter to whom you wish to offer the material.

This Agreement constitutes the entire agreement between us, and no other representations, warranties, or agreements have been made, and it is specifically understood that payment of the above finder's fee shall be in lieu of any and all other compensation you might claim in connection with above offering.

Very truly yours,
THE XYZ COMPANY

By_____
President

ACCEPTED AND AGREED TO

_____
Joe Finder

LETTER OF INTENT

The New Going Public Corporation
124 Street and 123 Avenue
New York, New York 10009

Gentlemen:

It is the purpose of this letter to summarize our recent conversations. You have transmitted to us five years' statements of income and surplus together with your last annual audited balance sheet as of the end of your last fiscal year and also an unaudited balance sheet for the last quarter and unaudited statements of income and surplus for the three months ended X.

You have represented to us that:

1. All of the outstanding common stock of the Company is owned by Messrs. A, B and C; and

2. The aforementioned financial statements fairly reflect the financial condition of the Company and the results of its operations at the dates and for the periods covered by the respective statements set forth above; and

3. None of the selling stockholders nor the Company know of any state of facts materially or adversely affecting the financial condition of the Company which is not fully disclosed in the above financial statements.

Based upon the aforementioned representations as well as on our appraisal of the general conditions in the securities market, we have discussed with you a proposed underwriting under which the Company would sell 200,000 shares of its 10 cent par value stock, and the present stockholders would sell 200,000 shares of their stock, so that, after registration of the shares under the Securities Act of 1933, there would be offered to the public through an underwriting group of which we would serve as the lead representative 400,000 shares of common stock—200,000 for the Company and 200,000 for the account of the selling stockholders. The Company would remain with 600,000 unissued but authorized shares of 10 cent par value common stock.

The Company undertakes to promptly prepare and file, at its own cost and expense, under the Securities Act of 1933, a registration statement relating to the shares discussed above contemplating their being sold through our underwriting group as set forth above. It is anticipated that the registration statement will be ready for filing not later than December 31, 197— and that certified financial statements in form satisfactory to us, our counsel and the SEC will be prepared by Messrs. Zilch and Filch, Certified Public Accountants, as part of the aforementioned SEC registration statement.

On the assumption that present market conditions are in effect as of the effective date of the registration statement under the SEC mentioned above, we anticipate that the common shares to be offered to the public will be in a price range between $1 and $1.25 per share. Based on that assumption, the underwriting discount relating to the shares purchased by the underwriting group will be not more than 10 percent of such public offering price.

The Company and the selling stockholders agree to pay the expenses of the proposed transaction, including all the fees and expenses of the Company's own counsel, together with all original issue and transfer taxes, SEC registration fees, printing fees and certified public accounting fees. In addition, the Company will pay an amount equal to $—, representing counsel fees for the underwriting group and $—, representing blue sky law qualification fees in other states. Additional expenses of underwriters which will not exceed $— will also be paid for by the Company.

The underwriting agreement will also provide that the Company and the selling stockholders will use their best efforts for a period of five (5) years to cause a person designated by us, as underwriter, to be elected to office and serve as a director of the Company, and, furthermore, we, as underwriters for the Company, shall have a right of first refusal with respect to any other public offering of securities by the Company during that period.

This letter of intent is accepted by the Company and the selling stockholders as a statement of our intention, at this time, to the effect that the transaction anticipated by the parties will close along the lines set forth herein; but it is to be clearly understood that this is merely a "letter of intent" and does not constitute any commitment on the part, either of the Company, the selling stockholders, or the underwriter, except as to mutual reimbursement of the expenses set forth above.

It is anticipated by the parties that until a firm underwriting agreement is entered into between us, that our sole liability to each other shall be to reimburse each other for the expenses set forth above.

If you agree that our understanding is as set forth above, please be good enough to indicate your consent in writing where indicated below.

Sincerely yours,
UNDERWRITER & CO.

By_____
President

ACCEPTED BY:
THE NEW GOING PUBLIC CORPORATION
By_____
President

_____
Joe Selling Stockholder

How to Draw Up an Effective Prospectus STEP-BY-STEP

(Form S-1)

Get Form S-1 and the instructions relating thereto from the SEC in Washington and read Regulation C (Rules 400 et seq.) carefully.

Bear in mind that your prospectus is a "disclosure" document. Some draw it so you go from paragraph to paragraph each more frightening than the one before - as one gloomy statement follows another.

Others - within the limits of what the SEC will permit - sprinkle the prospectus with "the company's management plans to ..." followed by "but there is no assurance that this will occur."

As in all endeavors - the best results are achieved by a skillful blend. It is best to reveal the bad but do **not** hide the good needed to counterbalance it.

Enough theory. Here is an example of how it is done - with the special language followed, in each case, by an example taken from an actual registration.

Item 1. *Distribution Spread.*

The information called for by the following table shall be given, in substantially the tabular form indicated, on the outside front cover page of the prospectus as to all securities being registered which are to be offered for cash (estimate, if necessary).

	Price to public	Underwriting discounts and commissions	Proceeds to registrant or other persons
Per unit	....	....	....
Total	....	....	....

Instructions. 1. The term "commissions" has the meaning given in paragraph (17) of Schedule A of the Act. Only commissions paid by the registrant or selling security holders in cash are to be included in the table. Commissions paid by other persons, and other considerations to the underwriters, shall be set forth following the table with a reference thereto in the second column of the table. Any finder's fees or similar payments shall be appropriately disclosed.

2. If it is impracticable to state the price to the public, the method by which it is to be determined shall be explained. In addition, if the securities are to be offered at the market, or if the offering price is to be determined by a formula related to market prices, indicate the market involved and the market price as of the latest practicable date.

3. If any of the securities being registered are to be offered for the account of security holders, refer on the first page of the prospectus to the information called for by Instruction 3 to Item 19.

	Subscription Price	Underwriting Commission		Proceeds to Company(2)(3)	
		Minimum	Maximum	Minimum	Maximum
Per Unit	$250	$15	$20	$230	$235
Total	$11,750,000	$705,000	$940,000	$10,810,000	$11,045,000

(1) The Company has agreed to sell to Representatives of the Underwriters 100,000 Stock Purchase Warrants at 5¢ per Warrant, permitting purchase of an aggregate of 100,000 shares of Class A Stock at any time on or before April 30, 1964, at $12.50 per share. The Representatives may resell some or all Stock Purchase Warrants at their cost to some or all of the other Underwriters herein, their officers, partners, employees, and members of their immediate families. These purchasers may be deemed Underwriters within Section 2(11) of the Securities Act of 1933 with respect to offering said securities. If any Underwriter resells such Warrant at a price higher than cost, and to the extent that such Warrants are exercised and shares purchased are resold at higher than the exercise price, a profit will be realized which may be deemed a gain in addition to the underwriting discounts or commissions noted above. See "Options to Purchase Securities" and "Underwriting". The afore-mentioned Underwriters and/or purchasers will not offer to sell Warrants or Shares issuable on exercise of said Warrants unless a Post-Effective Amendment has been filed and made effective setting forth the proposed method of distribution and terms of reoffering. The provisions of Rule 10(b)(6) of the Securities and Exchange Act of 1934 may be applicable to any subsequent distribution of the Warrants or the 100,000 underlying shares of Class A Stock.

(2) Before deducting expenses payable by the Company estimated at $147,826.66, including all accountable expenses of the Under-writers up to $40,000, not inclusive of $5,000 to be received by the Company from sale of Stock Purchase Warrants referred to in note (1) above, and not inclusive of any amounts received by the Company upon exercise of said Warrants.

(3) The Company has agreed to indemnify the Underwriters against certain liabilities, including liabilities under the Securities Act of 1933. Morris Cohon, senior partner of Morris Cohon and Co., is a member of the Board of Directors of the Company.

(4) 40,784 shares of Class A Stock are being registered for purposes of distribution in accordance with contract dated February 23, 1962 relating to the purchase by the Company of the KMBC Building. The Company heretofore issued 7,500 shares of Class A Stock as a portion of the consideration to purchase Pelham Park Apartments, to be held for investment purposes, and the holder has requested registration for purposes of sale in the reasonably foreseeable future. Reference is made to "The Company", "Application of Proceeds", "Properties". Such shares, from time to time, may be sold over-the-counter at prices prevailing at time of sale. The Company has undertaken to file and make effective a Post-Effective Amendment to the Registration Statement prior to any future public offering of such shares. The holders of such shares may be deemed to be "Underwriters" within the meaning of Section 2(11) of The Securities Act of 1933 and the profit, if any, on any such resales of such shares may be deemed "underwriting commissions".

Item 2. *Plan of Distribution.*

(a) If the securities being registered are to be offered through underwriters, give the names of the principal under-writers, and state the respective amounts underwritten. Iden-tify each such underwriter having a material relationship to the registrant and state the nature of the relationship. State briefly the nature of the underwriters' obligation to take the securities.

Instructions. All that is required as to the nature of the underwriters' obligation is whether the underwriters are or will be committed to take and to pay for all of the securities if any are taken, or whether it is merely an agency or "best efforts" arrangement under which the underwriters are required to take and pay for only such securities as they may sell to the public. Conditions precedent to the underwriters' taking the securities, including "market outs", need not be described except in the case of an agency or "best efforts" arrangement.

(b) State briefly the discounts and commissions to be allowed or paid to dealers, including all cash, securities, con-tracts or other consideration to be received by any dealer in connection with the sale of the securities.

Instruction. If any dealers are to act in the capacity of sub-underwriters and are to be allowed or paid any additional dis-counts or commissions for acting in such capacity, a general statement to that effect will suffice without giving the additional amounts to be so paid.

(c) Outline briefly the plan of distribution of any securities being registered which are to be offered otherwise than through underwriters.

UNDERWRITING

The Company has entered into an Underwriting Agreement (Exhibit 1.01 to the Registration Statement) whereby the Underwriters named below have severally agreed, subject to the terms thereof, to purchase from the Company, in the respective percentages set forth below, such of the 328,912 shares of Common Stock offered hereby as are not subscribed for pursuant to the Subscription Right or by the Trustee of the Pension Trust Fund for the Company's Employees' Retirement Plan, pursuant to its subscription privilege (herein called the "Unsubscribed Stock").

Name	Address	Percentage
Merrill Lynch, Pierce, Fenner & Smith Incorporated	70 Pine Street, New York 5, N. Y.	18.25%
The First Boston Corporation	15 Broad Street, New York 5, N. Y.	6.50
Kuhn, Loeb & Co. Incorporated	30 Wall Street, New York 5, N. Y.	6.50
Lehman Brothers	One William Street, New York 4, N. Y.	6.50
Eastman Dillon, Union Securities & Co.	15 Broad Street, New York 5, N. Y.	6.25

Merrill Lynch, Pierce, Fenner & Smith Incorporated, as Representative, is the managing underwriter. Under the Agreement the Underwriters do not have the option of purchasing less than all of the Unsubscribed Stock but in case some of the Underwriters default in their purchase, the Company, at its option, may nevertheless require the remaining Underwriters to purchase at least their respective percentages.

The Underwriting Agreement provides that the Underwriters will pay to the Company 50% of any excess of net proceeds realized by them on the sale of any shares of Unsubscribed Stock over the Subscription Price computed in the manner set forth in the Agreement.

Merrill Lynch, Pierce, Fenner & Smith Incorporated, the Representative of the Underwriters, has advised the Company that sales to certain dealers may be made at concessions not in excess of 75 cents per share and that Underwriters may allow and such dealers may reallow not in excess of 15 cents per share to certain other dealers.

Item 3. *Use of Proceeds to Registrant.*

State the principal purposes for which the net proceeds to the registrant from the securities to be offered are intended to be used, and the approximate amount intended to be used for each such purpose.

Instructions. 1. Details of proposed expenditures are not to be given; for example, there need be furnished only a brief outline of any program of construction or addition of equipment. If any substantial portion of the proceeds has not been allocated for particular purposes, a statement to that effect shall be made together with a statement of the amount of proceeds not so allocated.

2. Include a statement as to the use of the actual proceeds if they are not sufficient to accomplish the purposes set forth and the order of priority in which they will be applied. However, such statement need not be made if the underwriting arrangements are such that, if any securities are sold to the public, it can be reasonably expected that the actual proceeds of the issue will not be substantially less than the estimated aggregate proceeds to the registrant as shown under Item 1.

3. If any material amounts of other funds are to be used in conjunction with the proceeds, state the amounts and sources of such other funds. If any material part of the proceeds is to be used to discharge a loan, the item is to be answered as to the use of the proceeds of the loan if the loan was made within one year; otherwise, it will suffice to state that the proceeds are to be used to discharge the indebtedness created by the loan.

4. If any material amount of the proceeds is to be used to acquire assets, otherwise than in the ordinary course of business, briefly describe the assets and give the names of the persons from whom they are to be acquired. State the cost of the assets to the registrant and the principal followed in determining such cost.

PURPOSE OF ISSUE

The proceeds from the sale of the 328,912 shares of Common Stock offered hereby will be used by the Company to pay part of the expenditures incurred and to be incurred for additions and betterments to the physical properties of the Company as more fully set forth in "Construction Program" under "Busi- ness and Property" including the payment of any then existing bank loans (presently estimated at $3 million) which were used to finance temporarily part of the construction expenditures incurred in the latter part of 1961 and the early part of 1962.

Item 4. *Sales Otherwise than for Cash.*

If any of the securities being registered are to be offered other- wise than for cash, state briefly the general purposes of the dis- tribution, the basis upon which the securities are to be offered, the amount of compensation and other expenses of distribution, and by whom they are to be borne.

Instruction. If the distribution is to be made pursuant to a plan of acquisition, reorganization, adjustment or succession, describe briefly the general effect of the plan and state when it became or is to become operative. As to any material amount of assets to be acquired under the plan, furnish information corresponding to that required by Instruction 4 of Item 3. See also General Instruction F.

PURCHASE AND EXCHANGE OFFER

Terms

The Company hereby offers to acquire all, but not less than 51%, of the Capital Units of each partnership on the following terms and conditions.

(a) Set forth in the tabulation below is the name and State of organization of each limited partnership with respect to which the Offer is made, together with the number of shares of Class A Stock of the Company to be offered for each full Capital Unit of each partnership. A proportionate number of shares of Class A Stock will be offered for fractional Capital Units but no fractional shares of Class A Stock of the Company will be issued and all fractions will be settled by the issuance of the nearest number of full shares of Class A Stock.

Partnerships	State of Organi- zation	Year Organized	Total Capital Units	Book Value of Partnership Net Assets as at Dec. 31, 1958	Depre- ciated Average Book Value per Capital Unit as at Dec. 31, 1958	Total Shares of Class A Stock offered to be Exchanged therefor	Shares of Class A Stock offered to be Exchanged for each full Capital Unit	Profits (Loss) for Income Tax Purposes per Capital Unit since organization to December 31, 1958	Distri- butions per Capital Unit since organiza- tion to December 31, 1958
Mart Associates	California	1956	100	$ 618,924	$6,189	200,000	2,000	($411)	$4.800
3450 Associates	California	1956	100	1,607,716	16,077	290,000	2,900	359	6,281
Transamerican Associates	New York	1958	221½	1,824,122	8,235	365,475	1,650	601	1,192
Fawcett Associates	New York	1958	87	773,407	8,890	113,100	1,300	(56)	250
King Edward Associates	New York	1956	100	168,037	1,680	57,000	570	(64)	1,406
Thirty-Four Associates	New York	1957	400	3,043,849	7,610	560,000	1,400	(390)	1,375
Pratney Associates	New York	1957	562½	4,005,018	7,121	871,875	1,550	(613)	2,400

(b) If assignments to and of 51% or more of the total of the Capital Units with respect to each and every one of the above limited partnerships are deposited with the Purchase and Exchange Agent prior to the Expiration Date, then the Purchase and Exchange Offer with respect to the Capital Units of all such partnerships shall become binding on the Company on the Expiration Date; provided, however, that the Company shall not be obligated to accept Assignments to and of 51% or more of the Capital Units of any one or more partnerships unless at least 51% of the Capital Units of all partnerships are deposited but may, at its option, accept Capital Units of any one or more of the partnerships of which at least 51% of the Capital Units shall have been deposited. Assignments to and of Capital Units deposited between the effective date of this Prospectus and the Expiration Date may not be withdrawn.

Item 5. *Capital Structure.*

Furnish the information called for by the following table, in substantially the tabular form indicated, as to each class of securities of the registrant and each class of securities, other than those owned by the registrant or its totally-held subsidiaries, of all subsidiaries whose financial statements are filed with the registration statement on either a consolidated or individual basis:

Title of class	Amount authorized or to be authorized	Amount outstanding as of a specified date within 90 days	Amount to be outstanding if all securities being registered are sold

Instructions. 1. Securities held by or for the account of the issuer thereof are not to be included in the amount outstanding, but the amount so held shall be stated in a note to the table. Also set forth in a note to the table a cross reference to the note in the financial statements containing information concerning the extent of obligations under leases on real property.

2. Indebtedness evidenced by drafts, bills of exchange, bankers' acceptances or promissory notes may be set forth in a single aggregate amount under an appropriate caption such as "Sundry Indebtedness."

3. A registrant may, at its option, include in the table the capital share liability in dollars, as well as the amount, of each class of shares shown in the table, together with capital surplus and earned surplus. Surplus shall be shown in the same manner as in the balance sheet of the registrant, or in the consolidated balance sheet of the registrant and subsidiaries, if such a consolidated balance sheet is included in the prospectus.

CAPITALIZATION

The following table sets forth the debt and common stock of the Company at February 23, 1962 and as adjusted to give effect to the sale of the Debentures offered hereby, the sale of stock to the Underwriters, and the application of the proceeds (see "Underwriting"):

Title of Class	Amount Authorized	Amount Outstanding February 23, 1962	Amount Outstanding Adjusted as stated above
SENIOR INDEBTEDNESS			
Notes due 1963 (a)	$2,619,368	$1,703,122	$1,703,122
Due officers and organizations controlled by officers, due not prior to July, 1962 (b)	—	$ 795,596	$ 795,596
Mortgages	—	$ 393,917(c)	$ 393,917(c)
Due under land purchase contracts	See Note C to Financial Statements of the Company as at September 30, 1961		
Due Great Sweet Grass Oils Limited (d)	—	$ 110,921	$ 110,921
Sundry	—	$ 36,031	$ 36,031
SUBORDINATED INDEBTEDNESS			
6½% Convertible Subordinated Debentures due 1971	$2,000,000	$ —0—	$2,000,000
CAPITAL STOCK			
Common Stock, par value 10¢ per share	3,500,000 shs.	2,522,500 shs.(e)	2,522,500 shs.(f)

(a) Of this amount, $104,368 was borrowed from Chemical Bank New York Trust Company on December 26, 1961, which amount is repayable in 19 approximately equal monthly installments with the final installment due June 2, 1963, with interest at the rate of 5½% per annum. Such note is secured by a mortgage and deed of trust covering substantially all of the Company's oil properties in Oklahoma, and also by an assignment of the income from such properties to the extent necessary to pay the monthly installments of principal and interest. The balance represents the direct obligation of subsidiaries, guaranteed by the Company, and reference is made to the discussion under the caption "Zilkha Loan" for a description of the interest rate, security, payment provisions and other divisions thereof.

(b) This represents indebtedness accrued by the Rainbow Companies prior to the merger-acquisition and includes accrued interest through February 23, 1962. For interest rate, payment provisions and other terms, see "Transactions with Management".

(c) Of which $56,100 represents first and second purchase money mortgages on the Albuquerque office building, and $337,817 represents the unpaid balance of indebtedness under six purchase money mortgages given by the Rainbow Land Companies on acquisition of various sections of Rainbow Lakes Estates. For interest rates, security, payment provisions and other terms, see "Rainbow Lakes Estates".

(e) Including 22,500 shares issued in settlement of claims for commissions arising out of the merger-acquisition. See Note (d) above.

(f) Not including _____ shares reserved for issue upon exercise of Debentures, and not including an aggregate of 75,000 shares to be sold or optioned to Troster, Singer & Co. or its designees

Item 6. *Summary of Earnings.*

Furnish in comparative columnar form a summary of earnings for the registrant or for the registrant and its subsidiaries consolidated, or both, as appropriate, for each of the last five fiscal years of the registrant (or for the life of the registrant and its immediate predecessors, if less) and for any period between the end of the latest of such fiscal years and the date of the latest balance sheet furnished, and for the corresponding period of the preceding fiscal year. In connection with such summary, whenever necessary, reflect information or explanation of material significance to investors in appraising the results shown, or refer to such information or explanation set forth elsewhere in the prospectus.

Instructions. 1. Include comparable data for any additional fiscal years necessary to keep the summary from being misleading. Subject to appropriate variation to conform to the nature of the business or the purpose of the offering, the following items shall be included: net sales or operating revenues; cost of goods sold or operating expenses (or gross profit); interest charges; income taxes; net income; special items; and net income and special items. The summary shall reflect the retroactive adjustment of any material items affecting the comparability of the results. See Item 21(b).

2. If common stock is being registered, the summary shall be prepared to present earnings applicable to common stock. Per share earnings and dividends declared for each period of the summary shall also be included unless inappropriate.

3. A registrant which is engaged primarly (i) in the generation, transmission or distribution of electricity, the manufacture, mixing, transmission or distribution of gas, the supplying or distribution of water or in furnishing telephone or telegraph services or (ii) in holding securities in such companies, may, at its option, include a summary for a twelve months period to the date of the latest balance sheet furnished, in lieu of both the summary for the interim period between the end of the last

fiscal year and such balance sheet date and the summary for the corresponding period of the preceding fiscal year.

4. A registrant may, at its option, show in tabular form for each fiscal year or other period, the ratio of earnings (computed in accordance with generally accepted accounting principles after all operating and income deductions, except taxes based on income or profits and fixed charges) to fixed charges. The term "fixed charges" shall mean (i) interest and amortization of debt discount and expenses and premium on all indebtedness; (ii) an appropriate portion of rentals under long-term leases and, (iii) in case consolidated figures are used, preferred stock dividend requirements of consolidated subsidiaries, excluding in all cases, items eliminated in consolidation. In the case of utilities, interest credits charged to construction should be added to gross income and not deducted from interest. If the ratio is shown, the pro forma ratio of earnings to fixed charges adjusted to give effect to the issuance of securities being registered and to any presently proposed issuance, retirement or redemption of securities should be disclosed. Any registrant electing to show the ratio of earnings to fixed charges, in accordance with this instruction, shall file as an exhibit a statement setting forth in reasonable detail the computations of such ratios. For the purpose of this exhibit and the pro forma ratio referred to above, an assumed maximum interest rate may be used on securities as to which the interest rate has not yet been fixed, which assumed rate should be shown.

5. In connection with any unaudited summary for an interim period or periods between the end of the last fiscal year and the balance sheet date, and any comparable unaudited prior period, a statement shall be made that all adjustments necessary to a fair statement of the results for such interim period or periods, have been included. In addition, there shall be furnished in such cases, as supplemental information but not as a part of the registration statement, a letter describing in detail the nature and amount of any adjustments, other than normal recurring accruals, entering into the determination of the results shown.

6. If long term debt or preferred stock is being registered, there shall be shown the annual interest requirements on such long term debt or the annual dividend requirements on such preferred stock. To the extent that an issue represents refunding or refinancing, only the additional annual interest or dividend requirements shall be stated.

EARNINGS AND RETAINED EARNINGS OF SWINGLINE INC. AND CONSOLIDATED SUBSIDIARY
(Including Equity in Net Earnings of Wilson Jones Company)

The following consolidated statements of earnings and retained earnings should be read in conjunction with the other financial statements and related notes of Swingline Inc. included in this Prospectus. The statements for the years ended March 31, 1958 through 1960, and for the five month period ended August 31, 1960, have been examined by Kaufman & Mendelsohn, independent Certified Public Accountants, whose opinion with respect thereto is included elsewhere in this Prospectus. (In 1960 the Company changed its fiscal year end from March 31 to August 31.) The statements for the year ended August 31, 1961 have been examined by Lybrand, Ross Bros. & Montgomery, independent Certified Public Accountants, whose opinion with respect thereto is included elsewhere in this Prospectus. The statement for the year ended March 31, 1957 has not been audited, but the management of the Company believes that all adjustments (all of which were of a normal recurring nature) necessary to a fair statement of the results for such period have been made.

	Years Ended March 31,				Five Months Ended August 31, 1960	Year Ended August 31, 1961
	1957 (Unaudited)	1958	1959	1960		
Net sales (A)	$6,779,961	$8,380,961	$10,605,802	$12,402,849	$5,357,346	$12,360,529
Cost of sales (A and B)	4,369,363	5,132,244	6,064,719	7,148,939	2,936,980	6,351,332
Gross profit	2,410,598	3,248,717	4,541,083	5,253,910	2,420,366	6,009,197
Selling and administrative expenses..	1,635,753	1,991,821	2,313,314	2,588,391	1,106,081	2,687,821
	774,845	1,256,896	2,227,769	2,665,519	1,314,285	3,321,376
Other income (deductions):						
Equity in net earnings of Wilson Jones Company (C)				137,268(D)	159,893(D)	338,077(D)
Dividends (C)	20,454	21,466	25	46,845		
Interest earned on mortgage (E)	22,640	43,969	41,125	35,219	12,944	37,887
Interest expense	(620)	(34,455)	(13,369)	(43,957)	(28,806)	(13,583)
Gain or (loss) on sales of plant, property and equipment	77,677(E)	1,900	30,850	(12,142)	43,520	59,843
Miscellaneous income	100,203	61,241	74,886	125,712	50,363	93,742
Gain on sales of marketable securities						80,527
	220,354	94,121	133,517	288,945	237,914	596,493
Earnings before federal income tax	995,199	1,351,017	2,361,286	2,954,464	1,552,199	3,917,869
Provision for federal income tax	490,381	673,174	1,225,965	1,444,817	740,000	1,864,000
Net earnings	504,818	677,843	1,135,321	1,509,647	812,199	2,053,869
Special credit, equity in gain on sale of land and building by Wilson Jones Company, net of income tax						369,153
Net earnings and special credit						2,423,022
Retained earnings at beginning of period	2,880,429	3,375,247	4,040,090	5,160,411	6,655,058	7,467,257
	3,385,247	4,053,090	5,175,411	6,670,058	7,467,257	9,890,279
Cash dividends	10,000	13,000	15,000	15,000		245,094
	3,375,247	4,040,090	5,160,411	6,655,058	7,467,257	9,645,185
Amount transferred to capital stock in connection with recapitalization (F)						750,000
Retained earnings at end of period...	$3,375,247	$4,040,090	$ 5,160,411	$ 6,655,058	$7,467,257	$ 8,895,185
Per share information (G):						
Net earnings	$ .50	$ .68	$1.14	$1.51	$ .81	$1.99
Special credit	—	—	—	—	—	.36

(A) Includes sales of a product line discontinued by the Company in August 1960. For amounts and further details see "Transactions Between the Company and Certain Persons".
(B) See Note 2 to financial statements.
(C) See Note 1 to financial statements.
(D) Of these amounts, dividends of $47,491, $94,982 and $189,963 have been received in the year ended March 31, 1960, five months ended August 31, 1960, and year ended August 31, 1961, respectively.
(E) See Note 3 to financial statements.
(F) See Note 5 to financial statements.
(G) Based on average number of shares outstanding in the respective periods, giving retroactive effect to the recapitalization in the year ended August 31, 1961 (see Note 6 to financial statements). It is not practicable to determine dividends per share under the present capitalization.

Item 7. *Organization of Registrant.*

State the year in which the registrant was organized, its form of organization (such as "A corporation", "An unincorporated association" or other appropiate statement) and the name of the State or other jurisdiction under the laws of which it was organized.

THE COMPANY

The First Republic Corporation of America ("The Company") was organized under Delaware laws on February 14, 1961. Its principal offices are at 375 Fifth Avenue, New York 16, New York.

The Company was organized by Ira Sands, Jerome Wishner and George Gewanter to utilize the opportunities and advantages which they believe available to a corporation having the broad diversified activities in which the Company is now engaged . . . . including purchasing or otherwise acquiring, owning, developing, operating managing, selling, mortgaging and financing of office buildings, industrial parks, apartment developments, commercial properties, shopping centers, and other income-producing real estate and interests therein in the United States and other parts of the world.

Item 8. *Parents of Registrant.*

List all parents of the registrant showing the basis of control and, as to each parent, the percentage of voting securities owned or other basis of control by its immediate parent, if any.

Instructions. 1. Include the registrant and show the percentage of its voting securities owned or other basis of control by its immediate parent. In case any parent is a resident of, or a corporation or other organization formed under the laws of, any foreign country, give the name of such country for each such foreign parent, and, if it is a corporation or other organization, state briefly the nature of the organization.

2. If the securities being registered are to be issued in connection with or pursuant to a plan of acquisition, reorganization, readjustment or succession, indicate, so far as practicable, the status to exist upon consummation of the plan.

Recent example not available–but instructions as set forth above are simple and self-explanatory.

Item 9. *Description of Business.*

(a) Briefly describe the business done and intended to be done by the registrant and its subsidiaries and the general development of such business during the past five years. If the business consists of the production or distribution of different kinds of products or the rendering of different kinds of services, indicate, insofar as practicable, the relative importance of each product or service or class of similar products or services which contributed 15% or more to the gross volume of business done during the last fiscal year.

Instructions. 1. The description shall not relate to the powers and objects specified in the charter, but to the actual business done and intended to be done. Include the business of subsidiaries of the registrant only insofar as is necessary to understand the character and development of the business conducted by the total enterprise.

2. In describing developments, information shall be given as to matters such as the following: The nature and results of any bankruptcy, receivership or similar proceedings with respect to the registrant or any of its significant subsidiaries; the nature and results of any other materially important reorganization, readjustment or succession of the registrant or any of its significant subsidiaries; the acquisition or disposition of any material amount of assets otherwise than in the ordinary course of business; any materially important changes in the types of products produced or services rendered by the registrant and its subsidiaries; and any materially important changes in the mode of conducting the business, such as fundamental changes in the methods of distribution.

(b) Indicate briefly, to the extent material, the general competitive conditions in the industry in which the registrant and its subsidiaries are engaged or intend to engage, and the position of the enterprise in the industry. If several products or services are involved, separate consideration should be given to the principal products or services or classes of products or services.

HISTORY AND BUSINESS OF THE COMPANY

Swingline had its origin in a business founded in 1925 by Mr. Jack Linsky, which engaged in the distribution of stapling machines and staples. By 1930 the business (which had since been incorporated) had begun its own manufacture of such products. In 1939 the corporation was replaced by a partnership, Speed Products Co., of which Mr. and Mrs. Jack Linsky were the sole partners. In 1946 the present corporation was incorporated under the laws of the State of New York, under the name of Speed Products Co., Inc., to succeed to the business of the partnership. Recognizing the wide acceptance of its tradename "Swingline" (which had been applied to its products since 1935) the corporation changed its name to Swingline Inc. in 1956.

In 1957 a wholly owned subsidiary of the Company purchased, for a total consideration of $1,533.743, all the assets and assumed all the liabilities of Ace Fastener Corp., a manufacturer of staplers, staples and staple removers which had been in business for over 35 years. The new subsidiary acquired, among other things, its predecessor's name, trademarks and goodwill. Ace Fastener maintains its own sales force and manufacturing facilities

The Company also manufactures staple removers. The Rubber Products Division of the Company manufactures rubber components for staplers and also produces rubber bands and rubber fingertips. The Company's other products are brass paper fasteners, binder label holders, file fasteners, binder clips, erasing shields and looseleaf holders. These miscellaneous products account for approximately 9% of the Company's gross sales.

The Company has ceased manufacturing and selling a line of compressed-air-driven, heavy-duty, nail and staple guns for industrial purposes, which it had previously sold only to an affiliate of the Selling Shareholders. (See "Transactions Between the Company and Certain Persons.")

Trademarks

The principal trademarks of Swingline Inc. are Tot-50, No. 101 Compression Tacker, Swingline Staplers, Swingline Staples, Speedway File Fasteners, Parr Fingertips and Rubber Bands. Ace Fastener's principal trademarks are Pilot, Ace Clipper, Ace Cadet, Ace Liner, Ace Dart and Ace Staple Remover. All of these trademarks have been registered.

Research and Development

The Company maintains an engineering, development and research department employing about fifteen men. This group develops new products in the stapling field and applies modern production methods to the Company's manufacturing operations. Swingline and Ace Fastener own approximately eighty patents and have a number of new patent applications now pending. However, the expiration or loss of any of the patents now held, or the non-issuance of the patents for which applications are now filed by the Company, would not, in the opinion of management, materially affect the operations of the Company.

Marketing and Sales

The Swingline and Ace Fastener sales forces, totalling about sixty salesmen, sell directly to retailers and wholesalers throughout the United States and Canada, to government agencies, and for export. Approximately 54% of the Company's sales are to domestic retailers, 36% to domestic wholesalers, 6% to United States Government agencies and 4% for export account. The Company promotes its products through national magazines, trade papers and other advertising media.

The Company's products are in keen competition with those of other manufacturers. While no definitive comparative figures are available, management believes that the Company is currently one of the leaders in the United States in terms of both unit and dollar sales volume of office and home staplers. Three other companies are believed to be important suppliers of such products. The rubber and other miscellaneous products of the Company are believed to occupy only a minor segment of the market for such products. The Company expects to continue to encounter intense competition in all phases of its business.

Manufacturing

The manufacture of stapling machines by Swingline is a highly integrated operation. Practically all metal parts are stamped, formed, machined and assembled in Swingline's modern plant in Long Island City, New York, N. Y. In the manufacture of staples Swingline draws heavy gauge wire to the fine sizes required, and then forms the staples on machinery of the Company's own design. The Rubber Products Division produces all rubber parts used in the manufacture of staplers.

Products

The principal products of the Company, accounting for approximately 54% of gross sales, are manually operated stapling machines, including desk staplers, compression tackers and stapling pliers. The Company's line currently includes about 25 different models of stapling devices, adapted to various business, home or school uses. The desk staplers range from the miniature "Tot" to heavy-duty and long reach devices. Compression tackers are used in display, shipping, upholstering and home repair. Stapling pliers find their principal use in retail stores for sealing packages or attaching tags to merchandise. The Company also manufactures electrically operated desk staplers, designed for volume use, which are variously actuated by finger touch, foot pedal or paper contact. In its merchandising of its stapling machines, the Company has emphasized easy loading. jam-proof operation and, where appropriate, attractive appearance and convenient packaging.

Staples, accounting for approximately 37% of the Company's total dollar volume of sales, are also a major product of the Company. They are sold for use in the Company's own machines as well as in those of other manufacturers. Approximately sixty styles and sizes of staples are in the Company's line.

Item 10. *Description of Property.*

State briefly the location and general character of the principal plants, mines and other materially important physical properties of the registrant and its subsidiaries. If any such property is not held in fee or is held subject to any major encumbrance, so state and briefly describe how held.

Instructions. 1. What is required is information essential to an investor's appraisal of the securities being registered. Such information should be furnished as will reasonably inform investors as to the suitability, adequacy, productive capacity and extent of utilization of the facilities used in the enterprise. Detailed descriptions of the physical characteristics of individual properties or legal descriptions by metes and bounds are not required and should not be given.

2. In the case of an extractive enterprise, material information should be given as to production, reserves, locations, developments and the nature of the registrant's interest. Where individual properties are of major significance to the enterprise (i) more detailed information concerning these matters should be furnished, including the results of development in the area and significant geological structures and formations, where appropriate and (ii) appropriate maps should be used to disclose location data of significant properties except where numerous maps would be required. Where the report of an engineer or other expert is referred to in the prospectus, a copy of the full report normally should be furnished as supplemental information but not as a part of the registration statement.

PROPERTY

The operations of the Company are conducted from the nine plants and one space location listed below:

Location	Leased or Owned*	Building Area (square feet)	Type of Building and Use
Chicago, Illinois	Owned in fee	178,000	A modern, single-story building containing the Company's general offices, warehouse and distribution facilities and facilities for coffee roasting and some packaging operations
Indianapolis, Indiana	Owned in fee	200,000	A modernized and expanded single-story building, containing distribution center, warehouse and office facilities, and the Company's principal food preparation, processing and packaging facilities
Detroit, Michigan	Lease expiring 1966 with an option to renew for 5 years	100,000	A four-story building containing chemical compounding, blending and packaging facilities for the preparation of detergents and cleaning compounds and distribution center, warehouse and office facilities
Long Island City, New York	Owned in fee** (See below)	94,000	A multi-story building, containing distribution center, warehouse and office facilities and facilities for coffee roasting, tea blending and packaging and spice grinding and packaging
Dallas, Texas	Lease expiring in November 1961 (See below)	80,000	A seven-story building containing distribution center, warehouse and office facilities
San Francisco, California	Lease expiring 1973	75,000	A modern, single-story building containing distribution center, warehouse and office facilities and coffee roasting and some food processing and packaging facilities
Pittsburgh, Pennsylvania	Lease expiring 1978 with an option to renew for 20 years	64,200	A modern, single-story building containing distribution center, warehouse and office facilities and coffee roasting facilities
Atlanta, Georgia	Owned in fee	58,000	A modern, single-story building, containing distribution center, warehouse and office facilities and coffee roasting facilities
Newton, Massachusetts	Lease expiring 1964 with an option to renew for 5 years	31,000	A modern, single-story building containing distribution center, warehouse and office facilities
Philadelphia, Pennsylvania	Leased space, lease expiring 1965	45,750	The leased space contains distribution center, warehouse and office facilities

* For information concerning the obligations of the Company under leases on real property, reference is made to Note 8 to the Financial Statements.

** Owned in fee by Deeps, Inc., a wholly owned subsidiary of the Company.

All of the plants and the leased space listed above are considered by the Company to be well maintained, and, except for the Company's plant in Long Island City, New York, suited for the purposes for which they are being used.

In November 1961 the Company will move its present Dallas, Texas distribution center to a new center in the Dallas area. The new center is being constructed to the Company's specifications, will be a single story building of 60,000 square feet containing distribution center, warehouse and office facilities and will be leased for ten years with three five year renewal options.

The Company intends to replace its present plant in Long Island City, New York, with a new food distribution center, warehouse, office and food processing plant of 114,000 square feet now being constructed in Englewood, New Jersey. The new plant will be owned by Deeps, Inc., a wholly owned subsidiary of the Company, and leased to the Company. Deeps, Inc. has entered into an agreement to sell the Long Island City plant for a total sale price of $540,000. Under the agreement payment of the major portion of the sale price is to be made at the closing, now scheduled for February 1, 1962. To help finance construction of the Englewood plant, the Company has agreed to guarantee up to $1,400,000 of short-term construction loan notes of Deeps, Inc. It is anticipated that upon completion of construction of the Englewood plant, permanent financing will be obtained in the form of long-term debt obligations aggregating approximately $1,100,000 of Deeps, Inc., secured by a first mortgage on the new plant and guaranteed by the Company.

Equipment and machinery used in the Company's operations, consisting principally of food processing and packaging equipment and chemical compounding, blending and packaging equipment, are owned by the Company. Of a total of 112 trucks, tractors and trailers used in the Company's operations, 95 are owned by the Company and the remainder is leased. The Company owns all of the approximately 324 passenger cars used in its operations.

Item 11. *Organization within 5 years.*

If the registrant was organized within the past 5 years, furnish the following information:

(a) State the names of the promoters, the nature and amount of anything of value (including money, property, contracts, options or rights of any kind) received or to be received by each promoter directly or indirectly from the registrant, and the nature and amount of any assets, services or other consideration therefor received or to be received by the registrant. The term "promoter" is defined in Rule 405.

(b) As to any assets acquired or to be acquired by registrant from a promoter, state the amount at which quired or to be acquired and the principle followed or to followed in determining the amount. Identify the perso making the determination and state their relationship, if a: with the registrant or any promoter. If the assets were quired by the promoter within two years prior to their trans to the registrant, state the cost thereof to the promoter.

TRANSACTIONS WITH AFFILIATED PERSONS

Messrs. Sands, Wishner and Gewanter are the organizers of the Company. Prior to its organization, during the years 1958 to 1961, Messrs. Sands, Wishner and Gewanter received, individually or as partners or stockholders of various partnerships and corporations, cash profits and fees in connection with the formation of partnerships and acquisition and management of properties (which were parties to an Exchange Offer made by the Company on June 12, 1961) aggregating approximately $660,825 gross, before disbursements of costs, fees and expenses. They purchased by assignment of certain purchase contracts and real estate rights and with no cash consideration, limited participations in various partnerships for which they received 130,299 shares of Class A Stock upon consummation of the Exchange Offer.

Milton H. Bernstein (46%), Frederick Bernstein (36%) and Rosalind Rinzler (18%) (sister of Messrs. Bernstein) are sole stockholders of Hempstead Terrace Corp. which originally held a contract to purchase the land subsequently acquired by the Company for the Imperial Square Development. (Messrs. Sands, Wishner and Gewanter have no interest whatever in Hempstead Terrace Corp. or affiliates thereof.) Hempstead Terrace Corp. earned $875,000 on sale of this contract to a joint venture of Milton H. Bernstein (23%), Frederick Bernstein (18%), Samuel Bernstein (9%), George Gewanter (16⅔%), Ira Sands (16⅔%) and Jerome Wishner (16⅔%). This joint venture has undertaken to construct the buildings at Imperial Square with an estimated gross gain of $1,379,945. From this gross gain, the joint venture paid all expenses of syndication, including underwriting fees, legal and accounting fees, commissions, stationery, printing, postage, and all other miscellaneous costs. In addition, the joint venture is obligated to pay rent, taxes, mortgage interest, etc. . . . . It is estimated that at the conclusion of the joint venture there will be no net profit whatsoever . .

. Messrs. Bernstein are sole stockholders of corporate entities which have undertaken to construct these buildings as sub-contractors at actual cost . . . For the assignment of their interests in the said purchase contract without cash consideration, Messrs. Bernstein, Sands, Wishner and Gewanter received limited Participation Units for which upon consummation of the Exchange Offer, Messrs. Bernstein received 213,125 shares of Class A Stock and Messrs. Sands, Wishner and Gewanter received 106,875 shares, which latter amount is included in the total stated in the first paragraph of this section. The Company, as fee owner and landlord has a lease with the said joint venture as tenant. This lease may be assigned to Square Management Corp. as tenant on or before 120 days after the issuance of the final Certificate of Occupancy for the last building to be erected. The stockholders of Square Management Corp. are: Milton H. Bernstein (20%), Frederick Bernstein (20%), Samuel Bernstein (10%), Ira Sands (16⅔%), Jerome Wishner (16⅔%) and George Gewanter (16⅔%). Under the lease, estimated annual net profit will be approximately $96,410 to the tenant.

Messrs. Sands and Wishner had advanced $50,000 in cash toward actual expenses of organization and formation of the Company and its first Registration Statement. They have accepted a non-interest bearing note of the Company due July 1, 1963 in payment.

The following officers and directors had interests in purchase contracts which were acquired by them after extended negotiations, after a cash advance by them of $180,000 for guarantees of contract performance, and after undertaking personal liabilities under said contracts. The cash advances of $180,000 were returned to them upon such contract performance. Upon assignment of these contracts to the Company, which included assignment of certain rights relating to mortgage refinancing benefits, on a non-arms length basis, they received capital stock of the Company as follows: Milton H. Bernstein— 414 Shares Class A; Ira Sands—37,294 Shares Class A, 116,200 Shares Class A (limited), 57,659 Shares Class B-II; Jerome Wishner—37,293 Shares Class A, 116,200 Shares Class A (limited), 57,658 Shares Class B-II; George Gewanter—37,293 Shares Class A, 78,700 Shares Class A (limited), 57,658 Shares Class B-II; Charles J. Cohl—6,759 Shares Class A, 1,500 Shares Class B-I; Sam Wanger —500 Shares Class A (limited). (For a description of the limitations upon Shares of Class A (limited), see "Description of Capital Stock".)

Messrs. Sands and Wishner have, for many years, been equal partners in The First Republic Company, syndication underwriters. The Company may utilize the established trained brokerage, sales force and sales outlets of The First Republic Company in connection with its future syndication sales activities. The Company will pay for such services at prevailing rates for identical services by other similar firms. In connection with the recent intra-state syndicate offering of Video Film Center, New York City, such gross underwriting commissions will amount to $154,000, before mailing, and distribution charges, disbursement for representatives' commissions, costs and other expenses. Tri-Management Company of which Messrs. Sands, Wishner and Gewanter are equal partners, subscribed to 150 shares of Class B-II Stock at par value of $.50 per share in connection with certain loan transactions which shares were subsequently transferred equally to Messrs. Sands, Wishner and Gewanter. (Reference is made to Note (10) to the financial statements.)

Messrs. Sands, Wishner and Gewanter assigned to the Company the 99-year leasehold owned by Manhattan Parking Associates, a partnership in which they were the sole and equal partners, pertaining to the Meyers Bros.-44th St. Garage (formerly Velvex Mid-City Parking Center). In return for this assignment, they received 15,729 shares of Class A Stock. The stock of Waltham Management Corp., equally owned by Messrs. Sands, Wishner and Gewanter, and acquired with no cash consideration, was exchanged for 52,038 shares of Class A and 71,250 shares of Class B-I Stock in a non-arms length transaction. Waltham Management Corp. owned a 99-year net lease of Waltham Engineering and Research Center which is now owned in fee simple and operated by The First Republic Corporation of America.

During the years 1958, 1959, 1960 and 1961, Messrs. Benjamin Ellner and Sam Wanger, Directors of the Company, received $7,912 and $8,505 respectively, as commissions on the sale of Units of Participation in various syndication partnerships which were parties to the Exchange Offer of May 16, 1961. In connection with the liquidation of certain loans (Reference is made to Footnote 10 to the Financial Statements on Page 48), Mr. Wanger received 1,760 shares of Class A Stock and Messrs. Ellner and Wanger received, respectively, 375 and 265 shares of Class B-II Stock.

Morris Cohon is the senior partner of Morris Cohon & Co. which received approximately $66,080 and 8,497 shares of Class B-II Stock of the Company for commissions as Managing Underwriters in connection with the May 16, 1961 public stock offering of the Company.

Item 12. *Pending Legal Proceedings.*

Briefly describe any material pending legal proceedings, other than ordinary routine litigation incidental to the business, to which the registrant or any of its subsidiaries is a party or of which any of their property is the subject. Include the name of the court or agency in which the proceedings are pending, the date instituted and the principal parties thereto. Include similar information as to any such proceedings known to be contemplated by governmental authorities.

Instructions. 1. If the business ordinarily results in actions for negligence or other claims, no such action or claim need be described unless it departs from the normal kind of such actions.

2. No information need be given with respect to any proceeding which involves primarily a claim for damages if the amount involved, exclusive of interest and costs, does not ex-

ceed 15 percent of the current assets of the registrant and its subsidiaries on a consolidated basis. However, if any proceeding presents in large degree the same issues as other proceedings pending or known to be contemplated, the amount involved in such other proceedings shall be included in computing such percentage.

3. Notwithstanding Instructions 1 and 2, any material bankruptcy, receivership, or similar proceeding with respect to the registrant or any of its significant subsidiaries shall be described. Any material proceedings to which any director, officer or affiliate of the registrant, any security holder named in answer to Item 19(a), or any associate of any such director, officer or security holder, is a party adverse to the registrant or any of its subsidiaries shall also be described.

LITIGATION

On June 4, 1957, a stockholders' derivative action for the benefit of Ridgeway Corporation, entitled "*Lester K. Striker v. Florida Canada Corporation, et al.*" was instituted in the Chancery Court of New Castle County, Delaware, against the Company, Associated Artists Productions Corp., Universal Controls, Inc., Donnell & Mudge, Ltd., Yellowknife Bear Mines Limited and certain individuals who, with one exception, are present or former directors of the Company and one or more of the other corporate defendants. The complaint alleges that the various corporate defendants and their directors deprived Ridgeway Corporation of certain corporate opportunities during 1956 and early 1957 to the benefit of such corporate defendants, and seeks an accounting from the defendants, individual and corporate, for profits in an unspecified amount alleged to belong to Ridgeway Corporation. Similar actions seeking substantially the same relief were commenced by the same plaintiff in the United States District Courts for the District of Delaware and the Eastern District of Michigan, Southern Division, on June 21, 1957 and July 15, 1957, respectively.

The Company has been served, has entered an appearance and has filed motions to dismiss the complaint in the two Delaware cases. Such motions have not as yet been set for argument. The Company has not been served with process in the action pending in the United States District Court for the Eastern District of Michigan and believes that it is not amenable to service. Accordingly, it has not entered an appearance or filed any answer or other pleading in this action. In the opinion of Messrs. Paul & Sams, general counsel for the Company, the Company has good and sufficient defenses to the claims made in these actions.

On December 6, 1960 Robert L. Catlin, a former employee of the Company, instituted an action in the Circuit Court of Dade County, Florida, seeking specific performance of a stock option agreement entered into between him and the Company on April 21, 1958. The Company had refused to issue the stock covered by this agreement because Catlin had refused to enter into certain investment stipulations. By decree of April 10, 1961 the Court ordered the Company to deliver to Catlin a stock certificate for 25,000 shares of stock on receipt of $140,200 in payment therefor. The decree further provided that the shares are to be held by Catlin "for investment and not with a view to distribution and [Catlin] may not sell or distribute any of such shares otherwise than in compliance with the U. S. Securities Act of 1933, as amended, and the applicable rules and regulations thereto". The Company has appealed this decree because it did not provide for the endorsement on the stock certificate of an investment legend. The Company has tendered the stock certificate without an investment legend to Catlin's agent, but the tender has been refused. Catlin contends that the tender was conditional in that his agent had been notified prior to the tender that an appeal had been filed. The appeal is pending.

The Company has been notified by the tax assessor of Charlotte County, Florida, where the major portion of the Company's Port Charlotte development is located, that in accordance with the program of reassessing all real property in Charlotte County, the assessed valuation of the Company's real property there for the year 1961 has been fixed at approximately $23,251,000. This represents an increase of $21,365,000 over the 1960 assessment which was approximately $1,886,000.

The New Jersey Real Estate Commission has entered a cease and desist order against the sale of homesites at Port Malabar. See "Regulation".

Item 13. *Capital Stock Being Registered.*

If capital stock is being registered, state the title of the class and furnish the following information:

(a) Outline briefly (1) dividend rights; (2) voting rights; (3) liquidation rights; (4) pre-emptive rights; (5) conversion rights; (6) redemption provisions; (7) sinking fund provisions; and (8) liability to further calls or to assessment by the registrant.

(b) If the rights of holders of such stock may be modified otherwise than by a vote of a majority or more of the shares outstanding, voting as a class, so state and explain briefly.

(c) Outline briefly any restriction on the repurchase or redemption of shares by the registrant while there is any arrearage in the payment of dividends or sinking fund installments. If there is no such restriction, so state.

Instructions. 1. This item requires only a brief summary of the provisions which are pertinent from an investment standpoint. A complete legal description of the provisions referred to is not required and should not be given. Do not set forth the provisions of the governing instruments verbatim; only a succinct resume is required.

2. If the rights evidenced by the securities being registered are materially limited or qualified by the rights of any other class of securities, include such information regarding such other securities as will enable investors to understand the rights evidenced by securities being registered. If any securities being registered are to be offered in exchange for other securities, an appropriate description of such other securities shall be given. No information need be given, however, as to any class of securities all of which will be redeemed and retired, provided appropriate steps to assure such redemption and retirement will be taken prior to or upon delivery by the registrant of the securities being registered.

DESCRIPTION OF THE COMMON STOCK

The following statements are brief summaries of certain provisions contained in the Certificate of Incorporation of the Company, the Company's Note Agreements with The Prudential Insurance Company of America and The Ford Foundation and the Indenture under which the Company's 6% Convertible Subordinated Debentures were issued, copies of which have been filed as exhibits to the Registration Statement. These summaries do not purport to be complete and are subject in all respects to the detailed provisions of such documents.

Dividends

Subject to the dividend limitations imposed by the Note Agreements and the Indenture, cash dividends may be declared and paid on the Common Stock from time to time as may be determined by the Board of Directors out of funds legally available therefor. Of the retained earnings at May 31, 1961, there would have been available under the most restrictive of such limitations $855,000, for the payment of cash dividends on the Common Stock. In addition, the payment of cash dividends would be subject to certain provisions of the Note Agreements requiring the maintenance of certain cash reserves or balances. See "Note Agreements and Warrants" and "Convertible Subordinated Debentures".

General

The Common Stock has a par value of $1. Each holder of Common Stock has one vote per share. Upon liquidation, holders of the Common Stock are entitled to receive pro rata the assets of the Company remaining after the satisfaction of its liabilities. Such holders have no conversion or preemptive rights. The outstanding shares of Common Stock are fully paid and non-assessable. The Common Stock is listed on the American and Toronto Stock Exchanges.

Non-Cumulative Voting

The Common Stock does not have cumulative voting rights, which means that the holders of more than 50% of the shares voting for the election of directors can elect 100% of the directors if they choose to do so and in such event the holders of the remaining less than 50% of the shares voting for the election of directors will not be able to elect any person or persons to the Board of Directors.

Item 14. *Long-Term Debt Being Registered.*

If long-term debt is being registered, outline briefly such of the following as are relevant:

(a) Provisions with respect to interest, conversion, maturity, redemption, amortization, sinking fund or retirement.

(b) Provisions with respect to the kind and priority of any lien securing the issue, together with a brief identification of the principal properties subject to such lien.

(c) Provisions restricting the declaration of dividends or requiring the maintenance of any ratio of assets, the creation or maintenance of reserves or the maintenance of properties.

(d) Provisions permitting or restricting the issuance of additional securities, the withdrawal of cash deposited against such issuance, the incurring of additional debt, the release or substitution of assets securing the issue, the modification of the terms of the security, and similar provisions.

Instructions. 1. In the case of secured debt, there should be stated (i) the approximate amount of unbonded bondable property available for use against the issuance of bonds, as of the most recent practicable date, and (ii) whether the securities being registered are to be issued against such property, against the deposit of cash, or otherwise.

2. Provisions permitting the release of assets upon the deposit of equivalent funds or the pledge of equivalent property, the release of property no longer required in the business, obsolete property or property taken by eminent domain, the application of insurance moneys, and similar provisions, need not be described.

DESCRIPTION OF SECURITIES

DEBENTURES

General

The Debentures are to be issued under an Indenture, dated as of   , between the Company and Chemical Bank New York Trust Company, 30 Broad Street, New York 15, New York, as Trustee. The latter is also the Paying Agent and Conversion Agent for the Debentures. The Debentures will bear interest from   , 1962, payable on   1 and   1 in each year, and will be due   ; 1972, unless sooner redeemed or converted. The Debentures will not be secured.

The Debentures are limited in amount to $2,000,000, will be coupon Debentures registerable only as to principal, and will be issued in denominations of $100, $500 and $1,000.

There are no sinking fund provisions for the retirement of the Debentures.

The statements under this caption relating to the Debentures and the Indenture are summaries and do not purport to be complete, but the Company believes that they are fair summaries of the provisions summarized. Such summaries make use of terms defined in the Indenture and are qualified in their entirety by express reference to the Indenture, a copy of which is filed as an exhibit to the Registration Statement, and the cited provisions thereof.

Redemption Provisions

The Debentures are to be redeemable at any time at the option of the Company, as a whole or from time to time in part on not less than thirty days notice, unless at the time of first publication of such notice the Company shall be in default with respect to any Senior Indebtedness, as defined in the Indenture, at the following prices (expressed in percentages of the principal amount), together with interest accrued to the redemption date. If redeemed during the 12 month period beginning   1 of the years indicated below:

Year	Percentage of Principal Amount	Year	Percentage of Principal Amount
1962	105 %	1967	102½%
1963	104½	1968	102
1964	104	1969	101½
1965	103½	1970	101
1966	103	1971	100½

Conversion Provisions

The holder of any Debenture will have the right, at his option, at any time prior to maturity, to convert the principal of such Debenture into Common Stock at the initial conversion price of $ per share, except that such privilege shall terminate at the close of business on the second business day prior to any redemption date as to Debentures called for redemption on such date. The conversion privilege is protected against dilution, as provided in the Indenture, in case of the happening of any of the events therein specified, including the issuance of additional shares of Common Stock at a price less than the conversion price then in effect, the payment of stock dividends and similar events. No adjustments in respect of interest or dividends, other than stock dividends, will be made upon the conversion of the Debentures. No fractional shares will be issued but an adjustment in cash will be made based on the market price of the Common Stock on the date of conversion. (Article Five)

Subordination of Debentures

The payment of the principal of (and premium, if any) and interest on the Debentures is subordinated in right of payment, as set forth in the Indenture, to the prior payment in full of all Senior Indebtedness of the Company, whether outstanding on the date of the Indenture or thereafter incurred. Senior Indebtedness is defined to include (a) indebtedness (including purchase money indebtedness) of the Company, whether outstanding on the date of the Indenture or thereafter created, incurred, assumed or guaranteed, which is for money borrowed by the Company or for money borrowed by others for the payment of which the Company is responsible or liable, (b) indebtedness of the Company (including contingent obligations to make payments under contracts) hereafter incurred in exchange for rights to explore for, or bring to account interests in, petroleum or natural gas, and (c) renewals, extensions and refundings of any such indebtedness. No principal or interest payments may be made on the Debentures while there exists any default upon Senior Indebtedness, and upon any dissolution, wind up, total liquidation or reorganization of the Company, all Senior Indebtedness must be paid in full before the Debentures are entitled to any payment whatever. Upon completion of the sale of the Debentures being offered hereby, the aggregate amount of the indebtedness of the Company which will be superior to the Debentures will be approximately $

Item 15. *Other Securities Being Registered.*

If securities other than capital stock or long-term debt are being registered, outline briefly the rights evidenced thereby. If subscription warrants or rights are being registered, state the title and amount of securities called for, the period during which and the price at which the warrants or rights are exercisable.

Instruction. The instructions to Item 13 shall also apply to this item.

Item 16. *Directors and Executive Officers.*

List the names of all directors and executive officers of the registrant and all persons chosen to become directors or executive officers. Indicate all positions and offices with the registrant held by each person named, and the principal occupations during the past five years of each executive officer and each person chosen to become an executive officer.

Instructions. 1. If any person chosen to become a director or executive officer has not consented to act as such, so state.

2. For the purpose of this item, the term "executive officer" means the president, vice president, secretary and treasurer, and any other officer who performs similar policy-making functions for the registrant.

MANAGEMENT

The directors and executive officers of the Company are:

Name	Office Held
James H. R. Cromwell	Chairman of the Board and Director*
Irving W. Blum	President and Director†*
Chester Carity	Vice President, Treasurer and Director*
Henry L. Hoffman	Vice President and Director
Howard W. Friedman	Secretary, Comptroller and Director*
Robert Berger	Assistant Vice President and Director
Charles A. Willoughby	Assistant Vice President and Director
Herman B. Oberman	Director
Leonard Oberman	Director
Mitchell S. Roberts	Director

*Member of Executive Committee
†Chief Executive Officer

Mr. Cromwell, formerly the United States envoy to Canada, was for several years prior to 1957 a partner of Cromwell & Co., Industrial Consultants of Washington, D. C., and since October 1957, he has been President of Limited.

Irving W. Blum, the chief executive officer of the Company, is a Certified Public Accountant, but he has been primarily engaged in real estate development work for the past 20 years. Herman B. Oberman served as President and chief executive officer of the Company from the time of the merger-acquisition until January, 1962, when he resigned as President and ceased to act as chief executive officer because of illness. However, he continues to participate actively in the affairs of the Company. Mr. Oberman, since 1950, has been engaged in various real estate activities, primarily in Florida. For several years prior to 1959, Messrs. Oberman and Blum were engaged as principals in the development of real estate subdivisions similar to Rainbow Lakes Estates. Since 1959, they have devoted substantially all of their time to Rainbow Lakes Estates and, since the merger-acquisition, to the affairs of the Company.

Since 1954, Chester Carity and Henry L. Hoffman have been associated as principals in numerous organizations engaged in the advertising, development and sale of various products on a nationwide basis. Their activities have been concentrated on mail order merchandising of various products, buying and selling for their own account, as principals, and also as sales consultants to others. In addition, prior to 1959 they acted as sales consultants to various real estate developments, and since 1959 they devoted a major portion of their time to Rainbow Lakes Estates. Since the merger-acquisition, they have been vice-presidents of the Company.

Howard W. Friedman was a practicing certified public accountant for a number of years prior to 1957. In 1957 he became a partner in Schoenfeld, Friedman Company, certified public accountants, although he has not been active in its affairs. Since 1957 Mr. Friedman has been associated with Messrs. Carity and Hoffman in their various activities as controller and chief financial officer, under arrangements whereby he participates in the profits.

Robert B. Berger, a licensed professional engineer and certified public accountant, is President of Val-U Homes Corporation of Delaware, B-B Electrical Contractors, Inc. and Cross Construction Corporation, all of Paterson, New Jersey.

Charles A. Willoughby, Major General, United States Army, Ret., served with the Army from 1916-1951 and was the Chief of Intelligence for General MacArthur's Commands from 1941 until his retirement in 1951. He is a contributing editor to a number of national periodicals.

Item 17. *Remuneration of Directors and Officers.*

(a) Furnish the following information in substantially the tabular form indicated below as to all direct remuneration paid by the registrant and its subsidiaries during the registrant's last fiscal year to the following persons for services in all capacities:

(1) Each director, and each of the three highest paid officers, of the registrant whose aggregate direct remuneration exceeded $30,000, naming each such person.

(2) All directors and officers of the registrant as a group, without naming them.

Instructions. 1. This item applies to any person who was a director or officer of the registrant at any time during the period specified. However, information need not be given for any portion of the period during which such person was not a director or officer of the registrant.

2. The information is to be given on an accrual basis if practicable. The tables required by this paragraph and paragraph (b) may be combined if the registrant so desires.

3. Do not include remuneration paid to a partnership in which any director or officer was a partner, but see Item 20.

(A) Name of individual or identity of group	(B) Capacities in which remuneration was received	(C) Aggregate direct remuneration

Name of Individual or Identity of Group(1)	Capacities in Which Remuneration Was Received	Aggregate Direct Remuneration
Louis Chesler	Chairman of the Executive Committee, and Vice President	$ 75,000
All directors and officers as a group		$146,735

(1) Mr. Chesler is also entitled to reimbursement for reasonable expenses incurred in connection with his services to the Company not exceeding $30,000 per year.

(2) Mr. H. A. Yoars became Vice President of the Company as of January 1, 1961 at an aggregate direct remuneration of $75,000 per year. Mr. Yoars is being paid the same remuneration as President of the Company.

(3) Mr. Neil E. Bahr's aggregate direct remuneration as Vice-President was fixed at $45,000 per year on June 1, 1961. On the same date the aggregate direct remuneration of each of Adm. A. J. Fay as Executive Vice-President, Messrs. Thomas A. Ferris and James E. Vensel as Vice-Presidents, and Mr. William H. O'Dowd as Secretary-Treasurer was fixed at $35,000 per year.

Stock Options

At June 1, 1961, employees of the Company held restricted stock options, as defined in Section 421 of the Internal Revenue Code of 1954, to purchase an aggregate of 457,000 shares of the Company's Common Stock, as follows:

Name of Individual or Identity of Group	Number of Shares Covered by Options	Option Price Per Share	Expiration Date of Options
Frank E. Mackle, Jr.	87,500 *	$ 5.61 *	April 21, 1968
Robert F. Mackle	87,500 *	5.61 *	April 21, 1968
Elliott J. Mackle	87,500 *	5.61 *	April 21, 1968
H. A. Yoars	30,000	15.62	June 1, 1971
A. J. Fay	10,000	14.67	April 18, 1970
Neil E. Bahr	10,000	19.12	December 2, 1969
Thomas A. Ferris	25,000 *	5.61 *	April 21, 1968
James E. Vensel	25,000 *	5.61 *	April 21, 1968
William H. O'Dowd	25,000 *	5.61 *	April 21, 1968
All officers and directors as a group	337,500 *	5.61 *	April 21, 1968
	30,000	15.62	June 1, 1971
	10,000	14.67	April 18, 1970
	10,000	19.12	December 2, 1969
All other employees	12,500 *	5.61 *	April 21, 1968
	22,000	17.77	June 10, 1969
	10,000	22.21	December 30, 1969

* As adjusted in accordance with the terms of the options to reflect 1-for-4 and 1-for-1 Common Stock distributions on the Company's outstanding Common Stock which took effect on May 18, 1959.

(1) Mr. Orovitz, who ceased being an employee of the Company on June 1, 1961, held on that date an option, not included in the above figures, to purchase 25,000 shares of the Company's Common Stock at a price of $5.61 per share. He has since exercised his option.

The option price of each of the options when granted was 95% of the fair market value of the Common Stock on the date of grant. The options which expire on April 21, 1968 are presently exercisable as to all shares covered thereby. Those which expire on June 10, 1969, December 2, 1969, December 30, 1969 and April 18, 1970 will not become exercisable until June 10, 1964, December 2, 1964, December 30, 1964 and April 18, 1965 respectively, when they will become exercisable in full, and unless the optionees remain in the employ of the Company or one of its subsidiaries until such dates, the options will not be exercisable to any extent. The option which expires on June 1, 1971 will become exercisable as to 20% of the stock covered thereby on June 1, 1963 and as to an additional 20% on each succeeding June 1, and will be exercisable in full after June 1, 1967. All options other than that granted to Mr. H. A. Yoars have been approved by the stockholders.

Each of the outstanding options terminates three months after the optionee ceases to be an employee of the Company or a subsidiary except that in the event of the optionee's death, his heirs, executors or administrators may exercise the option at any time within the original option period, in the case of the options held by the Messrs. Mackle, or within six months after death, in the case of the remaining options. Each holder of an outstanding option has agreed to hold any shares acquired through the exercise of an option for investment and not with a view to distribution. No officer or director of the Company is currently eligible to receive an option under the Employee's Stock Option Plan referred to in the next succeeding paragraph, with the exception of Messrs. Fred W. Hooper, A. J. Fay and Neil E. Bahr. Messrs. Frank E. Mackle, Jr., Robert F. Mackle, Elliott J. Mackle, H. A. Yoars, Thomas A. Ferris, James E. Vensel and William H. O'Dowd would be eligible if they were to request the Company to cancel their outstanding options and the Committee should approve such requests. It is not anticipated that any of these persons will so request the cancellation of their outstanding options.

At the annual meeting held on May 16, 1961 the stockholders of the Company approved a Stock Option Plan under which restricted stock options, as defined in Section 421 of the Internal Revenue Code, may be granted to officers and key employees of the Company and its subsidiaries to purchase a total of not more than 150,000 shares of Common Stock. No individual may receive options under the Plan for more than 15,000 shares, subject, however, to proportionate adjustment in accordance with the anti-dilution provisions of the Plan. The purchase price of stock under each option will be fixed at $15.50 or 100% of the average fair market value of the shares on the date the option is granted, whichever is greater.

The Plan provides that the term of each option will be ten years from the date the option is granted, provided, however, that no option may be exercised more than three months after termination of employment. An option may be exercised as to 20% of the aggregate number of shares covered by such option after two years from the date of the grant of the option, as to an additional 20% of the aggregate number of shares covered by such option after each of the third, fourth and fifth years from the date of the grant of the option, and as to the entire number of shares covered by such option at any time, and from time to time, after the sixth year from the date of the grant, provided that no option may be exercised unless the optionee is then in the employ of the Company (or was in the employ of the Company within three months of the date of exercise) and shall have been continuously employed by the Company for two years from the date the option was granted. Upon the death of an optionee, the option may be exercised within a period of six months thereafter by his legal representative.

The Plan provides that no person who shall have exercised or who shall exercise an option not granted under the Plan is eligible to participate therein. It further provides that none of the persons currently holding options is eligible to participate therein, unless he shall file with the Company a request for the cancellation of all outstanding options theretofore granted to him and unless such request shall be approved by the Committee. The Committee may issue a new option to a person requesting cancellation of an option granted at a price higher than the price under the Plan only if the average fair market value of the Common Stock for the twelve months prior to the month in which the option is granted is less than 80% of the price of the Common Stock on the date on which that particular option was granted.

At its initial meeting on October 31, 1961 the Committee approved the requests of 9 persons, including Messrs. A. J. Fay and Neil E. Bahr, for the cancellation of options then held by them covering 44,500 shares and granted options to each of these persons and to 18 additional persons covering a total of 77,750 shares. Each of the options so granted is exercisable at the price of $15.50 per share. The new options granted to Messrs. A. J. Fay and Neil Bahr each covered 10,000 shares.

There were outstanding on November 1, 1961 options covering 464,750 shares of the Company's common stock. If all these options were to be immediately exercised, the number of shares issued under such exercise would be 6.61% of the then outstanding and issued common stock of the Company.

For a recent market price of the Common Stock see "Price Range of Common Stock and Dividends".

(b) Furnish the following information, in substantially the tabular form indicated below, as to all pension or retirement benefits proposed to be paid under any existing plan in the event of retirement at normal retirement date, directly or indirectly, by the registrant or any of its subsidiaries to each director or officer named in answer to paragraph (a) (1) above:

(A) Name of individual	(B) Amounts set aside or accrued during registrant's last fiscal year	(C) Estimated annual benefits upon retirement

Instructions. 1. The term "plan" in this item includes all plans, contracts, authorizations or arrangements, whether or not set forth in any formal document.

2. Column (B) need not be answered with respect to amounts computed on an actuarial basis under any plan which provides for fixed benefits in the event of retirement at a specified age or after a specified number of years of service.

3. The information called for by Column (C) may be given in a table showing the annual benefits payable upon retirement to persons in specified salary classifications.

4. In the case of any plan (other than those specified in Instruction 2) where the amount set aside each year depends upon the amount of earnings of the registrant or its subsidiaries for such year or a prior year, or where it is otherwise impracticable to state the estimated annual benefits upon retirement, there shall be set forth, in lieu of the information called for by Column (C), the aggregate amount set aside or accrued to date, unless it is impracticable to do so, in which case there shall be stated the method of computing such benefits.

(c) Describe briefly all remuneration payments (other than payments reported under paragraph (a) or (b) of this item) proposed to be made in the future, directly or indirectly, by the registrant or any of its subsidiaries pursuant to any existing plan or arrangement to (i) each director or officer named in answer to paragraph (a)(1), naming each such person, and (ii) all directors and officers of the registrant as a group, without naming them.

Instruction. Information need not be included as to payments to be made for, or benefits to be received from, group life or accident insurance, group hospitalization or similar group payments or benefits. If it is impracticable to state the amount of remuneration payments proposed to be made, the aggregate amount set aside or accrued to date in respect of such payments should be stated, together with an explanation of the basis for future payments.

Pensions and Other Remuneration

The Company has had in effect since January 1, 1953 a contributory Retirement Plan under a Pension Trust (Exhibits 11.09 to 11.12, inclusive), succeeding and supplemental to an insured retirement annuity plan (Exhibits 11.01 to 11.08, inclusive) which was in effect from June 1, 1940 to the effective date of the new Plan at which time contributions thereunder were discontinued. All eligible employees of the Company are enrolled in the Retirement Plan. During 1961, the cost to the Company for future service benefits amounted to approximately $600,000; and the cost for prior service benefits amounted to approximately $200,000, at which annual rate, costs for prior service benefits will be completed in 1964. The Company has reserved the right to discontinue payments to the Plan at any time. Supplemental payments to retired employees in 1961 aggregated approximately $40,000.

The Company has an insured group life insurance plan and an insured hospitalization and surgical plan. The gross premiums paid by the Company under these plans during 1961 amounted to approximately $250,000. Dividends paid to the Company by the insurers under these two plans during the past five years have averaged approximately $115,000 per annum.

Remuneration of Directors and Officers

The direct remuneration paid by the Company during 1961 to the following persons for services in all capacities and the estimated annual pension benefits of such persons are as follows:

Name of individual or identity of group	Capacities in which remuneration was received	Aggregate direct remuneration	Estimated annual benefits upon retirement*
D. S. Kennedy	As Chairman of the Board and President	$ 69,900	$ 28,389
All other directors and officers of the Company	As directors, officers or executives	227,042	80,801
Total		$296,942	$109,190

*The amounts listed in this column are estimates based on the assumption that the individual will remain in the employ of the Company until normal retirement (age 65), that the Company's Retirement Plan (part of the cost of which is borne by the Company and part by the employee) will continue in force in its present form, and that his salary will continue at the present level. The directors, as such, are not covered under the Plan.

Item 18. *Options to Purchase Securities.*

Furnish the following information as to options to purchase securities from the registrant or any of its subsidiaries, which are outstanding as of a specified date within 30 days prior to the date of filing.

(a) Describe the options, stating the material provisions including the consideration received and to be received for such options by the grantor thereof and the market value of the securities called for on the granting date. If, however, the options are "restricted stock options" as defined in Section 421 of the Internal Revenue Code of 1954 only the following is required: (i) a statement to that effect, (ii) a brief description of the terms and conditions of the options or of the plan pursuant to which they were issued, and (iii) a statement of the provisions of the plan or options with respect to the relationship between the option price and the market price of the securities at the date when the options were granted, or with respect to the terms of any variable price option.

(b) State (i) the title and amount of the securities called for by such options; (ii) the purchase prices of the securities called for and the expiration dates of such options; and (iii) the market value of the securities called for by such options as of the latest practicable date.

Instruction. In case a number of options are outstanding having different prices and expiration dates, the options may be grouped by prices and dates. If this produces more than five separate groups then there may be shown only the range of the expiration dates and the average purchase prices, i.e., the aggregate purchase price of all securities of the same class called for by all outstanding options to purchase securities or that class divided by the number of securities of such class so called for.

(c) Furnish separately the information called for by paragraph (b) above for all options held by (i) each director or officer named in answer to paragraph (a)(1) of Item 17 naming each such person, and (ii) all directors and officers as a group without naming them.

See material furnished at item 17 on stock options.

Item 19. *Principal Holders of Securities.*

Furnish the following information as of a specified date within 90 days prior to the date of filing in substantially the tabular form indicated:

(a) As to the voting securities of the registrant owned of record or beneficially by each person who owns of record, or is known by the registrant to own beneficially, more than 10 percent of any class of such securities. Show in Column (3) whether the securities are owned both of record and beneficially, of record only, or beneficially only, and show in Columns (4) and (5) the respective amounts and percentages owned in each such manner:

(1) Name and address	(2) Title of class	(3) Type of Ownership	(4) Amount owned	Percent of class (5)

(b) As to each class of equity securities of the registrant or any of its parents or subsidiaries, other than directors' qualifying shares, beneficially owned directly or indirectly by all directors and officers of the registrant, as a group, without naming them.

(1) Title of class	(2) Amount beneficially owned	(3) Percent of class

Instructions. 1. The percentages are to be calculated on the basis of the amount of outstanding securities, excluding securities held by or for the account of the issuer. In any case where the amount owned by directors and officers as a group is less than 1 percent of the class, the percent of the class owned by them may be omitted.

2. If the equity securities are being registered in connection with, or pursuant to, a plan of acquisition, reorganization, readjustment or succession, indicate, as far as practicable, the status to exist upon consummation of the plan on the basis of present holdings and commitments.

3. If any of the securities being registered are to be offered for the account of security holders, name each such security holder and state the amount of the securities owned by him, the amount to be offered for his account, and the amount to be owned after the offering.

4. If, to the knowledge of the registrant or any principal underwriter of the securities being registered, more than 10 percent of any class of voting securities of the registrant are held or are to be held subject to any voting trust or other similar agreement, state the title of such securities, the amount held or to be held and the duration of the agreement. Give the names and addresses of the voting trustees and outline briefly their voting rights and other powers under the agreement.

SHAREHOLDERS

Common Shares of the Company (a) held by the only person who as of September 1, 1961, owned of record, or, to the knowledge of the Company, owned beneficially, more than 10% of the outstanding Common Shares, and the name and address of such person and (b) owned beneficially by the directors and officers of the Company as a group, are set forth below:

Name and Address	Type of Owner- ship	Number of Common Shares Owned	Percentage of Common Shares Outstanding
E. A. Egan, A. H. Egan, E. F. Egan and W. Q. Egan c/o E. A. Egan 1710 Orrington Avenue Evanston, Illinois Trustees under three separate trusts	Record	115,488	15.5%
Officers and Directors as a Group	Beneficial*	123,894*	16.6%

*This amount (1) includes shares held by Crystal Wood Farm, Inc., a corporation controlled by Thomas G. Sexton, a Director of the Company, (2) excludes the remainder interest of A. H. Egan, Treasurer and a Director of the Company, in the three trusts named above and (3) excludes the interest of T. M. Sexton, President and a Director of the Company, in the estate of his father, Franklin Sexton (deceased).

The beneficiaries under the three trusts referred to above are, to the best of the Company's knowledge, Mrs. Helen Sexton Egan and, as remaindermen, her husband, their children (including her son, A. H. Egan, Treasurer and a Director of the Company) and the descendants of their children.

Item 20. *Interest of Management and Others in Certain Transactions.*

Describe briefly, and where practicable state the approximate amount of any material interest, direct or indirect, of any of the following persons in any material transactions during the last three years, or in any material proposed transactions, to which the registrant or any of its subsidiaries was, or is to be, a party:

(a) Any director or officer of the registrant;

(b) Any security holder named in answer to Item 19(a);

(c) Any associate of any of the foregoing persons.

Instructions. 1. See Instruction 1 to Item 17(a). Include the name of each person whose interest in any transaction is described and the nature of the relationship by reason of which such interest is required to be described. Where it is not practicable to state the approximate amount of the interest, the approximate amount involved in the transaction shall be indicated.

2. As to any transaction involving the purchase or sale of assets by or to the registrant or any subsidiary, otherwise than in the ordinary course of business, state the cost of the assets to the purchaser and the cost thereof to the seller if acquired by the seller within two years prior to the transaction.

3. This item does not apply to any interest arising from the ownership of securities of the registrant where the security holder receives no extra or special benefit not shared on a pro rata basis by all other holders of the same class.

4. No information need be given in answer to this item as to any remuneration not received during the registrant's last fiscal year or as to any remuneration or other transaction disclosed in response to Items 17 or 18.

5. Information should be included as to any material underwriting discounts and commissions upon the sale of securities by the registrant where any of the specified persons was or is to be a principal underwriter or is a controlling person, or member, of a firm which was or is to be a principal underwriter. Information need not be given concerning ordinary management fees paid by underwriters to a managing underwriter pursuant to an agreement among underwriters the parties to which do not include he registrant or its subsidiaries.

6. No information need be given in answer to this item as to any transaction or any interest therein where:

(i) the rates or charges involved in the transaction are fixed by law or determined by competitive bids;

(ii) the interest of the specified persons in the transaction is solely that of a director of another corporation which is a party to the transaction;

(iii) the transaction involves services as a bank depository of funds, transfer agent, registrar, trustee under a trust indenture, or other similar services;

(iv) the interest of the specified persons, including all periodic installments in the case of any lease or other agreement providing for periodic payments or installments, does not exceed $30,000;

(v) the transaction does not involve remuneration for services, directly or indirectly, and (A) the interest of the specified persons arises from the ownership individually and in the aggregate of less than 10% of any class of equity securities of another corporation which is a party to the transaction, (B) the transaction is in the ordinary course of business of the registrant or its subsidiaries, and (C) the amount of such transaction or series of transactions is less than 10% of the total sales or purchases, as the case may be, of the registrant and its subsidiaries.

7. Information shall be furnished in answer to this item with respect to transactions not excluded above which involve remuneration, directly or indirectly, to any of the specified persons for services in any capacity unless the interest of such persons arises solely from the ownership individually and in the aggregate of less than 10% of any class of equity securities of another corporation furnishing the services to the registrant or its subsidiaries.

8. This item does not require the disclosure of any interest in any transaction unless such interest and transaction are material.

TRANSACTIONS BETWEEN THE COMPANY AND CERTAIN PERSONS

In 1954 a corporation was formed by the Selling Shareholders under the name "Swingline Industrial Corp." ("Industrial"). The corporation engaged in the development and sale of a newly-designed line of compressed-air-driven, heavy-duty, nail, corrugated fastener and staple guns for industrial purposes, together with the nails, fasteners and staples required for such equipment. Mr. and Mrs. Jack Linsky were directors of Industrial and have at all times owned all its Class A voting stock. All the Class B non-voting stock (the only other stock outstanding) was and is owned by daughters and other relatives of Mr. and Mrs. Linsky. Mr. Alan Seff, then an officer of the Company, was also an officer of Industrial. The compressed-air guns, and the requisite nails, fasteners and staples, marketed by Industrial, were purchased or manufactured for it and sold to it by the Company. The net amounts of such sales were $100,964 during the fiscal year ending March 31, 1958; $195,154 during the fiscal year ending March 31, 1959; $846,198 during the fiscal year ending March 31, 1960; and $304,960 during the 5 month period ending August 31, 1960.

Since the compressed-air guns handled by Industrial were newly developed devices, in which neither the Company nor Industrial had previously dealt, and were in direct and intense price competition with other well-established products of other manufacturers, the Company realized virtually no profit on such sales.

In August, 1960, Industrial changed its corporate name from "Swingline Industrial Corp." to "Speedfast Corporation" ("Speedfast"). At about the same time, Speedfast established its own offices and manufacturing facilities in its own leased premises, where it commenced the manufacture of its own industrial compressed-air nail, fastener and staple guns, and the supplies therefor. These are being marketed under its own trademarks and trade names. It is not presently anticipated that the Company will have further transactions in significant amount with Speedfast (they amounted to $45,875 in the fiscal year ended August 31, 1961), but if such transactions occur they will be at competitive prices. The Company does not intend to continue the manufacture or sale of industrial compressed-air guns. In August, 1960 the Company sold to Speedfast certain machinery and equipment used in the manufacture of compressed-air guns and certain executive office furnishings for a total price of $126,675, and also sold to Speedfast the Company's inventory of compressed-air guns and of staples, parts, raw materials and supplies therefor, for $160,473. The resulting indebtedness to the Company of $287,148 has since been reduced, by payments, to $137,148, and Speedfast has undertaken to pay the balance by May 31, 1962. There was a capital gain of approximately $43,000 to the Company on these transactions. Mr. and Mrs. Linsky have resigned as directors and Mr. Seff has resigned as an officer of Speedfast. None of the present officers and directors of Swingline is an officer or director of Speedfast, although Mr. and Mrs. Linsky continue to own all of its voting stock.

The compressed-air guns, nails, corrugated fasteners and staples manufactured or sold by Speedfast, all of which are designed solely for heavy-duty industrial use, are not competitive with the products manufactured or sold by the Company.

The Company holds a first mortgage on the premises at 32-00 Skillman Avenue, Long Island City, New York, in which the Company's main office, factory and warehouse are located. The premises are owned by Lenmur, Inc., the stockholders of which are daughters of Mr. and Mrs. Linsky.

Item 21. *Financial Statements.*

Include in the prospectus all financial statements called for by the Instructions as to Financial Statements for this form, except as provided in paragraphs (a) and (b) below:

(a) All schedules to balance sheets and profit and loss statements may be omitted from the prospectus except (1) those prepared in accordance with Rules 12-16 and 12-32 of Regulation S-X which are applicable to balance sheets and profit and loss statements included in the prospectus, and (2) those prepared in accordance with Rule 12-27 in Regulation S-X which are applicable to a company's latest balance sheet included in the prospectus. All historical information required by Part E of the Instructions as to Financial Statements may also be omitted from the prospectus.

(b) If either the profit and loss or earned surplus statements required are included in their entirety in the summary of earnings required by Item 6, the statements so included need not be otherwise included in the prospectus or elsewhere in the registration statement.

Important: There follow herewith several abstracts from accountants' certifications and footnotes which were selected as illustrating common registration problems and how others have treated them.

Financial Statement Problems

OPINION OF INDEPENDENT CERTIFIED PUBLIC ACCOUNTANTS

Board of Directors
Goodway Printing Company, Inc.

We have examined the balance sheets of the corporations comprising Goodway Printing Company, Inc. and wholly owned subsidiaries as of February 28, 1961 and the separate statements of income for the three years ended February 28, 1961 of those business entities which comprise Goodway Printing Company, Inc. and wholly owned subsidiaries. These business entities and the periods of their existence are enumerated in Note 1 of Notes to the Financial Statements included in this Prospectus. The pro forma consolidated statements of income have been prepared for purposes of this Prospectus by consolidating such separate statements of income on the basis described in Note A thereto. Our examination, which included a review of the pro forma consolidated statements of income for the three years ended February 28, 1961, was made in accordance with generally accepted auditing standards and accordingly included such tests of the accounting records and such other auditing procedures as we considered necessary in the circumstances. Since we were not engaged to perform the examination until after February 28, 1961, it was not practicable to observe physical inventories at the fiscal year end dates. However, we satisfied ourselves as to reasonableness of the inventory amounts by other auditing procedures including (1) observation of physical inventories and extensive test counts subsequent to February 28, 1961, (2) reconciliation with quantities at February 28, 1961 by use of purchase, production, sales and shipping records, (3) review of gross profit ratios, (4) extended auditing procedures utilizing such records and ratios with respect to compilation and pricing of inventories recorded by the Company at that date and prior year ends.

In our opinion, the accompanying pro forma consolidated balance sheet presents fairly the pro forma consolidated financial position of Goodway Printing Company, Inc. and wholly owned subsidiaries at February 28, 1961 and the pro forma consolidated statements of income appearing elsewhere in this Prospectus present fairly the pro forma consolidated results of their operations, on the basis indicated in Note A, for the three years ended February 28, 1961 in conformity with generally accepted accounting principles applied on a consistent basis.

ACCOUNTANTS' REPORT

Board of Directors
Girltown, Inc.
Boston, Massachusetts

We have examined the accompanying combined balance sheet of Girltown, Inc. and affiliated companies (see Note 1) as of June 30, 1961 and the related statements of earnings and retained earnings for the three years then ended. Our examination was made in accordance with generally accepted auditing standards, and accordingly included such tests of the accounting records and such other auditing procedures as we considered necessary in the circumstances, except with respect to inventories of prior years as discussed below.

Because we were not engaged as auditors until 1961 we were not present to observe the physical inventories of Girltown, Inc. and affiliated companies at the beginning and end of each year in the two year period ended June 30, 1960; moreover, detail listings are not available with respect to the physical inventories taken as to all of the companies at June 30, 1958 and 1959 and certain of the affiliated companies at June 30, 1960. The inventories at the beginning and end of each of the two years were tested by us by means of sales and other operating data, and although there may be variations which would affect the reporting of earnings as between the aforementioned periods, such inventories appear to be reasonable.

In our opinion, the financial statements referred to above present fairly the combined financial position of Girltown, Inc. and affiliated companies at June 30, 1961, and, with the foregoing explanation about inventories, the combined results of their operations for the three years then ended, in conformity with generally accepted accounting principles applied on a consistent basis.

We were engaged during March, 1961 to examine the financial statements of the Company for the three years ended March 31, 1961. While we were present at the taking of the physical inventory at March 31, 1961, we were not in attendance to observe physical inventories taken at the beginning and end of the fiscal years 1959 and 1960. The inventories at dates prior to March 31, 1961 were tested by us by means of other auditing procedures. We test-checked the pricing and clerical accuracy of those earlier inventories and also made such analytical and statistical tests of related data as we deemed appropriate. Such inventories do not appear to be unreasonable.

We observed the taking of physical inventories at June 30, 1961 but we did not carry out this auditing procedure at prior dates because we were not engaged as auditors of the companies until after the close of the 1960 fiscal years. To review the reasonableness of inventory amounts at the ends of prior fiscal periods, we have carried out other auditing procedures, including tests of sales and purchases records and certain analytical and statistical tests. Nothing came to our attention as a result of these tests which in our judgment would indicate that the recorded inventory amounts are not reasonably stated.

We have examined the accompanying consolidated balance sheet of John Sexton & Co. and subsidiary company at June 30, 1961, the related consolidated statement of income and earned surplus for the three years then ended and the related consolidated summary of earnings for the five years then ended. Our examination was made in accordance with generally accepted auditing standards, and accordingly included such tests of the accounting records and such other auditing procedures as we considered necessary in the circumstances.

In our opinion, the statements mentioned above present fairly the consolidated financial position of John Sexton & Co. and subsidiary company at June 30, 1961 and the consolidated results of their operations for the three years then ended, and the consolidated summary of earnings presents fairly the summarized results of operations for the five years then ended, in conformity with generally accepted accounting principles applied on a consistent basis during the period.

EXCERPTS FROM AN "A" OFFERING

OFFERED AS A SPECULATION

(See Caption "Introductory Statement" for greater details)

	Offering Price to Public	Underwriting Discounts or Commissions	Proceeds to Issuer
Per Share	$5.00(1)	$.625(2)(3)	$4.375
Total	$300,000	$37,500	$262,500(2)(4)

(1) As this is the initial public offering of securities by the Company, there is no market for its Capital Stock. The price of the shares of Class A Stock being offered has been arbitrarily determined, and bears no relation to the present net assets or earnings of the Company.

(2) The Underwriter has agreed that for a period of thirty (30) days after the date of this Offering Circular, which period may be mutually extended for a like period, it will use its "best efforts" to sell the shares offered hereby. There is no assurance that all of the shares offered hereby will be sold. In the event that less than 60,000 shares are sold, no provision has been made for return of any funds to the subscribers thereof.

(3) The Underwriter will receive from the Company in addition to the commissions set forth, 12½¢ per share for each share sold, or a total of $7,500 if all the shares are sold, for its advertising, traveling, and other expenses in connection with the offering. If the Underwriter incurs expenses of less than $7,500, the difference between such actual expenses and the expense allowance received may be deemed additional underwriting compensation.

The Underwriting Agreement contains provisions for mutual indemnification between the Company and the Underwriter for certain civil liabilities under the Securities Act of 1933. The Underwriter, upon the sale of all of the shares offered hereunder will be entitled to nominate one (1) member to the Company's Board of Directors for a period of five (5) years. Additionally, upon the same condition and for the same period, the Underwriter is awarded a preferential right to underwrite or arrange future public financing for the Company.

The principal stockholders have granted the Underwriter an option to purchase from them, at 10¢ per share, a total of 9,000 shares of Class B Convertible Stock, par value 10¢ per share on the basis of three (3) shares for each twenty (20) shares sold for the account of the Company. Such options are exercisable during the period commencing thirteen (13) months from the Effective Date and terminating sixty (60) months from the Effective Date. Mr. Lew Prince and Mr. Ben Aaronson have acted as "Finders" herein. Mr. Prince is to receive from the Company a maximum of $7,500 on the basis of 12½¢ for each share sold for the account of the Company and options to purchase 1,500 shares of Class B Convertible Stock on the basis of one (1) share for each forty (40) shares sold for the account of the Company. Such options are exercisable at $1.50 per share during the period commencing thirteen (13) months from the Effective Date and terminating sixty (60) months from such date. Mr. Aaronson is to receive from the Company options to purchase 3,000 shares of Class B Convertible Stock, on the basis of one (1) share for each twenty (20) shares sold for the account of the Company, exercisable at the same price and during the same period as those options granted Mr. Prince. The Underwriter and the "Finders" may not sell, assign or transfer these options or the shares underlying such options for a period of thirteen (13) months from the date hereof. Thereafter such shares may be sold only after complying with all applicable provisions of the Securities Act of 1933, as amended. Any sums realized upon a sale of such shares in excess of cost may be deemed additional Underwriter's compensation. See "Description of Classes of Stock" for conversion rights of the holders of Class B Convertible Stock. (See also "Underwriting".)

(4) Proceeds are shown before deducting expenses of the offering payable by the Company estimated at $25,000 which amount includes legal fees of $5,000, accounting fees estimated at $1,500, printing of the Offering Circular estimated at $1,000, printing of stock certificates estimated at $600, finders' fee of $7,500, expenses of the Underwriter of $7,500 as set forth under footnote 1 hereof, and other miscellaneous expenses.

INTRODUCTORY STATEMENT

1. The Company has had nominal sales to date having been primarily in a formative and developmental stage and there is no assurance that its products will find general acceptance.

2. Prior to this offering there has been no market for the stock of the Company. The offering price of $5.00 per share has been arbitrarily determined and bears no relation to the book value of the Company's stock, nor is such price to be considered a representation that such shares could be sold at such price by the owners thereof.

3. At the conclusion of this offering, if all shares offered hereby are sold, $300,000 in cash will have been paid for 60,000 shares which will represent 33⅓% of the stock that will be outstanding. The 120,000 shares held by officers, directors and promoters will represent 66⅔% of the stock then outstanding which had a deficit of $10,805.39 or minus (.09) per share based on tangible net asset value at September 30, 1961.

Upon termination of this offering, the equity of officers, directors and promoters based on tangible net asset value will increase from minus (.09) per share to $1.26 per share without cost to them on 120,000 shares and the public's equity in the Company will decrease from the $5.00 per share offering price to $1.26 per share.

4. The principal stockholders have been granted options to purchase a total of 55,500 shares of the Company's Class B Convertible Stock at $1.50 per share during the period commencing 13 months from the Effective Date and terminating 60 months from such Effective Date; the Underwriter has been granted an option to purchase a total of 9,000 shares of Class B Convertible Stock from the principal stockholders at 10¢ per share during the period commencing thirteen (13) months from the Effective Date and terminating sixty (60) months from such Effective Date; and the "finders" will have options to purchase a total of 4,500 shares of the Company's Class B Convertible Stock from the Company, exercisable at the same prices and during the same period as those of the principal stockholders (See "Underwriting"). During the life of such options the Company might be deprived of favorable opportunities to produce additional equity capital needed for its business; and at any time when the holders of such options might be expected to exercise them (e.g. if the market price for the Class A Stock should exceed the exercise price of the options), the Company would probably be able to obtain equity capital by the sale of shares of its Class A Stock on terms more favorable to it than those fixed by the options.

5. Additionally, assuming the options to purchase all 60,000 shares are exercised, the equity which the public will have in the shares offered hereby will be further reduced while the equity of the principal stockholders, the Underwriter and the "finders" will be further increased with only nominal cost to them. If all such options are exercised the public will own 25% of all the stock then outstanding, while the principal stockholders, Underwriter and "finders" will own 75% of all the stock then outstanding.

6. Commencing on the Effective Date of this offering, officers' salaries will be increased from $7,800 paid between February 1, 1961 - September 30, 1961 to a sum equal to 5% of the gross sales of the Company but in no event shall such sum be less than $25,000. One year from the Effective Date salaries may be further increased in the sole discretion of the Board of Directors.

Only one of the Company's officers and directors will devote full time to the affairs of the Company.

7. With respect to the application of $117,500 for working capital, it is to be noted that to the extent that the Issuer has not committed itself to any plan, it has in effect a "blank check". This amount constitutes 52% of the net proceeds of this offering. No further authority will be required from stockholders as to the use of such funds, and there are no restrictions as to the discretion of management concerning the use of such funds.

The Company intends to submit audited annual financial statements to its stockholders.

Competition

The Company knows of no other product comparable to its "pk" process. Products similar to its "Paprotex" formula are presently being marketed by competitors who may have greater financial resources than the Company. As the Company has not yet commenced full scale marketing of "Paprotex" and will not do so until it receives the proceeds of this financing, its success in meeting competition cannot yet be predicted.

Backlog of Orders

As of November 15, 1961, the Company had unfilled orders on its books of $15,000 for its various products.

APPLICATION OF PROCEEDS

In the event that all the shares of stock offered hereby for the account of the Company are sold, the estimated net proceeds to the Company, after payment of the Underwriters commissions, expenses and the other costs of the offering will aggregate $237,500.00. It is anticipated that such proceeds will be utilized substantially as follows, in the order of priority listed:

1. Remuneration of Officers and Directors(1)	$ 25,000.00
2. Purchase and Installation of Wallpaper Coater Equipment......	30,000.00
3. Purchase of Inventory	10,000.00
4. Test Marketing and Development	10,000.00
5. Advertising and Sales Promotion Campaign	45,000.00
6. Addition to Working Capital(2)(3)	117,500.00
	$237,500.00

STATEMENT OF INCOME, EXPENSE AND RETAINED EARNINGS
From Incorporation on February 1, 1961 to September 30, 1961

SALES			$3,049.13
COST OF SALES:			
Purchases	$5,108.73		
Less: Inventory at September 30, 1961 (Note 2).......	3,503.71	$1,605.02	
Production labor		181.00	
Rent (Note 5)		200.00	1,986.02
Gross Margin on Sales			$1,063.11

OTHER EXPENSES:

Officer's salary (Note 5)	332.00	
Other	21.00	353.00
Net income before organization expense and federal tax provision...		$ 710.11
Organization expense (Note 7)		110.70
		599.41
Provision for Federal Taxes (Note 9)		399.70
NET INCOME FOR PERIOD, AND RETAINED EARNINGS AT SEPTEMBER 30, 1961		$ 199.71

Inventory Release
(on certification of inventories)
Accounting Series Release #90, ¶72112 CCH

It seems clear from the discussion above that if an accountant reports that his examination was made in accordance with generally accepted auditing standards, and accordingly included such tests of the accounting records and such other auditing procedures as he considered necessary in the circumstances, an exception as to failure to observe beginning inventories is contradictory and should be omitted. A middle paragraph explaining that the certificate covers a first audit is informative and in some cases is essential to describe the alternative procedures applied. A negative type conclusion to this paragraph appears to be a carry-over from wartime usage and is not acceptable. Lost and inadequate records may give rise to questions as to the reliability of the results shown in the financial statements and may make it impracticable to apply alternative audit procedures. Alternative procedures must be adequate to support an unqualified opinion as to the fairness of presentation of the income statements by years.

If, as a result of the examination and the conclusions reached, the accountant is not in a position to express an affirmative opinion as to the fairness of the presentation of earnings year by year, the registration statement is defective because the certificate does not meet the requirements of Rule 2-02 of Regulation S-X. If the accountant is not satisfied with the results of his examination he should not issue an affirmative opinion. If he is satisfied, any reference from the opinion paragraph to an explanatory paragraph devoted solely to the scope of the audit is inconsistent and unnecessary. Accordingly, phrases such as "with the foregoing explanation as to inventories" raise questions as to whether the certifying accountant intended to limit his opinion as to the fairness of the presentation of the results shown and should be omitted.

A "subject to" or "except for" opinion paragraph in which these phrases refer to the scope of the audit, indicating that the accountant has not been able to satisfy himself on some significant element in the financial statements, is not acceptable in certificates filed with the Commission in connection with the public offering of securities. The "subject to" qualification is appropriate when the reference is to a middle paragraph or to footnotes explaining the status of matters which cannot be resolved at statement date.

¶72,112 CCH _____ _____ A.S.R #90

FORM OF FIRM UNDERWRITING
AGREEMENT

----
as Representative of
the Several Underwriters

New York, N.Y. 10004

Dear Sirs:

1. Introductory: XYZ, INC. (the "Company"), a New York
corporation, proposes to issue and sell 50,000 shares of its authorized but unissued Class "A" stock ($1 par value), and Mr. and Mrs.
---- (the "Selling Shareholders") propose to sell 200,000 presently
outstanding shares of such class of stock to the public through the
Underwriters named in Schedule A annexed hereto. Each of the Selling Shareholders also grants an option to said Underwriters as provided herein to purchase up to 12,500 additional shares of such class
of stock. The 250,000 shares of Class "A" stock which the said Underwriters agree to purchase hereunder are herein sometimes called the
"Purchased Stock." The 25,000 additional shares are herein sometimes
called the "Option Stock," and the entire 275,000 shares of Class "A"
stock are herein sometimes together called the "Stock." Such Stock
is more fully described in the Registration Statement and the Prospectus hereinafter mentioned. The Company and the Selling Shareholders
hereby confirm their several agreements with you, acting as Representative of such Underwriters, as follows:

2.   Representations and Warranties of the Company and the
                      Selling Shareholders

A.   The Company and each of the Selling Shareholders severally
represent and warrant to each of the Underwriters that:

(a) The Company has been duly incorporated and is validly
existing as a corporation in good standing under the laws of New York
with power and authority to own its properties and conduct its business as described in the Prospectus hereinafter mentioned; and the
Company is qualified as a foreign corporation in all jurisdictions
in which the ownership or base of property requires such qualification.

(b) -------------- and -------------------- have been duly
incorporated and are validly existing as corporations in good standing under the laws, respectively, of Illinois and Massachusetts, with
power and authority to own their properties and to conduct their businesses as described in said Prospectus; and each of said ~~ppope~~ corporations is qualified as a foreign corporation in all jurisdictions
in which the ownership or base of property requires such qualification.

(c) The outstanding shares of Class "A" and Class "B" stock of the Company have been duly authorized and issued, are full paid and non-assessable and conform to the description thereof contained in the Prospectus; the 800,000 shares of Class "A" stock reserved for issuance upon the conversion of the Class "B" stock have been duly authorized and, when issued upon conversion, will be duly issued, full paid and non-assessable; and the 50,000 shares of Class "A" stock to be issued and sold by the Company pursuant to this Agreement have been duly authorized and, when issued and delivered pursuant to this Agreement, will be duly issued, full paid and non-assessable and will conform to the description thereof contained in the Prospectus.

(d) This Agreement has been duly authorized, executed and delivered on behalf of the Company and the Selling Shareholders and is a valid Agreement enforceable against the Company and the Selling Shareholders in accordance with its terms.

(e) A registration statement (File No   ) with respect to the Stock has been carefully prepared by the Company in conformity with the requirements of the Securities Act of 1933, as amended (the "Act") and the rules and regulations (the "Rules and Regulations") of the Securities and Exchange Commission (the "Commission") thereunder and has been filed with the Commission; and the Company proposes to file prior to the effective date of such registration statement an amendment to such registration statement. Copies of such registration statement and amendment, and of each related preliminary prospectus ("Preliminary Prospectus") and the final prospectus, have been delivered to you. Such registration statement and final prospectus, as finally amended and revised prior to the effective date of the registration statement, are herein respectively referred to as the "Registration Statement" and the "Prospectus".

(f) When the Registration Statement becomes effective and at all times subsequent thereto up to the Closing Dates hereinafter mentioned, the Registration Statement and the Prospectus and any amendments thereof or supplements thereto will contain all statements which are required to be stated therein in accordance with the Act and the Rules and Regulations and will in all respects conform to the requirements of the Act and the Rules and Regulations, and neither the Registration Statement nor the Prospectus, nor any amendment or supplement thereto, will include any untrue statement of a material fact or omit to state any material fact required to be stated therein or necessary to make the statements therein not misleading; provided, however, that neither the Company nor the Selling Shareholders makes any representations, warranties or agreements as to information contained in or omitted from the Registration Statement or the Prospectus or any such amendment or supplement in reliance upon, and in conformity with, written information furnished to the Company by any Underwriter for use in the preparation thereof.

(g) Subsequent to the respective dates as of which information is given in the Registration Statement and Prospectus and prior to the Closing Dates hereinafter mentioned, and except as contemplated in the Prospectus, (1) neither the Company nor any of its subsidiaries has incurred or will have incurred any liabilities or obligations, direct or contingent, nor has it entered or will it have entered into any material transaction, not in the ordinary course of business, (2) there has not been and will not have been any change in the Company's capital stock or funded debt or any material adverse change in the financial position or results of operations of the Company or any of its subsidiaries, (3) no loss or damage (whether or not insured) to the property of the Company or any of its subsidiaries has been or will have been sustained which materially and adversely affects the operations of the Company and its subsidiaries on a consolidated basis, and (4) no material legal or governmental proceeding, domestic or foreign, affecting the Company or any of its subsidiaries, or the transactions contemplated by this Agreement, has been or will have been instituted or threatened.

(h) The consummation of the transactions herein contemplated and the fulfillment of the terms hereof will not result in a breach of any of the terms and provisions of, or constitute a default under, any indenture, mortgage, deed of trust or other agreement or instrument to which the Company or the Selling Shareholders is a party or the charter or by-laws of the Company as presently in effect or, to the best of its knowledge, any order, rule or regulation applicable to the Company of any court or of any federal or state regulatory body or administrative agency or other governmental body, domestic or foreign, having jurisdiction over the Company or its properties.

(i) No approval, authorization, consent or other order of any public board or body (other than in connection with or in compliance with the provisions of the Act and the security or blue sky laws of various states) is legally required for the sale of the Stock.

(j) Messrs.
who have certified to certain of the financial statements filed with the Registration Statement, some of which are incorporated in the Prospectus, are independent public accountants as required by the Act and the Rules and Regulations.

B. Each Selling Shareholder severally represents and warrants to each of the Underwriters that on the Closing Dates hereinafter defined he or she will own, free and clear of all claims, encumbrances and defects in title, the shares of Stock then to be sold and delivered by him or her hereunder; there will be no restrictions on the sale or delivery of such shares by such Selling Shareholder to the Underwriters; and such Selling Shareholder shall have the right and power to sell and deliver all such shares in accordance with the terms hereof, and such sale and delivery will be valid in all respects.

3. *Representations of the Underwriters.* Each of the Underwriters represents and warrants to the Company and the Selling Shareholders that the information furnished to the Company in writing by such Underwriter expressly for use in the Registration Statement or the Prospectus does not, and any amendments thereof or supplements thereto thus furnished will not, contain an untrue statement of a material fact or omit to state a material fact required to be stated therein or necessary to make the statements therein not misleading. Each Underwriter has furnished to the Company in writing expressly for such use, the statements with respect to Underwriters in Item 22 of the Registration Statement and any statements relating to the offerings by the Underwriters on the cover page of and under "Underwriting" in the Prospectus.

4. *Covenants of the Company and the Selling Shareholders.*

A. The Company covenants and agrees with the several Underwriters that:

(a) The Company will use its best efforts to cause the Registration Statement to become effective and will advise you when it is effective, and the Company will not file any amendment to the Registration Statement of which you have not been advised and furnished with a copy, or to which you have reasonably objected in writing.

(b) The Company will advise you promptly of any request of the Commission for amendment of the Registration Statement or Prospectus or for additional information and of the issuance by the Commission of any stop order suspending the effectiveness of the Registration Statement or of the institution of any proceedings for that purpose, and the Company will use its best efforts to prevent the issuance of any such stop order and to obtain as soon as possible the lifting thereof, if issued.

(c) If, at any time when a Prospectus relating to this financing is required to be delivered under the Act within nine months after the effective date of the Registration Statement, any event occurs as a result of which the Prospectus as then amended or supplemented would include an untrue statement of a material fact, or omit to state any material fact necessary to make the statements therein, in the light of the circumstances under which they were made, not misleading, or if it is necessary at any time within nine months after the effective date of the Registration Statement to amend the Prospectus to comply with the Act, the Company promptly will prepare and file with the Commission an amendment or supplement which will correct such statement or omission or an amendment which will effect such compliance.

(d) Not later than fifteen months after the effective date of the Registration Statement, the Company will make generally available to its securityholders an earnings statement, covering a period of at least twelve months beginning not earlier than said date, which shall satisfy the provisions of Section 11(a) of the Act.

(e) The Company will furnish to you copies of the Registration Statement (two of which will be signed and will include all exhibits thereto), each Preliminary Prospectus, the Prospectus, and all amendments and supplements to such documents, in each case as soon as available and in such quantities as you request.

(f) The Company will furnish such information and execute such instruments as may be required to qualify the Stock for sale under the security or blue sky laws of such jurisdictions as you designate and will continue such qualifications in effect so long as required for distribution; provided, however, that such qualifications need not be continued in effect after nine months after the effective date of the Registration Statement.

(g) For a period of five years from the date of the Prospectus the Company will deliver to you and, upon request, to each of the other Underwriters, (i) as soon as practicable after the end of each fiscal year, balance sheets and statements of income and surplus of the Company and its consolidated susbidiaries and of   and its consolidated subsidiaries, as at the end of and for such year and the last preceding year, all in reasonable detail and certified by independent public accountants, (ii) as soon as practicable after the end of each quarterly fiscal period (except for the last quarterly fiscal period of each fiscal year), balance sheets and statements of income and surplus of the Company and its consolidated subsidiaries and of   and its consolidated susbidiaries, as at the end of and for such period and for the comparable period of the preceding year, all in reasonable detail, (iii) as soon as available, a copy of each report of the Company mailed to stockholders or filed with the Commission or any securities exchange, and (iv) such other information concerning the financial condition and operations of the Company and its consolidated subsidiaries and of Wilson Jones, and its consolidated subsidiaries, as you may from time to time reasonably request.

(h) The Company will apply the net proceeds from the sale of the Purchased Stock sold and delivered by it in the manner set forth in the Prospectus.

B. Each of the Selling Shareholders covenants and agrees with the several Underwriters that he or she will use his best efforts, including voting any capital stock he or she may hold, to cause the Company to carry out its covenants contained in Section 4A.

C. The Company and the Selling Shareholders will pay (a) all their costs and expenses in connection with the transactions herein contemplated, including, but not limited to, the fees and disbursements of counsel for the Company and the Selling Shareholders; the fees, costs and expenses of preparing, printing and delivering the certificates for the Stock; the fees, costs and expenses of the Transfer Agent and Registrar of the Company's Class "A" stock and their counsel, if any; accounting fees and disbursements; original issue taxes upon the issue of the Stock being issued by the Company; transfer taxes upon the sale of the Stock being sold by the Selling Shareholders; expenses in an amount not exceeding $5,500 in connection with the qualification or exemption of the Stock under State security or blue sky laws, including filing fees, counsel fees and disbursements in connection therewith; and the costs and expenses in connection with the preparation, printing and filing of the Registration Statement and Prospectus, the preparation and printing of this Agreement, and the furnishing to the Underwriters of such copies of each Preliminary and final Prospectus as the Underwriters may reasonably require, including copies required for use during the period of nine months after the date of public offering; and (b) the sum of $10,000 to you as Representative of the several Underwriters in partial reimbursement of expenses of the Underwriters. The Selling Shareholders will pay such expenses as are specified to be payable by them in Item 23 of the Registration Statement and their proportionate share of the amount to be reimbursed to you pursuant to the provisions of this Section 4C.

5. *Sale, Purchase and Delivery of Purchased Stock.* On the basis of the representations and warranties herein contained, but subject to the terms and conditions herein set forth, the Company and

the Selling Shareholders hereby agree to sell to the Underwriters, severally and not jointly, and each Underwriter, severally and not jointly, agrees to purchase from the Company and the Selling Shareholders the respective number of shares of Purchased Stock set opposite its name in Columns I and II on Schedule A hereto, at a price of $19.995 per share. Each Selling Shareholder and each Underwriter agree that the number of shares to be sold by such Selling Shareholder to such Underwriter and purchased by such Underwriter from him shall be one half the number of shares set forth opposite the name of such Underwriter in Column II in said Schedule A.

The Company and the Selling Shareholders will deliver the Purchased Stock to you for the accounts of the several Underwriters against payment of the purchase price therefor by certified or official bank check or checks in New York funds drawn to the respective orders of the Company and each of the Selling Shareholders, at the office of Manufacturers Trust Company, 55 Broad Street, New York, New York, at 10:00 A.M., Eastern Standard Time, on December 22, 1960, or at such other time not later than seven full business days thereafter as you and the Company shall determine, such time and place being herein referred to as the "First Closing Date". The certificates for the shares so to be delivered will be in such denominations and registered in such names as you may request. Such certificates will be made available for checking and packaging at the above office at least 24 hours prior to the First Closing Date.

6. *Granting and Exercise of Options With Respect to Option Stock.* On the basis of the representations and warranties herein contained, but subject to the terms and conditions herein set forth, each of the Selling Shareholders hereby grants an option to the several Underwriters to purchase, in the aggregate, up to 12,500 shares of Option Stock at a price of $19.995 per share. The options granted hereunder may be exercised on the First Closing Date or at any other time within 30 days after the effective date of the Registration Statement upon four full business days' prior written notice by you to the Selling Shareholders setting forth the number of shares of Option Stock as to which the several Underwriters intend to exercise the options, the names and denominations in which the certificates for such shares are to be registered and the time and place at which such options will be exercised, such time and place (unless it is the First Closing Date) being herein referred to as the "Second Closing Date". The Selling Shareholders will deliver the Option Stock to you for the accounts of the several Underwriters against payment of the purchase price therefor by certified or official bank check or checks in New York funds drawn to the respective orders of each of the Selling Shareholders. The number of shares of Option Stock to be purchased by each Underwriter shall be the same percentage of the total number of shares of Option Stock being purchased by the several Underwriters as such Underwriter is purchasing of Purchased Stock, and shall be purchased in equal numbers from each of the Selling Shareholders, all adjusted by you in such manner as to avoid fractional shares.

The options with respect to the Option Stock granted hereunder may not be exercised unless the Purchased Stock has been sold and delivered to the Underwriters pursuant to the terms of this Agreement.

7. *Offering by Underwriters.* The several Underwriters agree that they will offer the Stock to the public as set forth in the Prospectus.

8. *Conditions of the Obligations of the Underwriters.* The obligations of the several Underwriters to purchase and pay for the Purchased Stock and the Option Stock (after the requisite notice has been given pursuant to Section 6 hereof) shall be subject to the accuracy of the representations and warranties on the part of the Company and the Selling Shareholders herein as of the date hereof and the respective Closing Dates, to the accuracy of the statements of Company officers and the Selling Shareholders made pursuant to the provisions hereof, to the performance by the Company and the Selling Shareholders of their obligations hereunder and to the following additional conditions:

(a) The Registration Statement shall have become effective not later than 6 P.M., New York Time, on the day following the date of this Agreement, or such later date as shall have been consented to by you; and no stop order suspending the effectiveness of the Registration Statement shall

have been issued and no proceedings for that purpose shall have been instituted or shall be pending, **or, to** the knowledge of the Company, the Selling Shareholders or you, shall be contemplated by the **Commission.**

(b) You shall not have advised the Company that the Registration Statement or Prospectus **or any** amendment or supplement thereto contains an untrue statement of fact which, in the opinion **of Messrs.** Beekman & Bogue, counsel for the Underwriters, is material, or omits to state a fact **which, in** the opinion of such counsel, is material and is required to be stated therein or is necessary **to make** the statements therein not misleading.

(c) On the First Closing Date you shall have received the following:

(i) An opinion of Messrs. Aranow, Brodsky, Bohlinger, Einhorn & Dann, counsel for the Company and the Selling Shareholders, dated said Closing Date, to the effect that:

(aa) The Company has been duly incorporated and is validly existing as a corporation **in good** standing under the laws of New York with power and authority to own its properties and conduct its business as described in the Prospectus; and the Company is qualified **as a** foreign corporation in all jurisdictions in which the ownership or lease of property **requires** such qualification.

(bb) have been duly incorporated and are validly existing as **corporations** in good standing under the laws, respectively, of Illinois and Massachusetts, **with power** and authority to own their properties and to conduct their businesses as **described** in the Prospectus.

(cc) The outstanding shares of Class "A" and Class "B" stock of the Company, including the shares of Purchased Stock being purchased from the Company, have been duly **authorized** and issued, are full paid and non-assessable and conform to the description **thereof** contained in the Prospectus.

(dd) This Agreement has been duly authorized, executed and delivered on behalf of **the** Company and the Selling Shareholders and is a valid Agreement enforceable against the Company and the Selling Shareholders in accordance with its terms.

(ee) The Registration Statement has become effective under the Act, and, to the best **of the** knowledge of such counsel, no stop order suspending the effectiveness of the Registration Statement has been issued and no proceedings for that purpose have been instituted **or are** pending or contemplated under the Act, and the Registration Statement and Prospectus, and each amendment thereof or supplement thereto (except for the financial **statements** and other financial data included therein as to which such counsel need express **no opinion)** comply as to form in all material respects with the requirements of the Act **and the** Rules and Regulations; such counsel has no reason to believe that either the Registration Statement or the Prospectus, or any such amendment or supplement, contains **any untrue** statement of a material fact or omits to state a material fact required to be stated **therein** or necessary to make the statements therein not misleading; the descriptions in the Registration Statement and Prospectus of statutes, legal and governmental proceedings and **contracts** and other documents are accurate and fairly present the information required to **be shown;** and such counsel does not know of any legal or governmental proceedings, **domestic** or foreign, required to be described in the Prospectus which are not described **as required,** nor of any contracts or documents of a character required to be described in **the** Registration Statement or Prospectus or to be filed as exhibits to the Registration Statement which are not described and filed as required.

(ff) To the best of the knowledge of such counsel, the consummation of the transactions herein contemplated and the fulfillment of the terms hereof will not result in a breach of any of the terms and provisions of, or constitute a default under, any indenture, mortgage, deed of trust or other agreement or instrument to which the Company is a party or the charter or by-laws of the Company as presently in effect or any order, rule or regulation applicable to the Company of any court or of any federal or state regulatory body or administrative agency or other governmental body, domestic or foreign, having jurisdiction over the Company or its properties.

(gg) All legally required proceedings in connection with the sale of the Purchased Stock then being purchased from the Company and the Selling Shareholders by the Underwriters in the manner set forth herein have been had; and the authorization of the transactions related thereto, and all approvals, authorizations, consents or other orders of such public boards or bodies, domestic or foreign, as may be legally required with respect to all or any of such matters (other than under state security or blue sky laws) have been obtained.

(hh) Title to the shares of Stock then being purchased from the Selling Shareholders has been duly and legally transferred to the purchasers thereof, and, to the best of the knowledge of such counsel, such shares are free and clear of all claims, encumbrances and defects of title and there are no restrictions on the sale and delivery of such shares by the Selling Shareholders.

(ii) Such opinion or opinions of Messrs.   counsel for the Underwriters, dated said Closing Date, with respect to the sufficiency of all corporate proceedings and other legal matters relating to this Agreement, the validity of the Stock then being purchased, the accuracy and completeness of the Registration Statement and the Prospectus, and such other related matters as you may reasonably require, and the Company and the Selling Shareholders shall have furnished to such counsel such documents as they request for the purpose of enabling them to pass upon such matters.

(iii) A certificate of the President or a Vice-President and a principal financial officer of the Company and of each of the Selling Shareholders, dated said Closing Date, to the effect that:

(aa) The representations and warranties of the Company and the Selling Shareholders in Section 2A of this Agreement are true and correct as of said Closing Date, and the Company and the Selling Shareholders have complied with all the agreements and satisfied all the conditions on their part to be performed or satisfied at or prior to said Closing Date.

(bb) No stop order suspending the effectiveness of the Registration Statement has been issued and no proceedings for that purpose have been instituted or are pending or, to the knowledge of the respective signers of the certificate, are contemplated under the Act.

(iv) A certificate of each of the Selling Shareholders, dated said Closing Date, to the effect that his or her representations and warranties in Section 2B of this Agreement are true and correct as of said Date.

(v) A certificate or letter of Messrs.   dated said Closing Date, confirming that they are independent public accountants within the meaning of the Act and the Rules and Regulations, and stating that, in their opinion, (i) the financial statements and related schedules examined by them and included in the Registration Statement and Prospectus on their authority as experts comply as to form in all material respects with the pertinent requirements of the Act and the Rules and Regulations, and (ii) on the basis of a limited review (which need not constitute an examination in accordance with generally accepted auditing standards) of the latest available interim financial statements and minute books of the Company and its consolidated subsidiaries and inquiries and discussions with officers responsible for financial and accounting matters of said corporations and other pertinent inquiries as to transactions and events subsequent to August 31, 1960, they have no reason to believe that during the period from such date to a specified date not more than 5 days prior to said Closing Date there has been any change in the capital stock or funded debt of the Company or any material adverse change in the financial position or results of operations of the Company and its consolidated subsidiaries, except as set forth or contemplated in the Registration Statement.

(vi) A certificate or letter of Messrs.   dated said Closing Date, confirming that they are independent public accountants within the meaning of the Act and the Rules and Regulations, and stating that, in their opinion, (i) the financial statements and related schedules examined by them and included in the Registration Statement and Prospectus on their authority as experts comply as to form in all material respects with the pertinent requirements of the Act, and the Rules and Regulations, and (ii) on the basis of a limited review (which need not constitute an examination in accordance with generally accepted auditing standards) of the latest available interim financial statements and minute books of Wilson Jones and its consolidated subsidiaries and inquiries and discussions with officers responsible for financial and accounting matters of said corporations and other pertinent inquiries as to transactions and events subsequent to August 31, 1960, they have no reason to believe that during the period from such date to a specified date not more than 5 days prior to said Closing Date there has been any change in the capital stock or funded debt of Wilson Jones or any material adverse change in the financial position or results of operations of Wilson Jones and its consolidated subsidiaries, except as set forth or contemplated in the Registration Statement.

(d) On the Second Closing Date (or on the First Closing Date, if Option Stock is then being purchased) you shall have received the following:

(i) An opinion of Messrs.   dated said Closing Date, to the same effect as the opinions called for by Subsections (c)(i)(ee) and (hh) of this Section 8, and to the further effect that:

(aa) The outstanding shares of Class "A" and Class "B" stock of the Company, including the shares of Option Stock being purchased from the Selling Shareholders, have been duly authorized and issued, are full paid and non-assessable and conform to the description thereof contained in the Prospectus.

(bb) All legally required proceedings in connection with the sale of the Option Stock then being purchased from the Selling Shareholders by the Underwriters in the manner set forth herein have been had; and the authorization of the transactions related thereto, and all approvals, authorizations, consents or other orders of such public boards or bodies, domestic or foreign, as may be legally required with respect to all or any of such matters (other than under state security or blue sky laws) have been obtained.

(ii) Opinions, certificates and letters, each dated said Closing Date, similar in scope to the opinions, certificates and letters, respectively called for by Subsections (c)(ii), (iii) and (iv) of this Section 8.

(e) Prior to each Closing Date, the Company and the Selling Shareholders shall have furnished to you such further certificates and documents as you may reasonably request.

In rendering the foregoing opinions Messrs.   and Messrs   may, as to matters of foreign law, rely upon the opinion of local counsel satisfactory to you, but in such case a signed copy of such opinion shall be furnished to you. All such opinions, certificates, letters and documents will be in compliance with the provisions hereof only if they are in all material respects reasonably satisfactory to you and to Messrs. Beekman & Bogue, counsel for the Underwriters. The Company and the Selling Shareholders will furnish you with such conformed copies of such opinions, certificates, letters and documents as you request.

If any condition of the Underwriters' obligations hereunder to be satisfied prior to either Closing Date is not so satisfied, this Agreement may be terminated by you, by written or telegraphic notice to the Company, without liability on the part of any Underwriter or the Company or the Selling Shareholders, except for the expenses to be paid or reimbursed by the Company and the Selling Shareholders pursuant to Section 4C.

9. *Agreements Relating to Class "B" stock.* The Selling Shareholders agree that

(a) During the first twelve month period following the date of this Agreement they will not, without the consent of the Representative, convert, sell or transfer any shares of Class "B" stock except that:

(i) they may each convert up to 12,500 shares to obtain shares of Option Stock for delivery to the Underwriters;

(ii) they may each convert up to 15,000 shares to obtain shares of Class "A" stock for delivery to employees of the Company and Ace in accordance with the Company's Employee Stock Purchase Plan described in the Prospectus; and

(iii) they may transfer Class "B" stock to any child or grandchild or the spouse of any child or grandchild of the Selling Shareholders, or to a trustee or trustees of one or more inter vivos trusts for the benefit of either of the Selling Shareholders or any child, grandchild or spouse of a child or grandchild of the Selling Shareholders, or to any firm or corporation directly or indirectly controlled by any of the foregoing or by the Selling Shareholders (any such transfer being hereinafter referred to as a "Family Transfer").

(b) During the second twelve month period following the date of this Agreement they will not, without the consent of the Representative, convert, sell or transfer more than 200,000 shares of Class "B" stock except that:

(i) they may transfer any of such shares in a Family Transfer; and

(ii) they may dispose of any of such shares in any statutory merger or consolidation of corporations, or transfer any of such shares to another corporation, or to any stockholder of another corporation, in exchange for the issuance or delivery of more than 30% of the stock or of a major portion or all of the assets of such corporation to the Selling Shareholders or to any person, firm or corporation designated by them.

(c) The restrictions on the conversion, sale or other transfer of shares of Class "B" stock provided for in Subsections (a) and (b) above shall terminate (i) upon the death of either of the Selling Shareholders or the holder (other than as trustee) of any shares received in a Family Transfer, as to all such shares held by such Selling Shareholder or holder, or (ii) at the time of transfer, as to any of such shares transferred to any person, firm or corporation in any transaction authorized by Subsection (b)(ii) above; but such restrictions shall be binding upon the transferee of shares of Class "B" stock in any Family Transfer; and each such transferee in a Family Transfer shall agree with you and the Selling Shareholders to abide by the provisions of this Section 9.

(d) Notwithstanding the foregoing all restrictions on the conversion, sale or other transfer of shares of Class "B" stock shall terminate at the end of the twenty-four month period following the date of this Agreement.

10. *Cancellation of Agreement.* At any time prior to the Registration Statement becoming effective, the Company and the Selling Shareholders may, by notice to you, cancel this Agreement; and at any time

prior to such time, you, as Representative of the Underwriters, may, by notice to the Company and the Selling Shareholders, cancel this Agreement. You, as Representative of the Underwriters, may also, by notice to the Company and the Selling Shareholders, cancel this Agreement on or after the effective date of the Registration Statement and prior to the First Closing Date if during such period there shall have occurred any general suspension of trading in securities on the New York Stock Exchange or there shall have been established by the New York Stock Exchange or by the Commission or by any federal or state agency or by the decision of any court any limitation on prices for such trading or any restrictions on the distribution of securities, all to such a degree as in your judgment would restrict materially a free market for the Stock, or if there shall have been such a material change in general economic or financial conditions, or if the effect of international conditions on the financial markets of the United States shall be such as, in any such case, in your judgment, makes it impracticable for the Underwriters to enforce contracts for the sale of the Stock.

In the event of such cancellation no Underwriter shall be under any liability to the Company or the Selling Shareholders, nor shall the Company nor any Selling Shareholder be under any liability to any Underwriter, except that in the event of such cancellation by the Company and the Selling Shareholders they shall be liable for the expenses to be paid or reimbursed by them pursuant to the provisions of Section 4C, and except that in the event of such cancellation by the Underwriters the Company and the Selling Shareholders shall be liable only for the expenses to be paid or reimbursed by them pursuant to the provisions of Section 4C(a).

11. *Indemnification.* (a) The Selling Shareholders and the Company will indemnify and hold harmless each Underwriter and each person, if any, who controls any Underwriter within the meaning of the Act against any losses, claims, damages or liabilities, joint or several, to which such Underwriter or such controlling person may become subject, under the Act or otherwise, insofar as such losses, claims, damages or liabilities (or actions in respect thereof) arise out of or are based upon any untrue statement or alleged untrue statement of any material fact contained in the Registration Statement, the Preliminary Prospectus, the Prospectus, or any amendment or supplement thereto, or arise out of or are based upon the omission or alleged omission to state therein a material fact required to be stated therein or necessary to make the statements therein not misleading, and will reimburse each Underwriter and each such controlling person for any legal or other expenses reasonably incurred by such Underwriter or such controlling person in connection with investigating or defending any such loss, claim, damage, liability or action; provided, however, that neither the Company nor the Selling Shareholders will be liable in any such case to the extent that any such loss, claim, damage or liability arises out of or is based upon an untrue statement or alleged untrue statement or omission or alleged omission made in the Registration Statement, the Preliminary Prospectus, the Prospectus or such amendment or such supplement, in reliance upon and in conformity with written information furnished to the Company by any Underwriter specifically for use in the preparation thereof. This indemnity agreement will be in addition to any liability which the Company or the Selling Shareholders may otherwise have.

(b) The Selling Shareholders will indemnify and hold harmless the Company, each of its directors and each of its officers who has signed the Registration Statement against any losses, claims, damages or liabilities to which the Company or any such director or officer may become subject, under the Act or otherwise, insofar as such losses, claims, damages or liabilities (or actions in respect thereof) arise out of or are based upon any untrue statement or alleged untrue statement of any material fact contained in the Registration Statement, the Preliminary Prospectus, the Prospectus, or any amendment or supplement thereto, or arise out of or are based upon the omission or the alleged omission to state therein a material fact required to be stated therein or necessary to make the statements therein not misleading, in each case to the extent, but only to the extent, that such untrue statement or alleged untrue statement or omission or alleged omission was made in the Registration Statement, the Preliminary Prospectus, the Prospectus, or such amendment or such supplement, in reliance upon and in conformity with written information furnished to the Company by the Selling Shareholders specifically for use in the preparation thereof; and will reimburse the Company or any such director or officer for any legal or other expenses reasonably incurred by them in connection with investigating or defending any such loss, claim, damage, liability or action. This indemnity agreement will be in addition to any liability which the Selling Shareholders may otherwise have.

(c) Each Underwriter will indemnify and hold harmless the Company, each of its directors, each of its officers who has signed the Registration Statement, and each of the Selling Shareholders against any losses, claims, damages or liabilities to which the Company, any such director, officer or Selling Shareholder may become subject, under the Act or otherwise, insofar as such losses, claims, damages or liabilities (or actions in respect thereof) arise out of or are based upon any untrue statement or alleged untrue statement of any material fact contained in the Registration Statement, the Preliminary Prospectus, the Prospectus, or any amendment or supplement thereto, or arise out of or are based upon the omission or the alleged omission to state therein a material fact required to be stated therein or necessary to make the statements therein not misleading, in each case to the extent, but only to the extent, that such untrue statement or alleged untrue statement or omission or alleged omission was made in the Registration Statement, the Preliminary Prospectus, the Prospectus, or such amendment or such supplement, in reliance upon and in conformity with written information furnished to the Company by such Underwriter specifically for use in the preparation thereof; and will reimburse the Company or the Selling Shareholders for any legal or other expenses reasonably incurred by them in connection with investigating or defending any such loss, claim, damage, liability or action. This indemnity agreement will be in addition to any liability which such Underwriter may otherwise have.

(d) Promptly after receipt by an indemnified party under this Section of notice of the commencement of any action, such indemnified party will, if a claim in respect thereof is to be made against the indemnifying party under this Section, notify the indemnifying party in writing of the commencement thereof, but the omission so to notify the indemnifying party will not relieve it from any liability which it may have to any indemnified party otherwise than under this Section. In case any such action is brought against any indemnified party, and it notifies the indemnifying party of the commencement thereof, the indemnifying party will be entitled to participate in, and, to the extent that it may wish, jointly with any other indemnifying party, similarly notified, to assume the defense thereof, with counsel satisfactory to the indemnifying parties, and after notice from the indemnifying party to such indemnified party of its election so to assume the defense thereof, the indemnifying party will not be liable to such indemnified party under this Section for any legal or other expenses subsequently incurred by such indemnified party in connection with the defense thereof other than reasonable costs of investigation.

12. *Default of Underwriters.* If any Underwriter or Underwriters default in their obligations to purchase the Stock hereunder, and the Stock which such defaulting Underwriter or Underwriters shall have agreed to purchase does not exceed 27,500 shares, and arrangements satisfactory to you, the Company and the Selling Shareholders, evidenced by a writing or writings signed by you and all of them, for the purchase of such Stock by other persons are not made within twenty-four hours after such default, the remaining Underwriters shall be obligated proportionately to take up and pay for such shares of the Stock as all of such defaulting Underwriters failed to purchase. If any Underwriter or Underwriters default in their obligations to purchase the Stock hereunder, and the Stock which such defaulting Underwriter or Underwriters shall have agreed to purchase exceeds 27,500 shares, and arrangements satisfactory to you, the Company and the Selling Shareholders, evidenced by a writing or writings signed by you and all of them, for the purchase of such Stock by other persons are not made within twenty-four hours after such default, the Company and the Selling Shareholders shall have the right within an additional period of twenty-four hours to require such remaining Underwriters, irrespective of the default as aforesaid, to purchase the respective shares of Stock which they originally agreed to purchase hereunder. If the Company and the Selling Shareholders do not notify you within such twenty-four hours of the exercise of such right, this Agreement will terminate without liability on the part of any non-defaulting Underwriter, the Company or the Selling Shareholders, but the Company and the Selling Shareholders shall be liable only for the expenses to be paid or reimbursed by them pursuant to the provisions of Section 4C(a).

If any such default occurs, either you or the Company and the Selling Shareholders shall have the right to postpone the First Closing Date for not more than three business days from the date first specified in Section 5 hereof in order that the necessary changes in the Registration Statement, Prospectus and any other documents, as well as any other arrangements, may be effected. As used in this Agreement, the term "Underwriter" includes any person substituted for an Underwriter under this Section. Nothing herein will relieve a defaulting Underwriter from liability for its default.

13. *Representations and Indemnities to Survive Delivery.* The respective indemnities, agreements, representations, warranties, and other statements of the Company, its officers, the Selling Shareholders and the several Underwriters set forth in or made pursuant to this Agreement will remain in full force and effect, regardless of any investigation made by or on behalf of any Underwriter, the Company or any of its officers or directors or any controlling person, or the Selling Shareholders and will survive delivery of and payment for the Stock.

14. *Notices.* All communications hereunder will be in writing and if sent to the Underwriters will be mailed, delivered or telegraphed and confirmed to you, at   or, if sent to the Company or the Selling Shareholders, will be mailed, delivered or telegraphed and confirmed at   attention the President of the Company.

15. *Successors.* This Agreement will inure to the benefit of and be binding upon the parties hereto and their respective successors and the officers and directors and controlling persons referred to in Section 11, and no other person will have any right or obligation hereunder.

16. *Representation of Underwriters.* You and only you will act for the several Underwriters in connection with this financing. You represent that you are authorized by each of the Underwriters to execute this Agreement and to take such action as you deem advisable in connection with its performance, including the purchase of the Purchased Stock and the exercise of the options with respect to all or any part of the Option Stock, and any action under or in respect of this Agreement taken by you will be binding upon all the Underwriters.

If the foregoing is in accordance with your understanding of our agreement, kindly sign and return to us the enclosed duplicate hereof, whereupon it will become a binding agreement between the Company, the Selling Shareholders and the several Underwriters in accordance with its terms.

Very truly yours,

By ....
President

Selling Shareholders:

....

....

The foregoing Purchase Agreement is hereby confirmed
and accepted by us, acting on behalf of ourselves and
as the Representative of the several Underwriters
named in Schedule A attached hereto
as of the date first above written.

By ....
A General Partner

SOME FULL SEC PROSPECTUSES

A useful device in drafting your own prospectus is to examine any number of recent prospectuses in your own industry. These are obtainable from the Public Reference Room of the Securities and Exchange Commission, in Washington, D.C. They may be ordered by mail, and xerox copies are charged to you at a nominal price (a few cents a page) plus postage.

In some cases, prospectuses are obtainable from local underwriters or stock brokers, but the complete filing in Washington, D.C. contains many exhibits which are ordinarily not available from the broker's offering circular which is commonly obtained from brokerage firms.

We reproduce herewith the "cover" of each of two different offerings or registration statements, the first of which is an industrial company under S-1, and the second of which is a real estate offering under S-11. By taking a look at the cross reference sheet in each case you can see how industrial offerings differ from real estate offerings.

The SEC has a wealth of information obtainable in its Public Reference Room in Washington, D.C., and all prospective offerors should familiarize themselves with that material, either directly or through their attorneys or underwriters.

As filed with the Securities and Exchange Commission on April 28, 1972

Registration No. 2-42470

SECURITIES AND EXCHANGE COMMISSION
WASHINGTON, D. C. 20549

AMENDMENT No. 2
TO
FORM S-1

REGISTRATION STATEMENT
UNDER
THE SECURITIES ACT OF 1933

ARNEX INDUSTRIES CORP.

(Exact name of Registrant as specified in charter)

48 West 48th Street
New York, N. Y. 10036
(Address of principal executive offices)

ARNOLD B. FUCHS, President **ARNEX INDUSTRIES CORP.** 48 West 48th Street New York, N. Y. 10036	**BERNARD JAY COVEN P.C.** 250 West 57th Street New York, New York 10019

(Name and address of agents for service)

Copies to:

**MESSRS. FINK, WEINBERGER,
LEVIN & CHARNEY**

551 Fifth Avenue
New York, N. Y. 10017

Approximate date of commencement of proposed sale to the public:
As soon as practicable after this Registration becomes effective.

The registrant hereby amends this registration statement on such date or dates as may be necessary to delay its effective date until the registrant shall file a further amendment which specifically states that this registration statement shall thereafter become effective in accordance with Section 8(a) of the Securities Act of 1933 or until the registration statement shall become effective on such date as the Commission, acting pursuant to said Section 8(a), may determine.

ARNEX INDUSTRIES CORP.

CROSS REFERENCE SHEET

Item in Form S-1	Prospectus Caption
1. Distribution Spread	Cover Page, Underwriting
2. Plan of Distribution	Cover Page, Underwriting
3. Use of Proceeds to Registrant	Use of Proceeds
4. Sales Otherwise than for Cash	Certain Transactions
5. Capital Structure	Capitalization
6. Summary of Earnings	Statement of Income
7. Organization of Registrant	Introductory Statement— The Company, Certain Transactions
8. Parents of Registrant	Principal Stockholders
9. Description of Business	Introductory Statement— The Company, Business—General
10. Description of Property	Plant and Equipment
11. Organization Within Five Years	*
12. Pending Legal Proceedings	*
13. Capital Stock Being Registered	Description of Securities — Common Stock
14. Long-Term Debt Being Registered	*
15. Other Securities Being Registered	Cover Page, Underwriting
16. Directors and Executive Officers	Management
17. Remuneration of Directors and Officers	Management — Remuneration
18. Options to Purchase Securities	*
19. Principal Holders of Securities	Principal Stockholders
20. Interest of Management and Others in Certain Transactions..	Certain Transactions
21. Financial Statements	Financial Statements

---

* Not applicable or answer is in the negative.

As filed with the Securities and Exchange Commission on November 12, 1971.

Registration No. 2-41343

SECURITIES AND EXCHANGE COMMISSION
WASHINGTON, D. C. 20549

AMENDMENT No. 1

to

FORM S-11

REGISTRATION STATEMENT

Under

THE SECURITIES ACT OF 1933

DFD Equity Limited Partnership
(Exact name of registrant as specified in charter)

3443 North Central Avenue
Phoenix, Arizona 85012
(Address of principal executive offices)

DOUGLAS E. FRANK, President
DOUG FRANK DEVELOPMENT CORP.
General Partner
3443 North Central Avenue
Phoenix, Arizona 85012
(Name and address of agent for service)

The Commission is requested to send copies of all communications to:
DANIEL S. BERMAN, Esq.

Fink, Weinberger, Levin & Charney
551 Fifth Avenue
New York, New York 10017

Approximate date of commencement of proposed sale to public:
As soon as practicable after registration becomes effective.

CALCULATION OF REGISTRATION FEE

Title of Each Class of Securities Being Registered	Amount Being Registered	Proposed Maximum Offering Price Per Unit	Proposed Maximum Aggregate Offering Price	Amount of Registration Fee
Limited Partnership Interests	410 Units	$10,000	$4,100,000	$820

DFD EQUITY LIMITED PARTNERSHIP

Cross Reference Sheet Pursuant to Rule 404(c)

Registration Statement Item Number and Caption	Caption in Prospectus
1. Distribution Spread	Cover Page
2. Plan of Distribution	Method of Distribution and Subscription Agreement
3. Use of Proceeds to Registrant	Use of Proceeds
4. Sales Otherwise Than for Cash	Not Applicable
5. Capital Structure	Capitalization
6. Summary Financial Data	Not Applicable
7. General Information as to Registrant	Introductory Statement; Concerning the General Partner; Terms of Limited Partnership Agreement
8. Policy with Respect to Certain Activities	Terms of Limited Partnership Agreement; Proposed Business—Investment and Other Policies
9. Investment Policies of Registrant	Use of Proceeds—Proposed Investments; Proposed Business—Investment and Other Policies
10. Description of Real Estate	Use of Proceeds—Proposed Investments
11. Operating Data	Not Applicable
12. Tax Treatment of Registrant and its Security Holders	Federal Income Tax Consequences
13. Description of Shares Being Registered	Cover Page; Terms of Limited Partnership Agreement; Limited Partnership Agreement
14. Long-Term Debt Being Registered	Not Applicable
15. Other Securities Being Registered	Not Applicable
16. Pending Legal Proceedings	Not Applicable
17. Parents of Registrant	Concerning the General Partner
18. Persons Owning Securities of Registrant	Interest of Management and Others in Certain Transactions
19. Directors and Executive Officers	Concerning the General Partner
20. Remuneration of Directors and Officers	Method of Distribution and Depreciation Policy
21. Options to Purchase Securities	Not Applicable
22. Selection and Management of Registrant's Investments	Concerning the General Partner
23. Policies With Respect to Certain Transactions	Interest of Management and Others in Certain Transactions
24. Interest of Certain Persons in Transactions with Registrant	Interest of Management and Others in Certain Transactions
25. Limitations of Liability	Terms of Limited Partnership Agreement
26. Financial Statements	Accountants' Reports; Financial Statements

INDEX